the best book of
LISTS
Ever!

the best book of
LISTS
Ever!

Over 275 fascinating lists to amaze and entertain you and your friends

COMPILED BY GEOFF TIBBALLS

CARLTON

This is a Carlton book

Text and design copyright © Carlton Books Limited 1999

This edition published 1999 by Carlton Books Limited, 20 St
Anne's Court, Wardour Street, London W1V 3AW

ISBN 1 85868 344 0

Printed and bound in Great Britain

CONTENTS

INTRODUCTION

Most of us are slaves to lists — whether it be shopping lists, lists of jobs to do, lists of things to take on holiday or lists of places to see when we get there. Only the Leaning Tower of Pisa has a greater list than the average Briton. And if we're not making lists, we're reading lists compiled by other people — checking the music charts, seeing who's top of the batting averages, flicking through the magazine listings or monitoring our children's education via the school league tables.

Books of lists have been popular since The Domesday Book. So why are people so fascinated with them? It is principally because they present information in an easily-digestible format and contain the sort of quirky material not found in standard reference books. The BEST BOOK OF LISTS *EVER!* follows in that noble tradition, offering a wealth of readily-accessible trivia on every major topic under the sun — including sport, the cinema, natural history, music, inventions, television, crime, history, transport, language and geography. Here you'll find lists to start and end arguments. What better way of passing an evening in the pub than to ask your friends to name 20 songs where the title doesn't appear in the lyrics? It's not as easy as it sounds. Or how about ten songs with a fruit in the title? Ten famous people who suffered from piles? Ten celebrities who once had soccer trials? Or, for the true afficionado, ten names for Colonel Mustard in foreign versions of Cluedo?

With some 300 lists in total, it is a book you can dip into any time, anywhere. Keep a copy on the bedside table or in the loo for those quiet moments of meditation. But be warned: you could be locked in there for hours as your thirst for useless knowledge knows no bounds.

Geoff Tibballs.

CHAPTER

PEOPLE

20 FIRST JOBS OF THE FAMOUS

1. SYLVESTER STALLONE – lion-cage cleaner.

2. WARREN BEATTY – rat-catcher.

3. ERROL FLYNN – sheep-castrator.

4. SEAN CONNERY – French polisher for coffin-maker.

5. CYNDI LAUPER – dog-kennel cleaner.

6. MICK JAGGER – porter at a mental hospital.

7. BETTE MIDLER – pineapple-chunker.

8. ROD STEWART – grave-digger.

9. JEFFREY ARCHER – deckchair attendant.

10. BILL WITHERS – aircraft toilet seat manufacturer.

11. RUSS ABBOTT – hearse driver.

12. MICHAEL DOUGLAS – petrol-pump attendant.

13. JON BON JOVI – Christmas decoration-maker.

14. JACK NICHOLSON – mailing boy.

15. OZZY OSBOURNE – slaughterhouse labourer.

16. ROCK HUDSON – vacuum cleaner salesman.

17. STING – filing clerk with the Inland Revenue.

18. BURT LANCASTER – lingerie salesman.

19. EDITH PIAF – wreath-maker.

20. JOE COCKER – gas fitter.

Warren Beatty's big theatre break came when he was 17 – but it was actually outside the theatre, in the alleyway. The National Theater, Washington DC, had been plagued by rats. Equity pressed the management to hire an official rat-catcher and young Beatty, desperate for a job in the theatre, landed the role.

20 CELEBRITY SACKINGS

1. GEORGE MICHAEL. Sacked from his Saturday job at British Home Stores for not wearing a shirt and tie in the stockroom.

2. MADONNA. Sacked from New York fast-food restaurant Dunkin' Donuts for squirting jam at a customer.

3. MICKEY ROURKE. Sacked from his job as a cinema usher after getting into a brawl with a colleague.

4. ELVIS PRESLEY. Sacked from his $30-a-week job at the Precision Tool Company, Memphis, in 1951 when his bosses discovered that, although his long hair suggested he was much older, he was really only 15 and therefore under-age.

5. VIC REEVES. Sacked from his job on a pig farm near Darlington because he wasn't strong enough to carry two hundredweight of corn. The farmer replaced him with a stronger lad. Vic's erratic tractor-driving may also have contributed to his downfall. He once demolished 100 yards of fencing and on another occasion reversed into a pig-sty.

6. BOY GEORGE. Sacked from his job as a shelf-stacker at Tesco for wearing the store's carrier bags. Tesco deemed his appearance 'disturbing'.

7. VINCENT VAN GOGH. Sacked from his job as assistant to a Paris art dealer for sneaking off to Holland at Christmas and for being rude to customers.

8. ROGER MOORE. Sacked as office boy with London cartoon-makers Publicity Picture Productions after a bad day at the office. He forgot to carry out an important errand, made a costly mistake on some celluloid and, to top it all, the tea he made was cold.

9. ROSEANNE BARR. Sacked from her job as a salad lady at Chuckarama in Salt Lake City for refusing to enter the walk-in freezer after a painful visit to the dentist.

10. ERIC SYKES. Sacked from a cotton mill for singing Bing Crosby's 'In the Blue of the Night' with an empty bucket on his head.

11. DUSTY SPRINGFIELD. Sacked from sales job at Bentalls for making a mess of a demonstration and fusing the store's entire lighting system.

12. PETER FINCH. Sacked as copyboy on the *Sun,* Sydney's leading newspaper of the 1930s, for emptying a jug of water over the editor's head.

13. BARRY MANILOW. Sacked from a New York brewery for failing to shut the large rolltop doors of the delivery truck. As the truck turned a corner, crates and bottles flew everywhere and the street was flowing with frothy beer.

14. DUSTIN HOFFMAN. Sacked from serving at the counter at Ridley's Restaurant, New York, for eating away the profits – six steaks in one sitting.

15. RINGO STARR. Sacked from his job as a barman on a charter boat to North Wales for being cheeky to the boss after a drunken all-night party.

16. SIDNEY POITIER. Sacked from his job parking cars because he couldn't drive! He got first gear mixed up with reverse and crashed into another car.

17. ROBERT MITCHUM. Sacked from a car factory in Toledo for refusing to wear socks.

18. DANNY KAYE. Sacked from an insurance job for unwittingly adding an extra nought to a payout so that the recipient received $40,000 instead of the intended $4,000. By the time the mistake was discovered, the man had taken the money and run.

19. ANDRE PREVIN. Sacked from his after-school job playing the piano for silent films in a small Hollywood theatre. For one film which kept switching rapidly between Biblical times and the 1920s, Previn started playing the Charleston and forgot to look up at the screen. When he did look up, he was playing 'Twelfth Street Rag' to the Crucifixion...

20. ALEXEI SAYLE. Sacked as assistant caretaker at a school in Fulham for dodging off home early. He was shopped by the school's lollipop man.

10 FAMOUS HYPOCHONDRIACS

1. ADOLF HITLER.

2. KENNETH WILLIAMS.

3. HANS CHRISTIAN ANDERSEN.

4. JOHN KEATS.

5. ARNOLD BENNETT.

6. MARCEL PROUST.

7. NICCOLO PAGANINI.

8. WILLIAM COWPER.

9. DR. SAMUEL JOHNSON.

10. PERCY BYSSHE SHELLEY.

Carry On star Kenneth Williams was obsessed with his bowels. He suffered dreadfully from piles and as a result harboured a deep distrust of other people's lavatories. Whenever he moved into a theatre for a play, he always had his own personal toilet, for his exclusive use. For the same reason, visitors to his London flat were never allowed to use the lavatory there – Williams insisted that they use the public toilets at nearby Tottenham Court Road tube station. Smoking was also forbidden in his flat which was described by one caller as being like a 'spotless, pristine, monk's cell.'

10 PEOPLE BORN ON CHRISTMAS DAY

1. SIR ISAAC NEWTON, scientist (1642).

2. WILLIAM COLLINS, poet (1721).

3. CONRAD HILTON, hotelier (1887).

4. DAME REBECCA WEST, novelist (1892).

5. CAB CALLOWAY, jazz singer (1907).

6. ANWAR SADAT, statesman (1918).

7. LITTLE RICHARD, singer (1935).

8. KENNY EVERETT, disc jockey (1944).

9. ANNIE LENNOX, singer (1954).

10. SHANE MCGOWAN, singer (1957).

The most widely-perpetuated myth about Christmas Day births is that Humphrey Bogart was among them. In fact he was born on 23 January 1899 but Warner Bros, sensing publicity possibilities, later changed it to 25 December 1900. Among those who died on Christmas Day were W.C. Fields in 1946 and Charlie Chaplin in 1977. On leaving school in Aberdeen, the only job Annie Lennox could find was at the local Findus fish products factory. The stench was appalling. She remembers: 'I used to wrap my work clothes in a plastic bag each night and fall flat on my face when I opened it the next morning. Working on the plaice-filleting machine made me want to throw up all the time. Yet, looking back, I suppose it was beneficial in discovering exactly what I NEVER wanted to do again.' Moving south, she got a job as a waitress at Pippins restaurant in Hampstead where one of the customers was her future musical partner Dave Stewart.

10 FAMOUS PEOPLE AND THEIR PETS

1. LORD BADEN-POWELL – a hyrax (a small nocturnal mammal) called Hyrie.

2. CHARLES BAUDELAIRE – a bat in a cage on his desk.

3. ROBERT BURNS – a ewe called Poor Mailie. He wrote two poems about her.

4. LORD BYRON – a bear. He kept one at Cambridge University because dogs weren't allowed.

5. HENRIK IBSEN – kept a pet scorpion on his desk.

6. FLORENCE NIGHTINGALE – kept a small owl in her pocket, even while serving in the Crimean War.

7. GEORGE ORWELL – a goat called Muriel.

8. ROBERT LOUIS STEVENSON – a donkey called Modestine.

9. ALFRED, LORD TENNYSON – a pony named Fanny which used to pull Tennyson's wife in a wheelchair.

10. VIRGINIA WOOLF – a marmoset called Mitz.

Edward Lear kept a striped tomcat called Foss, a creature with a curious stub tail. In 1881, Lear had to move to a new house in Italy because the building of a hotel blocked the view and ruined the light for Lear's painting. To make sure that Foss felt at home, Lear had his new house, the Villa Tennyson, built as an exact replica of their previous abode. Distinguished actor Sir Ralph Richardson used to ride his motorcycle to the theatre even when in his seventies, sometimes arriving with his pet parrot, José, on his left shoulder. He also kept a ferret called Eddie and, to the horror of his leading ladies, would often secrete a white mouse in his pocket.

10 FAMOUS INSOMNIACS

1. THE EMPEROR CALIGULA.

2. JOSEPH CONRAD.

3. MARLENE DIETRICH.

4. ALEXANDRE DUMAS.

5. W.C. FIELDS.

6. SCOTT FITZGERALD.

7. GALILEO.

8. HERMANN GOERING.

9. RUDYARD KIPLING.

10. ALEXANDER POPE.

Alexandre Dumas suffered terribly from insomnia and tried all sorts of remedies. His most inventive attempt at a cure was to eat an apple under the Arc de Triomphe. It didn't work. Perhaps he should have tried the Eiffel Tower. W.C. Fields used to wrap himself in towels and lie back in a barber's chair because had always found a trip to the barber's relaxing. On other occasions, he would go out into the garden in the dead of night and turn on the hose so that the spray of the water gently soaked him. Apparently he had always found rain therapeutic.

10 FAMOUS PEOPLE AND THEIR PHOBIAS

1. SID CAESAR – tonsurphobia, a fear of haircuts.

2. QUEEN CHRISTINA OF SWEDEN – fleas.

3. ELIZABETH I – anthophobia, a fear of roses.

4. SIGMUND FREUD – siderodromophobia, a fear of train travel.

5. KATHARINE HEPBURN – dirty hair.

6. HOWARD HUGHES – mysophobia, a fear of germs.

7. MADONNA – brontophobia, a fear of thunder.

8. MARILYN MONROE – agoraphobia, a fear of public places.

9. RICHIE VALENS – aerophobia. He died in a plane crash.

10. NATALIE WOOD – hydrophobia, a fear of water. She died by drowning.

Queen Christina ruled Sweden in the 17th century and was so terrified of fleas that she ordered the construction of a tiny 10cm-long cannon so that she could spend hours firing miniature cannonballs at the fleas which infested the royal bedchamber. Katharine Hepburn's phobia about dirty hair meant that when she was at Twentieth-Century Fox she apparently used to tour the set sniffing people's hair to make sure that it had been washed. Eccentric millionaire Howard Hughes' obsession with health and hygiene was legendary. Nobody else was permitted to touch his food and any visitors had to stand in a chalk square drawn outside the house and be inspected before being allowed near the front door. His own doctor could only examine him from the other side of the room and, as an added insurance, Hughes would touch nothing without first wrapping his hand in a paper tissue. When he stayed in a hotel, the windows were always darkened and taped. He developed food crazes – eating nothing but ice cream for weeks on end – and only visited a barber twice in ten years.

20 SELF-CONFESSED ATHEISTS AND AGNOSTICS

1. DOUGLAS ADAMS.

2. WOODY ALLEN.

3. BILLY BRAGG.

4. MARLON BRANDO.

5. MICHAEL CRICHTON.

6. QUENTIN CRISP.

7. AMANDA DONOHOE.

8. BRIAN ENO.

9. JODIE FOSTER.

10. BILL GATES.

11. MIKHAIL GORBACHEV.

12. BILLY JOEL.

13. STANLEY KUBRICK.

14. SIR IAN McKELLEN.

15. RANDY NEWMAN.

16. JACK NICHOLSON.

17. ROMAN POLANSKI.

18. TERRY PRATCHETT.

19. MICHAEL STIPE.

20. GORE VIDAL.

20 FAMOUS NICKNAMES

1. CALAMITY JANE – Martha Jane Canary, 19th-century U.S. cowgirl. She was surrounded by misfortune, 11 of her 12 husbands meeting untimely deaths.

2. THE ACCIDENTAL PRESIDENT – John Tyler, who only became U.S. President in 1841 after William Henry Harrison's sudden death a month after taking office.

3. SHARON – Elton John, so named by Rod Stewart. In turn, Elton nicknamed Rod 'Phyllis'.

4. THE BALD EAGLE OF FOGGY BOTTOM – Robert Lovett, President Truman's Secretary of Defence. He was bald and had previously worked in the State Department which was nicknamed 'Foggy Bottom' because of the confusion it created.

5. THE BULLFROG OF THE PONTINE MARSHES – Italian dictator Benito Mussolini, a derogatory label from Churchill.

6. FLUFF – Alan Freeman. The veteran disc jockey acquired the nickname from an old pullover he once wore to a party. He'd had it dry-cleaned beforehand and it had gone fluffy.

7. THE BULL MOOSE – Theodore Roosevelt. He had told a supporter in 1900: 'I am as strong as a bull moose.'

8. OLD SLOW HAND – Eric Clapton, on account of his distinctive twangy guitar-playing.

9. THE ILLINOIS BABOON – Abraham Lincoln, an uncomplimentary description of his appearance.

10. STING – Gordon Sumner was christened 'Sting' at the age of 16 because he often wore a wasp-striped T-shirt.

11. THE MAN ON THE WEDDING CAKE – Governor Thomas E. Dewey of New York. He was the Republican challenger to Truman in the 1948 Presidential election but his chances were irreparably damaged by a remark that, with his moustache, Dewey looked like the man on a wedding cake.

12. THE HUNCHFRONT OF LIME GROVE – Sabrina, the busty blonde bombshell who featured in Arthur Askey's TV shows in the 1950s.

13. OLD FUSS AND FEATHERS – 19th-century U.S. General Winfield Scott, referring to his vanity and pomposity.

14. THE BOUNCING CZECH – Crooked newspaper proprietor Robert Maxwell, born in Czechoslovakia.

15. THE FLANDERS MARE – Anne of Cleves, Henry VIII's fourth wife. The nickname was given to her by her husband. Not surprisingly, the marriage didn't last long.

16. LITTLE MISS DYNAMITE – Brenda Lee, energetic American singer.

17. OLD ROUGH AND READY – U.S. President Zachary Taylor, hero of the Mexican War. His troops called him this because of his informal dress and 'lack of military pretension.'

18. PRETTY FANNY – British statesman Lord Balfour, because his fastidiousness veered towards effeminacy.

19. THE THINKING MAN'S CRUMPET – TV presenter Joan Bakewell, doyenne of *Late Night Line-Up*, as described by Frank Muir.

20. THE TURNIP-HOER – George I, who suggested turning St. James's Park into a turnip-field.

10 SUPERSTITIOUS PEOPLE

1.   WALT DISNEY used to wash his hands 30 times an hour.

2.   GEORGE II was a stickler about timekeeping. At one minute to nine every night, he would stand outside his mistress's bedroom, fob-watch in hand. At precisely nine, he would enter, pull down his breeches and have sex – often without taking off his hat.

3.   CHARLES DICKENS always touched things three times for luck.

4.   ARNOLD SCHOENBERG was superstitious about the number 13. Fittingly, the composer died on Friday the 13th at 13 minutes to midnight.

5.   HANS CHRISTIAN ANDERSEN always turned back twice after leaving a room to ensure that all candles were out. When staying in hotels, he always took with him a coil of rope in case of fire.

6.   LOUIS XIV hated washing and only took three baths in his whole life.

7.   LORD BADEN-POWELL was obsessed with washing his entire body daily.

8.   EDWARD VII had been told by a palmist that the numbers 6 and 9 would guide his life. He married in 1863 (when split this makes 9+9) to a bride, Alexandra, whose name had nine letters, as did that of her father, Christian IX. Edward's coronation took place on 9 August and he reigned for nine years before dying at the age of 69.

9.   GEORGE V kept the hundreds of clocks at Sandringham House, Norfolk, 30 minutes fast so that he would never be late for an appointment.

10. PETER ILICH TCHAIKOVSKY, while conducting, used to hold his chin with his left hand and conduct with his right because he was afraid his head would roll off his shoulders.

SEPARATED AT BIRTH: 20 PAIRS WHO SHARE THE SAME BIRTHDAY

1. STEPHEN STILLS and VICTORIA PRINCIPAL (3 January 1945).

2. GEORGE FOREMAN and LINDA LOVELACE (10 January 1949).

3. PRINCESS MARGARET and JANIS JOPLIN (19 January 1943).

4. FEDERICO FELLINI and DEFOREST KELLEY (20 January 1920).

5. NEIL DIAMOND and RAY STEVENS (24 January 1941).

6. EARTHA KITT and ROGER VADIM (26 January 1928).

7. ERIC IDLE and JOHN MAJOR (29 March 1943).

8. MARLON BRANDO and DORIS DAY (3 April 1924).

9. GENE WILDER and JACKIE STEWART (11 June 1939).

10. LINDSAY WAGNER and MERYL STREEP (22 June 1949).

11. SYLVESTER STALLONE and BURT WARD (6 July 1946).

12. JAMES CAGNEY and ERLE STANLEY GARDNER (17 July 1899).

13. DANNY GLOVER and DON HENLEY (22 July 1947).

14. CHRISSIE HYNDE and JULIE KAVNER (7 September 1951).

15. LUCIANO PAVAROTTI and JOAN RIVERS (12 October 1935).

16. MARGOT KIDDER and GEORGE WENDT (17 October 1948).

17. MANFRED MANN and GEOFF BOYCOTT (21 October 1940).

18. KATE CAPSHAW and ROSEANNE BARR (3 November 1953).

19. DAVID HEMMINGS and JULIET MILLS (21 November 1941).

20. JOHN DENVER and BEN KINGSLEY (31 December 1943).

Yes, it's true. Burt Ward, who played Boy Wonder Robin in the Batman TV series, was born on the same day as Sylvester Stallone. Holy coincidence!

10 PEOPLE WHO HAVE HAD ROSES NAMED AFTER THEM

1. THORA HIRD.

2. ANGELA RIPPON.

3. ANNA FORD.

4. FELICITY KENDAL.

5. MAUREEN LIPMAN.

6. HANNAH GORDON.

7. SUE LAWLEY.

8. INGRID BERGMAN.

9. CARDINAL HUME.

10. JACQUELINE DU PRÉ.

Thora Hird is 'thorny' while Angela Rippon found herself to be prone to black spot. Maureen Lipman was intrigued by her description – 'good against a wall'.

10 PEOPLE WHO SUFFERED FROM PILES

1. CASANOVA.

2. CARDINAL RICHELIEU.

3. WILLIAM WORDSWORTH.

4. CHARLES DICKENS.

5. KENNETH WILLIAMS.

6. GEORGE II.

7. HENRI DE TOULOUSE-LAUTREC.

8. NAPOLEON I.

9. ANTON CHEKHOV.

10. FYODOR DOSTOEVSKY.

10 FAMOUS DYSLEXICS

1. ANTHEA TURNER.

2. WALT DISNEY.

3. TOM CRUISE.

4. SUSAN HAMPSHIRE.

5. WHOOPI GOLDBERG.

6. THOMAS EDISON.

7. HENRY WINKLER.

8. CHER.

9. BRIAN CONLEY.

10. LEONARDO DA VINCI.

20 PEOPLE KNOWN BY THEIR MIDDLE NAME

1. DANIEL LOUIS ARMSTRONG.

2. RUZ FIDEL CASTRO.

3. EDWARD MONTGOMERY CLIFT.

4. ALFRED ALISTAIR COOKE.

5. DOROTHY FAYE DUNAWAY.

6. WILLIAM CLARK GABLE.

7. SAMUEL DASHIELL HAMMETT.

8. NORVELL OLIVER HARDY.

9. JAMES PAUL McCARTNEY.

10. TERENCE STEVE McQUEEN.

11. KEITH RUPERT MURDOCH.

12. PATRICK RYAN O'NEAL.

13. ELDRED GREGORY PECK.

14. HELEN BEATRIX POTTER.

15. ROBERT OLIVER REED.

16. ERNESTINE JANE RUSSELL.

17. EDITH NORMA SHEARER.

18. MARIE DIONNE WARWICK.

19. HOWARD ANDY WILLIAMS.

20. MARIE DEBRA WINGER.

10 FAMOUS STAMMERERS

1. ARNOLD BENNETT.

2. LEWIS CARROLL.

3. PATRICK CAMPBELL.

4. KING CHARLES I.

5. WINSTON CHURCHILL.

6. THE EMPEROR CLAUDIUS.

7. CHARLES DARWIN.

8. KING GEORGE VI.

9. SOMERSET MAUGHAM.

10. BRUCE WILLIS (as a child).

10 PAIRS OF PEOPLE WHO HAD THE SAME JOB

1. NORMAN TEBBIT and TONY HANCOCK – assistants in menswear shops.

2. JIM BOWEN and FRANZ SCHUBERT – schoolteachers.

3. JACK NICHOLSON and 'DIDDY' DAVID HAMILTON – mailing boys.

4. DUSTY SPRINGFIELD and IMELDA MARCOS – record shop assistants.

5. MARLON BRANDO and DR. DAVID OWEN – sewage workers.

6. RONNIE BARKER and TERRY WOGAN – bank clerks.

7. HARRY HILL and ANTON CHEKHOV – doctors.

8. BOB HOLNESS and MARK TWAIN – printer's apprentices.

9. ABRAHAM LINCOLN and ROCK HUDSON – postmen.

10. FRANK SINATRA and PETER O'TOOLE – sports journalists.

10 FAMOUS LAST WORDS

1. LUDWIG VAN BEETHOVEN, 1827: 'I shall hear in heaven!' (Beethoven was stone-deaf).

2. ANDREW BRADFORD, the publisher of Philadelphia's first newspaper, 1742: 'O Lord, forgive the errata!'

3. W.C. FIELDS, who had been flicking through the Bible on his deathbed, 1946: 'I'm looking for a loophole.'

4. NEVILLE HEATH, the murderer who requested a glass of whisky as his last wish before being hanged, 1946: 'You might make that a double.'

5. HENRIK IBSEN, when his wife suggested that the playwright was looking a little better, 1906: 'On the contrary.'

6. LIBERACE, when asked if he wanted to go to church, 1986: 'I wish I could. I'll just stay here and watch my shows.'

7. KARL MARX, after his housekeeper had asked whether he had a final message for the world, 1883: 'Go on, get out! Last words are for fools who haven't said enough.'

8. VISCOUNT PALMERSTON. The former British Prime Minister's last words in 1865 displayed his sense of irony. 'Die, my dear doctor? That's the last thing I shall do.'

9. JAMES W. RODGERS, the Utah murderer when asked if he had any last requests before facing the firing squad, 1960: 'Yes – a bullet-proof vest.'

10. OSCAR WILDE, summoning a final champagne, 1900: 'I am dying, as I have lived, beyond my means.'

10 ROYAL IMPOSTERS

1. ANNA ANDERSON (Anastasia, daughter of Russian Czar Nicholas II).

2. STELLA CHIAPPINI (Marie Etoile d'Orléans, Queen of France).

3. HORACE COLE (Emperor of Abyssinia).

4. HARRY DOMELA (Grandson of Kaiser Wilhelm).

5. JIM MORAN (Crown Prince of Arabia).

6. KARL WILHELM NAUNDORFF (Louis XVII, heir to French throne).

7. OTREFIEF (Dmitri, younger son of Ivan the Terrible).

8. LAMBERT SIMNEL (Edward, Earl of Warwick).

9. PERKIN WARBECK (Richard, Duke of York).

10. SARAH WILSON (Princess Susanna Caroline Matilda, sister of Charlotte, wife of George III).

Caught stealing from Queen Charlotte, Sarah Wilson, a humble royal maid, was exiled to the United States in 1771 where she convinced Americans that she was Charlotte's sister and thus genuine royalty. As such, she was wined and dined wherever she went. Her exploits pale in comparison to those of Horace Cole who, in 1910, set out to play a trick on the Royal Navy. Socialite Cole had a telegram sent to the Navy, warning of the imminent arrival of the Emperor of Abyssinia at Weymouth. In false beards and rented costumes, Cole and his cohorts (among them the future novelist Virginia Woolf) received a formal gun salute and the playing of the Zanzibar national anthem (the Navy didn't know where Abyssinia was) before being piped aboard the Dreadnought. When questioned, they replied 'Bunga-bunga!' to everything. They got away with it despite one joker's moustache slipping and their make-up running in the rain.

10 REIGNS WHICH LASTED UNDER A YEAR

1. EDMUND (England) – murdered 1016.

2. HAROLD II (England) – killed in battle 1066.

3. DUNCAN II (Scotland) – murdered 1094.

4. WILLIAM III (Sicily) – murdered 1194.

5. GÜNTHER (Holy Roman Emperor) – died after just three weeks as Emperor 1349.

6. ELEANOR DE FOIX (Navarre) – died from natural causes 1479.

7. EDWARD V (England) – put in Tower of London by uncle Richard, Duke of Gloucester 1483. Presumed murdered.

8. FEODOR II (Russia) – murdered by a Moscow mob after reigning for only two months 1605.

9. LOUIS XIX (France) – abdicated 1830.

10. EDWARD VIII (UK) – abdicated 1936 after less than 11 months on the throne.

The dubious honour of the shortest proper reign in history goes to Louis XIX who was king of France from breakfast until tea-time on 2 August 1830, at which point he abdicated. With revolution in the air, his nephew and successor, Henri V, the last of the Elder Bourbon line, fared little better, lasting only a week from 2 August to 9 August. Louis does have a rival in Crown Prince Luis Filipe of Portugal who technically ruled his country as Dom Luis III for 20 minutes on 1 February 1908, the time between the death of his father, fatally shot in Lisbon, and his own demise, having been wounded in the same attack.

10 REIGNS OF OVER 55 YEARS

1. PEPI II (Egypt) c.2294 BC-c.2200 BC.

2. VICTORIA (UK) 1837-1901.

3. ALFONSO I (Portugal) 1112-85.

4. LOUIS XIV (France) 1643-1715.

5. FRANZ JOSEF I (Austria) 1848-1916.

6. CHRISTIAN IV (Denmark, Sweden, Norway) 1588-1648.

7. GEORGE III (Great Britain and Ireland) 1760-1820.

8. LOUIS XV (France) 1715-74.

9. WILHELMINA (Netherlands) 1890-1948.

10. HENRY III (England) 1216-72.

Pepi II partly owed his long life to his novel way of discouraging nasty insects. To deter flies from landing on the royal personage, he always kept a supply of naked slaves nearby, their bodies smeared with honey. Towards the end of her reign, Queen Victoria was so weak that family photographs became something of an ordeal. She was afraid of dropping babies and thus required hidden support. So when, in 1900, she was pictured surrounded by grandchildren and sitting with her great-grandson the infant Duke of York on her lap, the camera did not reveal the presence of a royal maid positioned out of sight beneath Victoria's vast dress to hold the baby firmly in place. Only female servants were encouraged to apply for this duty...

10 GAY MONARCHS (ALLEGEDLY)

1. WILLIAM II of England (1087-1100).

2. RICHARD I of England (1189-99).

3. EDWARD II of England (1307-27).

4. JOHN II of France (1350-64).

5. JAMES III of Scotland (1469-88).

6. HENRI III of France (1574-89).

7. JAMES I of England (James VI of Scotland) (1603-25).

8. LOUIS XIII of France (1610-43).

9. MARY II of England, Scotland and Ireland (1688-94).

10. ANNE of Great Britain and Ireland (1702-14).

Louis XIII of France's sexual preferences are thought to have stemmed from an incident at the age of 14 when he was allowed an attempt at carnal relations with his bride-to-be, Anne of Austria. It was a disaster and filled Louis with such a repugnance for physical love that it was another three years before the marriage was finally consummated. While Louis lavished his devotion on his friend the Marquis de Cinq-Mars, his visits to Anne's bed were isolated incidents. So it was almost by chance that they produced a son, the future Louis XIV. Their second son, Philippe, Duke of Orléans, was forced to wear pretty dresses and to play with dolls because Anne had longed for a daughter. Not surprisingly, he too turned out to be somewhat effeminate.

10 MAD ROYALS

1. GEORGE III of Great Britain and Ireland was being driven through Windsor Great Park when he ordered his carriage driver to stop. The King got out, walked over to an oak tree, shook hands with one of its branches and talked to it for several minutes. He thought he was talking to the King of Prussia. He ended up in a strait-jacket.

2. PRINCESS ALEXANDRA of Bavaria was convinced that as a child she had swallowed a full-size grand piano. Nothing could ever shake her from this belief.

3. LUDWIG II of Bavaria (1846-86) was Alexandra's nephew. His reign was notable for his decision to reverse night and day. He had a moon painted on his bedroom ceiling and embarked on epic mountain journeys in the dead of night in a golden sleigh, accompanied by coachmen who were forced to dress in the style of Louis XIV. Known as the 'Dream King', he built fairy-tale castles before finally being declared unfit to rule.

4. OTTO, younger brother of Ludwig II, decided the only way to preserve his own sanity was to shoot a peasant a day. Every morning he would start taking pot-shots at the peasants working in the royal garden. As staff numbers diminished, one servant was given the task of loading the king's pistol with blanks while another dressed as a peasant and pretended to fall down dead when Otto shot him.

5. CATHERINE THE GREAT of Russia (1729-96), discovering that she had dandruff, imprisoned her hairdresser in an iron cage for three years to stop the news spreading. Enchanted by a primrose in the royal garden, she posted a sentry to guard the plant day and night.

6. QUEEN JUANA of Spain worshipped her husband Philip, who died in 1506, so much that she refused to allow him to be buried and had his coffin accompany her wherever she travelled.

7. FERDINAND II of Sicily (1810-59) would only allow the country to have its own postage stamps as long as his portrait was not marred by an unsightly franking mark.

8. PHILIP, Prince of Calabria, the eldest son of Charles XIII of Spain (1716-88), was mad about gloves and was known to wear 16 pairs at any one time.

9. CHARLES VI of France (1368-1422) was convinced he was made of glass. So he hated travelling by coach in case the vibration caused him to shatter into a thousand pieces. He also started prowling the corridors of the royal palace, howling like a wolf, much to the consternation of Queen Isabeau. Deciding that she no longer wished to share the King's bed, Isabeau came up with a humble lookalike, Odette de Champdivers, to take her place. Every night for 30 years, Odette wore the Queen's clothes in the royal bed and Charles never once spotted the deception.

10. HENRY CHRISTOPHE, King of Northern Haiti (1767-1820), ordered his guards to prove their loyalty to him by marching over a 200ft-high cliff. Those who obeyed plunged to their deaths; those who refused were tortured and executed. Henry Christophe ended up shooting himself.

10 CURIOUS ROYAL DEATHS

1. EDWARD II of England (1307-27) met a painful end in Berkeley Castle, Gloucestershire, when three assassins, hired on the orders of his Queen, Isabella, and her lover Roger Mortimer, rammed a long, open-topped deer's horn up the King's backside. With this firmly in position, the red-hot tip of a long-handled poker was inserted through the horn and deep into Edward's bowels. The poker was then withdrawn, reheated and reinserted at least once more. Edward's screams resounded through the castle but, with no marks on his body, death was ascribed to natural causes.

2. ALEXANDROS I of Greece (1917-20) died from blood poisoning after being bitten by his pet monkey.

3. HENRY I of England (1100-35) died after eating a surfeit of lampreys (small eel-like creatures) at a banquet in France.

4. CHARLES VIII of France (1483-98) was noted for his manners. On entering a tennis court at the Chateau d'Amboise, he bowed to his wife and allowed her to proceed first, but, as he raised his head from his magnanimous gesture, he crashed it against a low wooden beam, fracturing his skull and killing him.

5. MITHRIDATES VI of Pontus in Asia Minor (132 BC-63 BC) took small doses of poison throughout his life to develop a resistance should anyone try to poison him. He built up such a strong immunity that when he tried to take his own life to escape the approaching Romans, the poison he took had no effect. Instead he ordered a slave to kill him with a sword.

6. HAAKON VII of Norway (1905-57) slipped on the soap in his marble bath and struck his head fatally on one of the taps.

7. QUEEN ELEANOR, dutiful wife of Edward I of England (1272-1307), was so distressed to see her husband lying gravely ill after poison had set into a battle wound that she personally sucked all the poison from the wound. Her brave deed saved the King's life but killed her. Edward was so moved by her sacrifice that he ordered large crosses – subsequently known as 'Eleanor crosses' – to be erected at each of the 12 places where her coffin stopped during its coach journey from Nottinghamshire to London.

8. KING JOHN of England (1199-1216) died in an East Anglian abbey after a sumptuous banquet, laid on for him by grateful subjects. The townsfolk of Lynn

had just been awarded a handsome contract to supply the royal garrisons and, to repay the King, they rounded off the banquet with his favourite dessert, peaches in cider. Alas, he consumed such a great amount that he suffered violent stomach pains and died a few days later.

9. MARGARET, 'Maid of Norway', was nominally declared Queen of Scotland in 1286 but it was not until 1290 that the seven-year-old Queen sailed from Norway to claim her new kingdom. Alas, on the journey across the North Sea, she suffered terrible sea-sickness and died in the Orkneys before ever setting foot on the Scottish mainland.

10. EDMUND IRONSIDE, King of Southern England, for just eight months, was murdered in 1016 while sitting on the toilet. He sat on the long wooden lavatory box in his house to empty his bowels, little knowing that an enemy knight, Edric Streona, was lurking in the pit below. As poor Edmund sat down, Streona twice thrust a sword into him.

10 CHILD RULERS

1. ALFONSO XIII of Spain (1886-1931) became King at birth. He survived several assassination attempts before fleeing the country in 1931 at the threat of civil war. When General Franco took charge in 1936, Alfonso was reinstated as a 'private citizen', but never returned to Spain alive and died in Rome in 1941.

2. JOHN I of France (1316) also became King at birth, but died five days later.

3. MARY, QUEEN OF SCOTS (1542-67) became Queen at the age of one week. She also experienced widowhood early, losing her husband when she was just 18.

4. HENRY VI of England (1422-61) became King at eight months old.

5. PETRONILLA of Aragon (1137-63) was less than a year old when she came to the throne.

6. ALFONSO XI of Leon and Castile (1312-50) was King at a year. He died from the Black Death.

7. JAMES V of Scotland (1513-42) became King aged one.

8. SIGURD II and his half-brother INGE I of Norway became joint rulers in 1136 at the ages of two and one respectively.

9. ISABELLE, daughter of Charles VI of France, was only seven when she married England's 29-year-old King Richard II in 1396. Three years later, she was a widow.

10. SHIH HUANG TI came to power in China as a 13-year-old boy in 222 BC. He built a network of 270 palaces, linked by tunnels, and was so afraid of assassination that he slept in a different palace each night.

20 RARELY-INVOKED PATRON SAINTS

1. APOLLONIA – toothache.

2. FIACRE – venereal disease and taxi drivers.

3. ANTHONY CLARET – savings banks.

4. GABRIEL – postal services.

5. SEBASTIAN – neighbourhood watch.

6. GENGULF – unhappy marriages.

7. JOHN THE BAPTIST – motorways.

8. LOUISE DE MARILLAC – social workers.

9. JEROME – librarians.

10. VERONICA – laundry workers.

11. MARTIN DE PORRES – hairdressers.

12. JOSEPH OF ARIMATHEA – grave-diggers and funeral directors.

13. CLARE – embroiderers.

14. VITUS – comedians and mental illness.

15. LUKE – butchers.

16. BERNARD OF CLAIRVAUX – beekeepers.

17. ADRIAN NICOMEDIA – arms dealers.

18. BONA – air hostesses.

19. MATTHEW – accountants.

20. BERNARDINO OF SIENA – advertising executives and hoarseness.

10 WEDDING-DAY DISASTERS

1.   The wedding of Jason Adams to Andrea Sims at St. Mary's Church, Arnold, Nottingham, in 1993 was marred when the arrival of the groom's uninvited mother, Ruth Baird-Parker, sparked a brawl in the aisle. When the vicar asked the congregation whether it could show any just cause or impediment, Mrs. Baird-Parker shouted that the bride was a trollop and not good enough for her son. When the vicar then asked whether the bride, forsaking all other, would keep herself only unto her man, so long as they both should live, Mrs. Baird-Parker interjected: 'That will be the first time!' As tempers became frayed, police officers (who, tipped off about possible trouble, had been keeping watch outside from behind bushes) leapt into action. Although the ceremony went ahead, the vicar described it as 'A very sad day for all concerned.'

2.   A French bride was arrested at her wedding reception in 1995 for stabbing her new husband with the knife they had just used to cut the wedding cake.

3.   Best man Albert Muldoon found himself married to the bride following a mix-up at a church at Kileter, County Tyrone, in the 1920s. Albert walked up to the altar with the groom but, instead of standing to the right of the groom, he stood on his left. Seeing Albert in that position, the priest addressed all the questions to him and Albert duly replied. The slip-up was only discovered when the real groom demanded to sign the register too. A second ceremony was hastily arranged, this time with Albert on the right. Albert said afterwards: 'The groom was so nervous that he didn't seem able to speak, so I thought I had better answer for him.'

4.   Bride Susan Baird was handcuffed and arrested along with the groom and 12 other guests who clashed with police officers at her wedding reception in September 1985. While her new husband Stephen spent the night in a police cell Mrs. Baird, who admitted obstructing the police and assaulting a WPC at Fulham police station, was fined £150.

5.   Minutes before he was due to conduct a wedding at Normanton Parish Church, West Yorkshire, in October 1996, Father Rodney Chapman tripped over a Bible, crashed into the aisle and broke his foot. With blood pouring down his face, he managed to marry Scott Niesyty and Paula Dunn before going to hospital.

6.   The wedding of the future George IV to Princess Caroline of Brunswick in

1795 was a sorry affair. So drunk that he had to be carried to the altar by his two ushers, the groom rose at one point in the ceremony as if trying to escape. His father, 'Mad' King George III, quickly left his seat and firmly pressed him down again. When asked by the Archbishop if there was any impediment to the marriage, the groom began to cry. That night, after briefly visiting the marital bed, he fell asleep in the fireplace.

7.   Newly-wed Kal Thorpe left All Saints' Church, Erdington, Birmingham, in August 1986 to discover that the wedding car had been stolen.

8.   At a wedding at Kingston, Surrey, in 1973, the vicar went sick and a replacement had to be found at short notice. Then the bride fainted when the groom placed the ring on her finger and, despite attempts to revive her, remained unconscious for 20 minutes. She was finally able to complete the ceremony and the happy couple headed for their car, which contained a cement mixer – for the honeymoon hotel had burnt to the ground and bride and groom were going to spend the time building a septic tank instead.

9.   Uninvited father of the bride Geoffrey Lloyd was about to deliver his speech to 100 guests at Eastnor Castle, Hereford and Worcester, in July 1995 when two police officers, summoned by the best man and the bride's brother, arrested him and marched him from the premises. 'He was arrested to prevent a breach of the peace,' explained a police officer. 'He came reasonably quietly.'

10. Princess Maria del Pozzo della Cisterno would never forget the day of her wedding to Amadeo, the Duke D'Aosta, son of the King of Italy, in Turin on 30 May 1867. Her wardrobe mistress hanged herself; the palace gatekeeper cut his throat; the colonel leading the wedding procession collapsed from sunstroke; the stationmaster was crushed to death under the wheels of the honeymoon train; the King's aide was killed falling from his horse; and the best man shot himself. Otherwise, it all went smoothly...

10 SHORT-LIVED MARRIAGES

1. Actress EVA BARTOK's third marriage (her first had been at 15) was to film publicist William Wordsworth, a descendant of the poet. She left him immediately after the wedding ceremony.

2. ATTILA THE HUN died on the night after his wedding in 453. It is rumoured that his desire to consummate the marriage proved fatal.

3. Former child star PATTY DUKE stayed married to Michael Tell for just 13 days.

4. In January 1994, a Barnsley couple split up 12 hours after the ceremony following a wedding-night row over the bride's ex-boyfriend.

5. Minor actress Jean Acker left RUDOLPH VALENTINO on their wedding night.

6. Silent movie star DAGMAR GODOWSKY decided to split from her second husband when, immediately after the ceremony, he put his arm around her and asked possessively: 'Who do you belong to now?' She got him to buy her dinner and then she left him.

7. Actress GREER GARSON was married to Edward Snelson for a mere five weeks.

8. One of the shortest royal marriages was that between HENRY VIII and ANNE OF CLEVES. Henry thought she was ugly and had the marriage declared void after six months. He also ordered Thomas Cromwell, who had recommended Anne as a suitable bride, to be beheaded.

9. U.S. actress JEAN ARTHUR split from husband Julian Anker after one day.

10. An hour after getting married at Kensington in November 1975, KATHRYN SLUCKIN stunned new husband Jerzy and his relatives by announcing at the reception: 'It won't work.' She went to live in a Finchley commune.

10 ODD COUPLES

1.   6ft 2in-tall Fabien Pretou towered over his 3ft 1in bride Natalie Lucius at their wedding at Seysinnet-Pariset, France, in April 1990.

2.   Harry Stevens, aged 103, married his cousin, 84-year-old Thelma Lucas, at a Wisconsin retirement home in 1984.

3.   6ft 7in Nigel Wilks married 3ft 11in Beverly Russell at Hull in 1984.

4.   In 1871, Captain Martin van Buren Bates married Anna Hanen Swan in London. She was 7ft 5 1/2in. tall and he was 7ft 2 1/2in.

5.   When Ruth and Kevin Kimber married in 1990, she was 93 and he was 28.

6.   Wrestler Giant Haystacks weighed as much as 50 stone in his prime. By contrast, his bride Rita weighed a mere 7st 7lb at their wedding.

7.   Minnie Munro, aged 102, married 83-year-old Dudley Reid in New South Wales in 1991.

8.   In 1863, American dwarf Charles S. Stratton, better known as General Tom Thumb, married Lavinia Warren. He was 2ft 10in tall and she was 2ft 8in. In 1884, the widowed Lavinia then married Count Primo Magri who was two inches shorter than her first husband at 2ft 8in.

9.   In 1994, 26-year-old American supermodel Anna Nicole Smith married 89-year-old millionaire J. Howard Marshall. She was attracted by his kindness.

10. In 1995, following a courtship lasting several months, 100-year-old Samuel Bukoro took the plunge and married 12-year-old Nyamihanda in Uganda.

But these sights at the altar appeared positively normal compared to that at St. Philip's Church, Birmingham, in 1797 where the bride stood naked throughout the ceremony. The reason behind her forsaking a dress and all other clothing was a superstition which held that if a wealthy woman married a man with debts, the creditors would be unable to reclaim their money from her if she was married naked.

10 ACTS OF LOVERS' REVENGE

1. After his wife left him, spurned husband Donald Niblett wrecked their Manchester home with a bulldozer, causing £15,000 of damage. By 1985, Niblett and his wife had been married for eight years but when they split up, he saw red, took the bulldozer from his workplace and began demolishing the house. Before he could complete the job, neighbours called the police. Niblett was bound over to keep the peace for two years.

2. When her husband Sir Peter Moon set up home in a Berkshire love-nest with a younger woman, Lady Sally Moon poured white gloss paint over his BMW, cut the sleeves off 32 of his £1,000 suits and distributed 70 of the finest bottles from his wine cellar on the doorsteps of her love rival's village.

3. In 1993, Lorena Bobbitt sliced off the penis of her husband, John Wayne Bobbitt, claiming that it was an act of retaliation following years of abuse. She was fêted by women all over America.

4. Following their marriage in 1688, Prince Antoine of Monaco was so incensed by his unfaithful wife, Marie de Lorraine, that he made straw effigies of all of her lovers. He then hanged them from the walls of the palace and made a humiliated Marie walk beneath them.

5. In 1988, an Egyptian belly-dancer paid back her unfaithful husband by going on a massive spending spree at his expense. She took his gold Ferrari and bought herself a fur coat and £46,000 of jewellery on his American Express card before flying to his villa in France and smashing the place up.

6. Divorced father Nigel Lambert dumped four lorries outside the Kent home of his ex-wife in 1995 following a dispute about maintenance payments.

7. On discovering that his wife, Queen Margaret, had entertained another man in her bed in 1315, French King Louis X arranged to have her smothered to death with a pillow on the same bed.

8. A year after installing a pretty air stewardess as his mistress in a London flat, a married pilot got fed up with her and ordered her to leave. The mistress asked for a few days to sort everything out, during which time the pilot set off on a

round-the-world flight. When he returned, the girl had gone and the flat was immaculately tidy except for the fact that the phone was off the hook. As he lifted the receiver, he heard an American voice endlessly repeating the time. Before departing, the irate mistress had dialled the speaking clock in Washington, D.C. The pilot was left with a phone bill for £1,200.

9.   Depressed following the break-up of his marriage, Raymond Orton burnt £100,000 in cash in the back garden of his Birmingham home in 1997 after withdrawing it from the joint account he shared with his ex-wife Brenda.

10. When Russian ruler Peter the Great (reigned 1682-1725) discovered that his wife Catherine had been unfaithful, he had the head of her lover, his own chamberlain William Mons, chopped off and inserted in a large jar of alcohol. He then placed the jar with its gruesome contents on Catherine's bedside table to remind her of her errant behaviour.

An unintentional, but nevertheless extremely effective, act of revenge was carried out by Czech housewife Vera Czermak. Distraught over her husband's unfaithfulness, she decided to throw herself out of the window of her third-floor Prague apartment, little realising that Mr. Czermak happened to be walking along the street below at precisely the same time. She landed directly on top of him, killing him outright. She survived.

10 INCOMPETENT CRIMINALS

1.   Three armed robbers, planning to raid a South Shields travel agents in July 1997, missed their intended target and burst into the optician's next door, waving a knife and an imitation sawn-off shotgun. Realising they were in the wrong shop, they made a hasty exit and finally made it to the travel agent's. They demanded to know where the safe was but lost their nerve and, instead of a £30,000 haul in traveller's cheques, they ended up with just a whisky bottle containing foreign coins donated to charity. Their getaway car then ran out of petrol and they abandoned it, leaving behind vital clues which led to their arrest. The judge described it as 'not a very efficient robbery'.

2.   In January 1998, a thief fled from the Yanmonoki Museum in central Japan with a 600-year-old Chinese platter dating from the Ming dynasty and worth an estimated £260,000. Making his escape, the thief dropped the priceless platter in the road, causing it to shatter into hundreds of pieces.

3.   In 1978, Charles A. Meriweather broke into a house in Baltimore and raped a woman occupant. He then demanded her money but when she told him she hadn't got much, he instructed her to write a cheque. She asked to whom she should make the cheque out and he replied: 'Charles A. Meriweather'. He was arrested within hours.

4.   In September 1992, robbers in Las Vegas held up a van thought to contain gambling chips, only to find that it was carrying potato chips instead.

5.   Having seized £4,500 from the Co-operative Stores at Perivale, Middlesex, in 1978, two robbers ran to their getaway car. But the driver turned the ignition key the wrong way and jammed the lock. The pair then tried another car, but managed to repeat the feat. They were quickly arrested.

6.   In 1998, a guard was caught smuggling a wad of money in his underpants out of a bank in Atlanta when a tiny security-dye capsule exploded, blowing a hole in his trousers.

7.   In 1998, a would-be Texas grocery store robber went to the trouble of disguising his face with a balaclava but forgot to remove from his breast pocket a laminated badge which bore his name, place of employment and position within the company – an oversight spotted by at least a dozen witnesses.

8.   A 1975 raid on the Royal Bank of Scotland in Rothesay degenerated into

farce when, on the way in, the three would-be raiders got stuck in the bank's revolving doors and had to be helped free by the staff. Undeterred, they returned a few minutes later and announced that it was a robbery. The staff thought it was a practical joke and refused to pay up. While one of the men vaulted the counter and twisted his ankle on landing, the other two made their escape, only to get trapped in the revolving doors again.

9.   Finding his car had been broken into and his pager stolen, Bristol warehouse manager David Withers decided to leave a message on the missing pager, saying the owner had won £500 in a competition and giving a number to ring. Shortly afterwards, his mobile phone rang and the voice on the other end, belonging to builder Justin Clark, agreed to a meeting to collect his prize. When Clark turned up, the police arrested him for handling stolen property. Mr. Withers said: 'I could not believe anybody would be that stupid, but obviously I came up against a total dimwit.'

10. Police had no difficulty catching a man who stole a barge on the River Thames in 1972. There was a dock strike on that day and his was the only craft moving.

10 JACK THE RIPPER SUSPECTS

1. JOSEPH BARNETT. The lover of Mary Jane Kelly, the Ripper's fifth and final victim. Supporters of Barnett as the Ripper suggest that he killed the other girls to scare Kelly into abandoning prostitution and then butchered her when she discovered his terrible secret. He fitted the description witnesses gave of the Ripper and also an FBI psychological profile of the killer. He knew the Whitechapel area well (the Ripper lured his victims into secluded corners and made a clean escape) and he had a big row with Kelly on the night before her murder.

2. WILLIAM BURY. He was hanged in Dundee in April 1889, five months after the final killing, for murdering his wife Ellen, also a prostitute. He was similar in height, age and build to descriptions given by Ripper witnesses and was living in Bow in the East End of London in 1888. And the deep abdominal mutilations on the body of his wife were like those on the Ripper's victims. Furthermore, chalked on the door to his tenement were the words: 'Jack Ripper is at the back of this door.'

3. MONTAGUE DRUITT. Barrister and schoolmaster whose body was recovered from the Thames on 31 December 1888 but had been there at least a month. He had committed suicide, possibly immediately after the final killing in early November. He was thought to have been sexually insane and even his own family suspected him.

4. WILLIAM GRANT GRAINGER. Irish ship's fireman and East End drunk who associated with loose women. Was known to have attacked prostitutes and had once trained as a medical student.

5. SIR WILLIAM GULL. Royal physician and Freemason whom conspiracy theorists believe carried out the murders to cover up the scandal of the Duke of Clarence and his bastard child. Gull was said to have been seen in Whitechapel on the nights of some of the murders.

6. AARON KOSMINSKI. Polish Jewish hairdresser whose insanity was blamed on his love of masturbation. He lived in Whitechapel, hated prostitutes and had homicidal tendencies. He was finally put in an asylum in 1890.

7. JAMES MAYBRICK. Liverpool cotton-broker who was murdered by his

wife Florence in April 1889. A journal purporting to be Maybrick's was signed 'Jack the Ripper' and detailed the Ripper's activities. Its authenticity, however, is open to question.

8. WALTER SICKERT. British artist who expressed considerable interest in the Ripper murders and was able to describe the injuries graphically. Supporters of Sickert for the Ripper claim that he was part of the Masonic conspiracy and that the 'Dear Boss' letter allegedly sent by the Ripper to the police was in Sickert's disguised handwriting.

9. DR. FRANCIS TUMBLETY. Irish-born doctor who spent most of his life in the U.S. He was charged in London with indecent assault against four men in 1888 but fled to America before the trial. His private life was shrouded in secrecy although he was believed to have hated women. When he died in 1903, a collection of preserved uteruses was found among his possessions. The American press printed rumours at the time that Tumblety was a Ripper suspect, heightened by stories of an American who was said to have taken bloodstained shirts to be laundered in Whitechapel.

10. PRINCE ALBERT VICTOR. The Duke of Clarence, grandson of Queen Victoria, was thought to have suffered from syphilis of the brain which drove him to commit the murders. Exponents of this theory suggest that there was then a cover-up at the highest level to preserve the good name of the Royal Family.

10 CON-ARTISTS

1. PHILIP ARNOLD and JOHN SLACK. In 1872, these veteran prospectors bought some diamonds in Europe for $35,000 and scattered them on land in Wyoming. They managed to convince the Bank of California in San Francisco that they had discovered a diamond field. Banker William Ralston paid them off with $700,000, thinking he had struck a good deal.

2. HUGO BARUCH. Born to a German father and English mother, Baruch made his name as literary con-man Jack Bilbo. Using that pseudonym, he sold a book, *Carrying a Gun for Al Capone,* to a German publisher in 1930. It was supposed to be a true account of the gangster's life by one of his henchmen but 'Bilbo' had never even been to Chicago, let alone carried a gun. By the time the truth was revealed, he had made a fortune from the book.

3. ARTHUR FURGUSON. Within the space of a few months in 1923, Scotsman Furguson succeeded in selling three different London landmarks to gullible American tourists. He sold Big Ben for a £1,000 deposit, Buckingham Palace for £2,000 and Nelson's Column for a princely £6,000. He then fled to the United States where he leased the White House for 99 years to a Texan cattle-rancher at the knockdown rent of $100,000 a year – the first year's rent payable in advance. His downfall came when he told an Australian visitor that, because of a widening scheme for New York Harbour, the Statue of Liberty would have to be dismantled and sold. He suggested that the statue would be perfectly suited to Sydney Harbour and the businessman was well on the way to raising the required $500,000 when his bank became suspicious. Furguson was arrested and sentenced to five years in jail.

4. MAUNDY GREGORY. The son of a Hampshire clergyman, Gregory sold titles to the vain, charging £10,000 for a knighthood, £35,000 for a baronetcy and £50,000 for a peerage. After finally being arrested in 1932, he was fined £50 and spent two months in jail.

5. OSCAR MERRIL HARTZELL. From 1921, Hartzell began a scam selling fake shares in the estate of Sir Francis Drake. He contacted as many American families as he could find with the surname Drake and was eventually accused of defrauding 270,000 people. The hoax netted him over $2,000,000.

6. VICTOR LUSTIG. An Austrian employee at the French Ministry of Works,

Lustig teamed up in 1925 with a small-time American crook named Collins and succeeded in selling the Eiffel Tower for scrap. Posing as a French government official with Collins as his secretary, Lustig invited tenders but hinted that a back-hander was needed to smooth the transaction. One André Poisson took the bait and by the time he realised he had been conned, Lustig and Collins had fled the country.

7. J. BAM MORRISON. When Morrison arrived at Wetumka, Oklahoma, in 1950, he claimed to be the advance publicity man for Bohn's United Circus which, he maintained, was due to hit town in three weeks. He sold advertising space to local traders...for a circus which didn't exist.

8. JAMES ADDISON REAVIS. By forging signatures, Reavis perfected a property swindle by which he was able to claim that he was the legal owner of 17,000 square miles of Arizona, including the capital, Phoenix. Soon the Southern Pacific Railway were paying him $50,000 and the Silver King Mining Company were handing him $25,000 just so that they could remain on 'his' land. The enterprise raked in $300,000 a year until he was arrested in 1895 and sentenced to six years.

9. PHILIP RILEY. Posing as a high-ranking British secret service agent who had been sent on secret anti-Communist assignments, Riley conned £2,000 out of a sympathetic Reading priest, Father Garlick. When Riley turned up with fake gunshot wounds and said he needed to flee the country, the priest gave him £1,000 for a holiday in Spain with his wife and two children. The law caught up with Riley in 1975 and he was jailed for two years.

10. JOSEPH WEILL. The man who inspired 'The Sting' operated at the start of the 20th century. He had a whole range of scams, which earned him some $6,000,000, but was best known for the fake bank con, whereby he rented an abandoned bank, hired billiard-hall customers as tellers, filled cash bags with lead discs and convinced businessmen that he had set up a genuine bank. He then waited for enough people to deposit large sums of money before shutting up shop and moving on to the next town.

10 MURDEROUS DOCTORS

1. MORRIS BOLBER of Philadelphia masterminded the murder of some 30 Italian patients during the 1930s so that he could claim on the insurance. He used a sandbag to induce cerebral haemorrhage in his victims and make death look like natural causes.

2. PIERRE BOUGRAT was convicted of murdering Jacques Rumebe, one of his patients, at Marseilles in 1925. Heavily in debt, Bougrat gave him an overdose of mercuric chloride, beat him up and robbed him of 20,000 francs.

3. ROBERT BUCHANAN set up in practice in New York in 1886 where he murdered his second wife, brothel-proprietress Anna Sutherland, for a $50,000 inheritance by giving her morphine. He was electrocuted at Sing Sing in 1895.

4. THOMAS NEILL CREAM, the Lambeth Poisoner, murdered four prostitutes with strychnine. On the scaffold, he is alleged to have said, 'I am Jack the – ' just as the bolt was drawn.

5. WILLIAM HENRY KING of Brighton, Ontario, poisoned his wife with arsenic so that he could have affairs with his patients. He was hanged in 1859.

6. GEORGE HENRY LAMSON murdered his brother-in-law by feeding him a slice of Dundee cake spiced with aconite. He was executed at Wandsworth in 1882.

7. WILLIAM PALMER, the Staffordshire Poisoner, may have murdered as many as 14 people, mainly with antimony.

8. EDWARD PRITCHARD poisoned his wife and mother-in-law with antimony and was hanged in Glasgow in 1865 before a 100,000 crowd, the last public hanging in Scotland.

9. WALTER WILKINS bludgeoned his wife to death at their home in Long Beach, Long Island, in 1919. He blamed burglars but was found guilty of murder. He subsequently hanged himself in jail.

10. ALICE WYNEKOOP, a 62-year-old Chicago widow, was found guilty of shooting her daughter-in-law, Rheta, in 1933. She was sentenced to 25 years.

10 PEOPLE WHO MISSED THE TITANIC

1. JOHN PIERPONT MORGAN (owner of the *Titanic*: blamed his absence on ill-health).

2. ROBERT BACON (U.S. Ambassador to Paris: cited business priorities).

3. FRANK ADELMAN (his wife had a premonition of danger so they caught a later ship).

4. MR. SHEPHERD (his wife sent a cable begging him to take another ship).

5. HENRY C. FRICK (his wife sprained her ankle).

6. HORACE HARDING (preferred the faster *Mauretania*).

7. GEORGE W. VANDERBILT (his mother-in-law was worried about maiden voyages).

8. JAMES V. O'BRIEN (detained by a court case in Ireland)

9. BERTRAM SLADE (crew member: missed the ship after being held up at a Southampton level crossing by a passing goods train)

10. EDWARD W. BILL (his wife had a premonition of impending doom).

10 ACCURATE PREMONITIONS

1.   David Booth, a Cincinnati office manager, phoned American Airlines after having nightmares on ten successive nights about a DC-10 crash. Three days later, on 25 May 1979, an American DC-10 crashed at Chicago, killing 273 people.

2.   The night before his attempt to break the world water speed record in *Bluebird* on 4 January 1967, Donald Campbell told a journalist: 'I have the most awful premonition that I'm going to get the chop. I've had the feeling for days.' The following morning, Campbell was killed in a 300 mph crash aboard *Bluebird*.

3.   King Wilhelm I of Württemberg completed the building of Rosenstein Castle in 1829 but didn't move in for another 35 years because a gypsy had prophesied that the King would die there. He finally took up residence in the castle in 1864 and died five days later.

4.   In 1896, German psychic Madame de Ferriëm had a vision of an impending disaster. She saw bodies being carried out of a coal mine at Dux in Bohemia in bitterly cold weather. Her vision was published in a German newspaper in 1899. The following year, in a extremely cold spell, hundreds of people were killed by an explosion in a coal mine at Dux.

5.   In 1980, American actor David Janssen, former star of The Fugitive, had a dream in which he saw himself being carried out in a coffin after a heart attack. He consulted a psychic who advised him to go for a check-up, but it was too late. Two days later, Janssen died from a massive heart attack.

6.   As Napoleon's troops advanced into Russia in 1812 Countess Toutschkoff, the wife of a Russian general, dreamt that she was in a room at an inn in a strange town. In her dream, her father entered the room, holding her small son by the hand and told her that her husband had been killed by the French. 'He has fallen,' said the father. 'He has fallen at Borodino.' After having the same dream twice more, she told her husband and they consulted a map but could find nowhere called Borodino. On 7 September 1812 the Russians engaged the French in a fierce battle at a village called Borodino, west of Moscow. The Countess and her family stayed at a nearby inn while her husband commanded the reserve forces. The following morning, her father came into the room, holding her small son by the hand, and told her that her husband had been slain. 'He has fallen,' he said. 'He has fallen at Borodino.'

7.   In May 1812, a Cornish innkeeper had a dream on three successive nights about the shooting of a prominent politician in the House of Commons. He had no idea of the identity of the man in his dream but a friend said the description matched that of the Prime Minister, Spencer Perceval. Several days later, news reached Cornwall that Perceval had been shot dead in the lobby of the House of Commons.

8.   Nashville psychic Spencer Thornton correctly predicted the first three horses home in the 1959 Kentucky Derby. Four days before the race, he wrote the names on a piece of paper which was then sealed, unread, in an envelope and placed in a bank vault. The vault was opened after the race and the paper bore the names of the first three finishers.

9.   Julia Grant, wife of US General Ulysses S. Grant, woke on the morning of 14 April 1865 with a strong feeling that she and her husband should get out of Washington. General Grant had been due to attend the theatre with President Lincoln that night but his wife was so insistent that he pulled out. Leaving the city, the Grants passed John Wilkes Booth on his way to assassinate Lincoln at the theatre. Grant was also found to be on Booth's death list.

10. Half-way through a financial meeting, just before 5pm on 7 October 1571, Pope Pius V suddenly announced that there had been a Christian victory. Two weeks later on 21 October, a messenger from Venice rode into Rome with news that a Christian fleet had vanquished the Turks at Lepanto. The official report of the battle stated that victory had been confirmed shortly before 5pm on 7 October.

10 POSSIBLE CASES OF SPONTANEOUS HUMAN COMBUSTION

1. On the morning of 2 July 1951 Mrs. Mary Reeser, a 67-year-old widow from St. Petersburg, Florida, was found reduced to ashes in an apartment which showed little sign of damage. The only sign of fire was a small charred area in the middle of the floor in which there were blackened chair springs and Mrs. Reeser's remains. Tremendous heat must have been necessary to incinerate the body, yet only the chair and the table next to it were damaged. The carpet on which the chair stood had not even burned through. Part of the ceiling was coated with soot but a pile of newspapers in the room remained intact. Experts were unable to determine the cause of the fire. Dr. William M. Krogman, a physical anthropologist at the University of Pennsylvania, commented: 'They say truth often is stranger than fiction and this case proves it.'

2. In the summer of 1922 at Sydenham, South London, 68-year-old widow Euphemia Johnson returned home from a shopping trip and made a pot of tea. She carried the hot cup to a table near the window. Later she was discovered fallen from her chair, her body consisting of nothing more than a pile of bones inside clothes which weren't even burnt. The varnish on the chair had bubbled slightly from the heat but the table-cloth was undamaged.

3. On 1 March 1953 at Greenville, South Carolina, Waymon Wood was found 'crisped black' in the front seat of his closed car. Only the windscreen had been affected by the heat and there was half a tank of petrol in the car which hadn't ignited.

4. One evening in the late 1950s, 19-year-old Maybelle Andrews was dancing with her boyfriend Billy Clifford in a London dance-hall when she suddenly burst into flames. The fire raged from her back and chest, enveloping her head and igniting her hair. At the inquest, Billy Clifford said: 'I know it sounds incredible, but it appeared to me that the flames burst outwards, as if they originated within her body.' The verdict was 'death by misadventure, caused by fire of unknown origin.'

5. At Sowerby Bridge near Halifax in 1899, Sara Kirby found her four-year-old daughter Amy ablaze in her bed. There was no evidence of matches or charred paper. As a distraught Sara went to impart the sad news to her estranged husband who lived nearby, a messenger informed her that her other daughter,

five-year-old Alice, had also been found on fire in her bed at her father's house. The two fatal fires had broken out at precisely the same time.

6.   On 9 October 1980 Jeanna Winchester, riding in a car in Jacksonville, Florida, suddenly burst into bright yellow flames. Examination of the car revealed little or no fire damage. There was no spilt petrol, the victim wasn't smoking and the car widow was up so nobody could have thrown anything into the vehicle. A fire officer remarked: 'I've never seen anything like it in 12 years in the force.'

7.   In 1986 at Essex County, New York, a retired fireman was reduced to a pile of bones and 31/2lb of ash following an intense fire. Most of the damage to the house was caused by smoke and the blaze had been so localised that a box of matches, a few feet from his remains, hadn't ignited.

8.   In 1943 Madge Knight died in a Chichester hospital after a curious fire at her home. She had been lying in bed when something unknown had set fire to her back. Yet the bedclothes weren't even scorched.

9. Walking along a London street in 1985, a 19-year-old man caught fire from the waist up. He said it was like being doused in burning petrol, yet no traces were found.

10. At Bladeboro, North Carolina, in 1932, a cotton dress being worn by Mrs. Charles Williamson suddenly burst into flames. She was not standing near any fire nor had her dress been in contact with any flammable substance. Over the next few days, a pair of Mr. Williamson's trousers, hanging in the wardrobe, also mysteriously caught fire, followed by a bed and a pair of curtains in an unoccupied room. In each case, the items burned with bluish jet-like flames, yet adjacent objects remained unaffected. Experts were unable to shed any light on the fires.

10 MILITARY MISHAPS

1. The Prussian commanders of the 18th century seemed to suffer from poor eyesight. In 1757, a Prussian army was forced to abandon a safe escape route when they saw the road blocked by what they took to be batteries of Austrian artillery. It turned out to be nothing more deadly than a herd of cattle. In the same year, the Prussians failed to press home their advantage against the French when they mistook young fir trees for French infantry marching to the rescue.

2. In 1836, Mexican troops were engaged in skirmishes with the Texans. On the hot afternoon of 20 April of that year, Mexican General Antonio Lopez de Santa Anna ordered his troops to take a siesta, during which the entire Mexican army was routed by the Texans in just 18 minutes.

3. At the Battle of Karansebes in 1788, 10,000 Austrian soldiers were killed or injured by their own side when drunken comrades started shouting that the Turks were upon them. In the darkness and confusion, the Austrians began firing indiscriminately at each other.

4. When the pretender Sultan of Zanzibar, Said Khalid, refused to vacate the palace in 1896, the British fleet declared war. Thirty-eight minutes later, the war was over. Zanzibar's only warship, the ageing Glasgow, was sunk by just two shells and the palace was destroyed.

5. In 1916, the much-prized Fort Douaumont at Verdun in France was captured by a single German soldier after the French General Chrétien (pronounced 'cretin') forgot to pass on a message. His orders were to defend the fort to the last man, but when he went on leave he forgot to tell his successor and so the mighty fortress was manned by just a handful of gunners who were taken completely by surprise. Twenty were arrested while attending a lecture!

6. When relations with Bolivia soured in 1865, Queen Victoria ordered the Royal Navy to send six gunboats to Bolivia and sink its fleet. Her admirals quietly pointed out that Bolivia had no coast and therefore no fleet, whereupon the Queen sent for a map and a pair of scissors and cut Bolivia from the world.

7. When Viking leader Harald Hardrada invaded England in 1066, he quickly defeated the northern militia near York and waited for the big showdown with King Harold II who was on the south coast anticipating a Norman invasion. Not expecting the English troops for days, Hardrada and his men camped on

meadows either side of the River Derwent at Stamford Bridge and, since it was such a lovely day, many of the Vikings removed their armour and indulged in a spot of sunbathing. They didn't even rouse themselves when they saw approaching soldiers, presuming them to be a detachment of Vikings. By the time they realised it was the English army, it was too late. The Vikings were overwhelmed and Hardrada was killed.

8. During the Second World War, the Russians invented the 'dog mine'. The idea was to train dogs to associate food with the underneath of tanks and thus, with bombs strapped to their backs, to wreak havoc on the German Panzer divisions. Alas, the dogs associated food solely with *Russian* tanks and forced an entire Soviet division to retreat. The plan was quickly scrapped.

9. Famous American General Thomas 'Stonewall' Jackson was devoutly religious and considered fighting on a Sunday to be sinful. In 1862, at the height of the Battle of Mechanicsville in the American Civil War, he stood alone praying on a nearby hill, steadfastly refusing to speak to anyone all afternoon. With nobody to guide them, his Confederate troops suffered huge losses.

10. Japanese soldier Hiroo Onoda continued fighting the Second World War until 1974 from the remote Philippine island of Lubang. Resisting all attempts to make him surrender, he dismissed stories that the war was over as cunning American propaganda. Search parties were greeted with a hail of bullets and it was only when his old commanding officer, Major Yoshimi Taniguchi, flew out to Lubang and ordered him to lay down his arms that Onoda finally complied.

20 CHOICE POLITICAL INSULTS

1. 'A triumph of the embalmer's art' (GORE VIDAL on RONALD REAGAN).

2. 'He makes George Bush seem like a personality' (JACKIE MASON on JOHN MAJOR).

3. NANCY ASTOR: 'Winston, if I were your wife, I would put poison in your coffee.' WINSTON CHURCHILL: 'Nancy, if I were your husband, I would drink it.'

4. 'He is a sheep in sheep's clothing' (WINSTON CHURCHILL on CLEMENT ATTLEE).

5. 'A modest little man with much to be modest about' (CHURCHILL again on ATTLEE).

6. 'He has a bungalow mind' (Former U.S. President THOMAS WOODROW WILSON on his successor WARREN HARDING).

7. 'I feel certain that he would not recognise a generous impulse if he met it on the street' (WILLIAM HOWARD TAFT on his 1912 U.S. Presidential opponent THOMAS WOODROW WILSON).

8. 'He could not see a belt without hitting below it' (MARGOT ASQUITH on DAVID LLOYD GEORGE).

9. 'RICHARD NIXON impeached himself. He gave us Gerald Ford as his revenge' (U.S. politician BELLA ABZUG on Tricky Dickie).

10. 'Nixon's motto was, "If two wrongs don't make a right, try three"' (U.S. writer NORMAN COUSINS).

11. 'A semi-house-trained polecat' (MICHAEL FOOT on NORMAN TEBBIT).

12. 'A kind of walking obituary for the Labour Party' (CHRIS PATTEN on MICHAEL FOOT).

13. 'If a traveller were informed that such a man was the Leader of the House of Commons, he might begin to comprehend how the Egyptians worshipped an insect' (BENJAMIN DISRAELI on British Prime Minister LORD JOHN RUSSELL).

14. 'GERRY FORD is so dumb that he can't fart and chew gum at the same

time' (former U.S. President LYNDON B. JOHNSON).

15. 'He is not only a bore, but he bores for England' (MALCOLM MUGGERIDGE on ANTHONY EDEN).

16. 'I wouldn't say she is open-minded on the Middle East, so much as empty-headed. She probably thinks Sinai is the plural of sinus' (JONATHAN AITKEN on MARGARET THATCHER).

17. 'The self-appointed king of the gutter' (MICHAEL HESELTINE on NEIL KINNOCK).

18. WILLIAM EWART GLADSTONE: 'Mr. Disraeli, you will probably die by the hangman's noose or a vile disease.' BENJAMIN DISRAELI: 'Sir, that depends on whether I embrace your principles or your mistress.'

19. HARRY TRUMAN proves that old adage that any man can become President of the United States' (U.S. politician NORMAN THOMAS).

20. 'A shiver looking for a spine to run up' (HAROLD WILSON on EDWARD HEATH).

10 MAD MOTORISTS

1. Former traffic policeman William Alexander set out to drive the 15 miles from Hereford to Ross-on-Wye in 1996. He and his wife were found confused 36 hours later, after a 1,000-mile drive, going the wrong way down the M1 near Barnsley.

2. In 1992 Clive Richley was stopped by police for driving his Reliant Robin at 104 mph on the M20 in Kent.

3. A mix-up between the accelerator and the clutch caused Mrs. Beatrice Park to drive into the River Wey at Guildford during her 1969 driving test. She and the examiner climbed on to the car roof and waited to be rescued. He was later sent home in a state of shock. When Mrs. Park asked whether she had passed, she was told: ' We cannot say until we have seen the examiner's report.'

4. In 1994 a nun who said she was rushing an injured dog to the vet was fined for reckless driving after refusing to stop for armed police in New York State.

5. Assuming she had failed after clipping the kerb during her 1995 test at Lowestoft, Tcheeka Johnson punched the examiner on the leg, screeched to a halt and pushed her out of the passenger door.

6. In 1989, a rare red-crested pochard from Siberia was killed in a collision with a car driven by former police sergeant Paul Corney near Portsmouth. Corney was chased by irate twitchers waving binoculars.

7. Trying to test his oil level manually, a Wakefield motorcyclist got his finger stuck in the oil tank and had to summon the fire brigade to free him.

8. Leroy Linen, a scrap-metal dealer from the Bronx, was banned from driving 633 times between 1990 and 1994.

9. Helen Ireland of Auburn, California, failed her test in the first seconds when she drove straight into the wall of the test centre.

10. In 1996, Sue Evan-Jones from Yate, near Bristol, failed her first test – after taking 1,500 lessons over 26 years at a cost of more than £18,000.

10 PEOPLE WHO CLAIM TO HAVE SEEN THE LOCH NESS MONSTER

1. DUNCAN CAMPBELL (1527) said he saw a terrible beast on the loch shore.

2. E.H. BRIGHT (1880) said he saw a monster leave a wooded area at Drumnadrochit and waddle into the water on four legs.

3. WILLIAM MACGRUER (1912) said he saw a yellow, camel-like creature with long legs slide into Loch Ness at Inchnacardoch Bay.

4. ALFRED CRUICKSHANK (1923) said he was driving at Invermoriston when he saw a khaki-green creature with four webbed, elephant-like legs.

5. ELEANOR PRICE-HUGHES (1933) said she saw a large creature emerge from some bushes and vanish into the loch.

6. COLONEL L. FORDYCE (1933) said he was near Foyers when he saw a grey creature with a small head on a long neck and a hump on its back, a cross between a large horse and a camel.

7. GEORGE SPICER (1933) said he was driving between Dores and Foyers when the monster crossed the road in front of the car before sliding into the loch.

8. JEAN MACDONALD and PATRICIA HARVEY (1934) said they were at Inchnacardoch Bay when they saw the monster crossing a stream in the moonlight. They described it as having a dark body tapering towards the tail and with four thick short legs.

9. MARGARET MUNRO (1934) said she saw a dark grey creature with a large body and a giraffe-like neck.

10. TORQUIL MACLEOD (1960) saw a grey-black mass with an elephant-like trunk.

10 GREAT ECCENTRICS

1. Prussian Field Marshal Prince Gebhard Leberecht von Blücher, whose timely intervention sealed Wellington's triumph at Waterloo, was convinced that he was pregnant with an elephant, fathered on him by a French soldier. He saw French conspiracies everywhere and used to totter around his room on tiptoe in the belief that the French had heated the floor to a temperature greater than human flesh could endure.

2. 19th-century naturalist Frank Buckland used to serve the most bizarre meals to guests at his London home. Dishes included roast parrot, stewed sea slug and mice on buttered toast. He even tried to make elephant's trunk soup but, in spite of being boiled for several days, the trunk was still too tough to eat. Animals ran amok in the house – pet monkeys were given a glass of beer every night and a drop of port on Sundays – while one lady guest stumbled over a dead hippopotamus on the stairs.

3. Legendary French actress Sarah Bernhardt's travelling companion on tour was a silk-lined coffin. She used to learn her lines while lying in it and allegedly entertained her string of lovers in it too.

4. California rifle heiress Sarah Winchester was told by a medium that, in order to guarantee a long life, she must build a mansion and keep adding to it. So for the next 38 years, until her eventual death in 1922, she constantly enlarged Winchester House near San Francisco so that it finished up with 2,000 doors and 10,000 windows. She was also obsessed by the number 13, so the house had 13 bathrooms, 13 hooks in every cupboard and 13 candles in every chandelier. In the sewing-room, she insisted on there being 13 windows and 13 doors. There were even 13 parts to her will...which she signed 13 times.

5. The English-born Comtesse de Noailles (1824-1908) was obsessed with her health and, wherever she lived, always kept a herd of cows tethered near the windows because she thought their methane gas was beneficial. At night, she used to wrap a pair of socks stuffed with squirrel-fur around her head and cover her chest with the skin of a Norwegian wildcat – to ward off germs.

6. 19th century French poet Gérard de Nerval was in the habit of taking a lobster for a walk on the end of a length of ribbon through the Palais Royal gardens in Paris. He ended up hanging himself from a lamp-post.

7.   Greek General Hajianestis, who led his country in the 1921 war with Turkey, often refused to get out of bed because he thought his legs were made of glass or sugar and were so brittle they would collapse. On other occasions, he simply pretended to be dead. It came as little surprise when he was relieved of his duties.

8.   18th-century Shropshire squire Jack Mytton was a heavy drinker who used to go hunting stark naked. To the horror of guests, he once rode a bear into his dining-room. He also came up with an ingenious cure for hiccups – it was to set fire to his own night-shirt while still wearing it. He suffered serious burns but his hiccups had gone!

9.   Wealthy English landowner and author William Beckford (1760-1844) was an inveterate traveller and was accompanied everywhere by his personal doctor, cook, valet and baker, plus two dogs, three footmen, 24 musicians and a Spanish dwarf. On a trip to Portugal, he even took with him a flock of sheep – to improve the view from the window. He also took his own wallpaper and refused to occupy any bedroom until it had been redecorated to his taste.

10. William John Cavendish Bentinck Scott, the fifth Duke of Portland, never invited anyone to his Nottinghamshire home, Welbeck Abbey. Only his valet was allowed near him. In the event of illness, the doctor had to wait outside while the valet took the Duke's pulse. To deter conversation, the doors of each room in the house had double letter-boxes, one for incoming and one for outgoing notes. To avoid being seen by anyone, he built miles of tunnels beneath his estates through which his coach could pass in secret, as well as an underground ballroom, underground stables – and an underground roller-skating rink.

THE FIRST 10 WOMEN IN SPACE

1. VALENTINA TERESHKOVA (USSR) 1963, Vostok VI.

2. SVETLANA SAVITSKAYA (USSR) 1982, Soyuz T7.

3. SALLY RIDE (USA) 1983, STS-7 Challenger Shuttle.

4. JUDITH RESNIK (USA) September 1984, STS-41-D Discovery Shuttle.

5. KATHRYN SULLIVAN (USA) October 1984, STS-41-G Challenger Shuttle.

6. ANNA FISHER (USA) November 1984, STS-51-A Discovery Shuttle.

7. MARGARET SEDDON (USA) April 1985, STS-51-D Discovery Shuttle.

8. SHANNON LUCID (USA) June 1985, STS-51-G Discovery Shuttle.

9. LOREN ACTON (USA) August 1985, STS-51-F Challenger Shuttle.

10. BONNIE DUNBAR (USA) November 1985, STS-61-A Challenger Shuttle.

CHAPTER

2

ALL CREATURES
GREAT
AND SMALL

20 NATURALISED BRITISH BREEDS

1. RED-NECKED WALLABY (Australia).

2. MONGOLIAN GERBIL.

3. JAPANESE SIKA DEER.

4. CHINESE WATER DEER.

5. NORTH AMERICAN MINK.

6. COYPU (South America).

7. EDIBLE DORMOUSE (Europe).

8. GREY SQUIRREL (United States).

9. FALLOW DEER (Southern Europe).

10. BLACK RAT (South-East Asia).

11. BROWN RAT (South-East Asia).

12. SOAY SHEEP (Europe).

13. CANADA GOOSE.

14. MANDARIN DUCK (Eastern Asia).

15. EDIBLE FROG (Europe).

16. COMMON CARP (Central Asia).

17. MARSH FROG (Europe).

18. PHEASANT (Asia).

19. CAPERCAILLIE (Northern Europe).

20. RUDDY DUCK (United States).

10 BREEDS WHICH ARE EXTINCT IN THE UK

1. WILD OX (7th century BC).

2. ELK (c. 500BC).

3. PELICAN (5th century).

4. REINDEER (9th century).

5. BROWN BEAR (11th century).

6. BEAVER (12th century).

7. CRANE (16th century).

8. WILD BOAR (17th century).

9. WOLF (18th century).

10. GREAT AUK (19th century).

Beavers used to be plentiful in Wales and Yorkshire. Indeed the town of Beverley, near Hull, is said to have derived its name from the number of beavers found in the vicinity. But the creature's last stronghold was in Scotland. The wolf became extinct in England in the early 16th century but survived in Scotland until 1743 and in Ireland until around 1770. There were stories about packs of wolves attacking horses in County Kildare around 1720 but thereafter the numbers diminished, mostly shot by fearful locals. The bear population once straddled the country from Devon and Cambridgeshire right up to Scotland, and when the native species died out foreign bears were imported to perpetuate the cruel medieval sport of bear-baiting. As late as 1880 two Frenchmen were charged with 'exhibiting a bear in the streets, to the danger of the public' after they were seen with a bear at Catford Bridge, South London. The bear was dancing, turning somersaults, climbing a pole and terrifying passing horses. The magistrate freed the two men on condition that they and their bear left the country.

10 SPIDERS TO AVOID

1. BRAZILIAN HUNTSMAN.

2. SYDNEY FUNNELWEB (Australia).

3. RED-BACK SPIDER (Australia).

4. BLACK WIDOW (Europe and the Americas).

5. TARANTULA (Europe and the Americas).

6. BROWN RECLUSE SPIDER (Americas).

7. WHITE-TAILED SPIDER (Australia).

8. SPITTING SPIDER (The tropics).

9. WOODLOUSE SPIDER (Europe).

10. *SICARIUS HAHNII* (South Africa).

Although nearly all spiders are venomous, only a handful are dangerous to humans. The American black widow is 15 times more venomous than a rattlesnake but the strongest venom is thought to be that of the Brazilian huntsman, a particularly aggressive species. It likes to hide in shoes and clothes, and a huntsman is said to have killed two Brazilian children when it got into their bed one night. The legendary tarantula (a large wolf spider) gets its name from its links with the Italian town of Taranto. Its bite was believed to be fatal unless victims danced furiously until they dropped from sheer exhaustion. Tarantella dancing is still popular in Italy, although the tarantula has been much-maligned since its bite causes nothing more than a sharp pain. The deadly spider from legend was more than likely a different species altogether – the European black widow.

THE 10 MOST VENOMOUS SNAKES IN THE WORLD

1. THE FIERCE SNAKE (Australia).

2. ISLAND FER-DE-LANCE (Brazil).

3. BLACK MAMBA (Southern and Central Africa).

4. TAIPAN (Australia and New Guinea).

5. TIGER SNAKE (Australia).

6. COMMON KRAIT (Southern Asia).

7. DEATH ADDER (Australia).

8. BROWN SNAKE (Australia).

9. CARPET VIPER (Africa and Asia).

10. BEAKED SEA SNAKE (Pacific Ocean).

A single male fierce snake possesses enough venom to kill 250,000 mice. Fortunately it lives in the remotest part of the Australian outback where it hardly ever comes into contact with man. As a result, there have never been any human fatalities although a bite would undoubtedly be lethal if only because medical aid would take so long to arrive. The island fer-de-lance, which inhabits a small island off the coast of Brazil, feeds entirely on sparrows and must possess a strong venom so that a bitten bird falls near enough for the snake to eat it. The mainland fer-de-lance, whilst still a formidable adversary, has slightly less potent venom. Of the snakes which come into contact with man, the black mamba is probably the most feared on account of its size and speed. Yet the snake which is probably responsible for more human deaths than any other is the saw-scaled or carpet viper because it is relatively common and lives around highly-populated regions.

10 SNAKES WHICH EAT OTHER SNAKES

1. NORTH AMERICAN KINGSNAKE.

2. TEXAS CORAL SNAKE.

3. RING-NECKED SNAKE.

4. SHARP-TAILED SNAKE.

5. KING COBRA.

6. KRAIT.

7. ASIAN CORAL SNAKE.

8. BLACK-HEADED PYTHON.

9. PAPUAN PYTHON.

10. BURROWING ASP.

If the need arises, quite a few breeds of snake will eat other species – it is not unknown for a grass snake to devour an adder – but the above ten specialise in a diet of serpents. The North American kingsnake is particularly bold and will even attack a deadly rattlesnake since it has a degree of immunity from the rattlesnake's venom. The sharp-tailed snake feeds mainly on the crowned snake of Florida while the burrowing asp has specialised fangs which enable it to bite its prey in confined spaces. Thus it is particularly fond of other burrowing snakes, especially the slim-collared snake. Pythons are renowned for being able to devour huge animals – a pig is a mere snack to a fully-grown python – and a Papuan python was once found with a carpet python in its stomach.

20 CREATURES WHICH MATE FOR LIFE

1. GIBBON.

2. GORILLA.

3. ORANG-UTAN.

4. BEAVER.

5. HOODED SEAL.

6. BADGER.

7. FOX.

8. MONGOOSE.

9. TERMITE.

10. SWAN.

11. STORK.

12. ALBATROSS.

13. PENGUIN.

14. JACKDAW.

15. GREY GOOSE.

16. MONTAGUE'S HARRIER.

17. BUDGERIGAR.

18. LOVEBIRD.

19. VULTURE.

20. PIGEON.

10 CREATURES WITH THEIR OWN LIGHTS

1. FIREFLY.

2. GLOW-WORM.

3. SEA ANEMONE.

4. CORAL SHRIMP.

5. SQUID.

6. INDO-PACIFIC FISH.

7. BATHYSPHERE FISH.

8. HATCHET FISH.

9. LANTERN FISH.

10. ANGLER FISH.

The angler fish lives in the depths of the Atlantic where there is no light. Above its mouth is a bony projection and from this stretches a long, thin line like a fishing rod, the end of which is illuminated by bacteria. The angler fish waves this rod about, causing smaller fish to investigate in the belief that the moving light is food. All the while, the angler fish keep its body perfectly still...until the tiny fish come within eating distance. The hatchet fish emits greenish-white lights which, because they look like a row of teeth, deter predators, and the bathysphere fish is so-called because the pale blue, glowing spots along its sides resemble the portholes of a diving-bell. It has two long tentacles with luminous ends which attract the fish on which it feeds. Fireflies glow in the dark to attract mates but, placed inside perforated gourd lanterns, have been used as a form of cheap lighting in places like Brazil and China. The glow from six large fireflies provides enough light to read a book.

10 MASTERS OF CAMOUFLAGE

1. CHAMELEON.

2. STICK INSECT.

3. PRAYING MANTIS.

4. ELEPHANT HAWK MOTH.

5. LEAF INSECT.

6. COPPERBAND BUTTERFLY FISH.

7. KING PAGE BUTTERFLY.

8. CRANE-FLY.

9. HORNED TOAD.

10. ROCK PTARMIGAN.

When threatened, the caterpillar of the elephant hawk moth retracts its legs and rolls over to reveal a pair of false 'eyes' like a deadly pit viper. Wisely, the predator tends to keep its distance. The caterpillar of the king page butterfly has an equally effective although less intimidating disguise – bird droppings. The pupa of the crane-fly, which lives in tropical rain forests, camouflages itself as a drop of water and hangs from the edge of a palm leaf, while the leaf insect has markings which resemble the veins of a leaf. For added authenticity, it has blotches to look like the holes in a leaf and its body has a brown edging to suggest a dying leaf. Like the chameleon, the horned toad changes colour to blend in with its surroundings – in this case, desert rocks. The copperband butterfly fish is designed in such a way that an enemy will think its tail is its head and will therefore snap at the wrong end. The fish also has a false eye near the tail, its real eye being concealed in a dark vertical stripe.

10 UNUSUAL BIRDS

1. The hummingbird is the only bird that can fly backwards. It achieves this feat by beating its wings up and down at great speed (some species have a wing-beat of 80 per second).

2. The male bower-bird from Australia attracts a female by building an elaborate love bower. After building a little hut out of twigs, he decorates it with flowers and colourful objects such as feathers, fruit, shells and pebbles or sometimes glass and paper if the nest is near civilisation. One particular species (the atlas bower-bird) actually paints the walls by dipping bark or leaves into the blue or dark green saliva he secretes. The entire bower-building procedure can take months and the bird will often change the decorations until he is happy with them. When finally satisfied, he performs a love dance outside the bower, sometimes offering the female a pretty item from his collection.

3. The home of the Great Indian hornbill is a prison. When the female is ready to lay her eggs, she hides in a hole in a tree. The male then seals up the hole, leaving just a narrow slit through which he passes food. The female stays in there until the chicks are a few months old when she breaks out and helps the male with feeding duties.

4. The secretary bird may have long legs but it can't run. Instead it hops along the African scrubland in search of its staple diet of snakes and lizards. The bird gets its name from the 20 black crest feathers behind its ears which are reminiscent of the old quill pens once favoured by secretaries.

5. The eyes of the woodcock are set so far back in its head that it has a 360-degree field of vision, enabling it to see all round and even over the top of its head.

6. The quetzal from Central America has such a long tail (up to 3ft long) that it can't take of from a branch in the normal way without ripping its tail to shreds. So instead it launches itself backwards into space like a parachutist leaving an aircraft. The quetzal nests in hollow trees but has to reverse into the hole. Once inside, it curls its tail over its head and out of the hole.

7. The wandering albatross has the largest wing-span of any bird and can glide for six days without ever beating its wings. It can also sleep in mid-air.

8. The young hoatzin of the Amazon forests has claws on its wings to help it clamber through the dense undergrowth. The bird is a throwback to the prehistoric archaeopteryx which also had three claws on each wing.

9.   The kiwi is the only bird with nostrils at the tip of its beak. Whereas other birds hunt by sight or hearing, the national bird of New Zealand uses its beaky nostrils to sniff out food at night. Although the kiwi is roughly the same size as a chicken, it lays an egg which is ten times larger than a hen's.

10. The little tailorbird uses its sharp beak to pierce holes along the edges of two leaves. It then constructs a nest by neatly stitching the leaves together with pieces of grass.

10 CREATURES WITH ODD SEXUAL HABITS

1.   After mating, the male garter snake from North America seals up the female's sexual opening with a plug made from kidney secretions. This acts as a form of chastity belt, ensuring that the female is fertilised by the first male to mate with her.

2.   The male Darwin's frog, found on the southern coast of Chile, swallows the eggs his mate lays and keeps them in a sac under his chin. When the tadpoles are big enough, he opens his mouth and releases them.

3.   The seahorse is the only creature where the male becomes pregnant. When ready to breed, the female inserts a nipple-like appendage into the male and releases her eggs into a special pouch in his stomach. He then discharges his sperm over them and, once the eggs are fertilised, his belly takes on the rounded shape.

4.   For the mouthbrooder catfish, which lives off Mozambique, fertilisation takes place in the female's mouth. She releases her ova into the water and then turns round and swallows them. When the male swims by, she mistakes the distinctive spots on his anal fin for more eggs. As she opens her mouth to swallow them, she ends up catching his sperm instead. The young fish remain in the mouth until they have absorbed their egg yolk before finally venturing out to feed. Even then, they often return to the safety of the mouth at night or if they feel threatened.

5.   Since the female bedbug has no sexual opening, the male drills his own vagina, using his curved, pointed penis as a drill. The male then inserts his sperm and the blood-sucking female feeds on some of it when blood is in short supply.

6.   The female praying mantis eats her partner after sex. During copulation, the larger female hooks her deadly arms around him and begins nibbling away at him. Sometimes she doesn't even wait until copulation has finished before turning him into her next meal, but his sex drive is so strong that he can carry on even while being eaten.

7.   The male moth mite is born as a mature insect and at birth helps his mother by seizing his sisters as they emerge from the sexual cavity and dragging them out of the birth passage with his hind legs. He then mates with them and continues to hover around his mother's birth passage ready to snap up the next

batch of sisters.

8.   The legs of the male water mite sometimes double as sexual organs and can be used to penetrate the female. While mating, he pins the female to the ground with tiny hooks so that she can barely move. He also glues himself to her with a special secretion so that there is no escape.

9.   The male swamp antechinus, a mouse-like marsupial from Australia, is the only mammal which dies after mating. The males dedicate their lives to a round of non-stop copulation until they literally drop dead. The majority die of starvation because they have no time to feed between sex.

10.   The male tick doesn't have a penis so instead he pokes around in the female's vagina with his nose. When her opening is large enough, he turns around and deposits sperm from his rear on to the entrance of her orifice. He then uses his nose to push the sperm deeper into the vagina.

10 SEX MACHINES

1. DESERT RAT.

2. MULTIMAMMATE RAT.

3. COD.

4. MUSSEL.

5. LEMMING.

6. RABBIT.

7. PRAIRIE DOG.

8. MOLE RAT.

9. FRUIT FLY.

10. TERMITE.

The desert rat is the ultimate sex machine, a creature which makes the rabbit look positively celibate. For the desert rat has sex as often as 122 times per hour. Blessed with no fewer than 24 teats, the multimammate rat can give birth to up to 120 offspring per year. Even this is small fry compared to certain insects and sea creatures. A termite is capable of laying an egg every two seconds while a mussel can produce 25 million eggs at a time and a cod eight million at a time. You'd need a lot of chips to go with that! A pair of Indian pythons were once observed copulating for 180 days and stick insects aren't usually in much of a hurry either. They have been known to keep it up for 79 successive days. The poor old Scandinavian lemmings become so agitated by the number of young in the colony that a fear of overcrowding is thought to be the reason behind their mass march of self-destruction. Desperate to reach the wide-open spaces of the sea, many plunge headlong to their deaths over cliffs while others drown en route trying to cross rivers.

10 COUNTRIES WHERE SHEEP OUTNUMBER PEOPLE

1. FALKLAND ISLANDS.

2. NEW ZEALAND.

3. AUSTRALIA.

4. URUGUAY.

5. MONGOLIA.

6. SYRIA.

7. NAMIBIA.

8. ICELAND.

9. MAURITANIA.

10. SOMALIA.

Whoever has stayed awake long enough to count the world's sheep estimates that there are in the region of 1,200,000,000 which works out at an average of around one sheep for every four people. However, in certain countries the ratio is definitely in favour of the sheep – nowhere more so than the Falkland Islands with a human population of under 2,000 but a sheep population of 700,000, making 350 sheep for every person. In New Zealand, there are approximately 20 sheep per human and in Australia, around ten. Lower down the list, Iceland boasts a ratio of three sheep per person and even Ireland has 1.7 woolly-heads for every human specimen.

10 PECULIAR PLANTS AND TREES

1.   The sausage tree of Africa *(Kigelia africana)* gets its name from the long, thick fruits which hang from the tree like sausages. The fruits have a different connotation to the Ashanti people of Ghana who call it the 'hanging breast tree', comparing it to old tribeswomen whose life of unremitting breastfeeding results in very long breasts.

2.   The starfish flower *(Stapelia variegata)* from Africa looks like a brown and yellow starfish nestling in the sand. It also smells like a dead animal, as a result of which flies, thinking it's a lump of rotten meat, decide it is the perfect place to raise a family. As they lay their eggs on the surface, they inadvertently pollinate the flower at the same time.

3.   *Welwitschia mirabilis*, from the deserts of Namibia, can live for over 2,000 years, yet its central trunk never grows more than 3ft in height. Instead the energy is transmitted into its two huge leaves which never fall and continue growing throughout the plant's life. The leaves can be as long as 20ft.

4.   The banyan tree *(Ficus benghalensis)* of India has more than one trunk. When the tree attains a certain size, it sends down rope-like roots which, on reaching the soil, take root and then thicken to form additional trunks. So the tree can spread outwards almost indefinitely. A 200-year-old specimen in the Calcutta Botanic Gardens has over 1,700 trunks, whilst during Alexander the Great's Indian campaign 20,000 soldiers are said to have sheltered under a single banyan tree.

5.   The merest touch causes the sensitive plant *(Mimosa pudica)* to collapse in one-tenth of a second. The wilting pose deters grazing animals from eating it and ten minutes later, when the danger has passed, the plant reverts to its upright position.

6.   *Puya raimondii* of Bolivia can take up to 150 years to bloom. And once it has flowered, it promptly dies. Although it's a herbaceous plant, it is built like a tree with a stem strong enough to support a man.

7.   The grapple tree *(Harpagophytum procumbens)* of South Africa produces a fearsome fruit called the 'Devil's Claw' which has been known to kill a lion. The fruit is covered in fierce hooks which latch on to passing animals. In trying to shake the fruit off, the animal disperses the seeds but at the same time, the hooks sink deeper into the creature's flesh. If the animal touches the fruit with

its mouth, the fruit will attach itself to the animal's jaw, inflicting great pain and preventing it from eating. Antelopes are the usual victims.

8.   The national flower of South Africa, the sugarbush *(Protea repens)*, depends on forest fires for survival. When its seeds have been fertilised, they are encased inside tough fireproof bracts which don't reopen until they have been scorched by fire. When the fire has passed, the seeds emerge undamaged.

9.   As it reaches upwards, the trunk of California's boojum tree *(Idris columnaris)* gradually reduces to a series of long, tentacle-like protuberances. Sometimes these droop down to the ground and root so that the tree forms a complete arch. The tree has no branches but is instead covered with thorny stems.

10. When the fruit of the South American sandbox tree *(Hura crepitans)* is ripe, it explodes with such force that the seeds can be scattered up to 15ft from the main trunk. The explosion is so loud that it can scare the life out of unsuspecting passers-by.

20 PLANTS AND THEIR MEANINGS

(as stated in an 1845 American Floral Vocabulary)

1. ANEMONE: frailty.

2. BARBERRY: sourness.

3. BASIL: hatred.

4. BINDWEED: humility.

5. BLUEBELL: constancy.

6. BUTTERCUP: ingratitude.

7. CARNATION: disdain.

8. DAHLIA: dignity.

9. DAISY: innocence.

10. HAREBELL: grief.

11. JONQUIL: desire.

12. LARKSPUR: fickleness.

13: LETTUCE: cold-heartedness.

14. LILY: purity.

15. LUPIN: sorrow.

16. NETTLE: slander.

17: POLYANTHUS: confidence.

18: YELLOW ROSE: infidelity.

19: ST. JOHN'S WORT: animosity.

20. VENUS FLY TRAP: deceit.

The moral is simple. If you want to impress your loved one, never present her with a lettuce as a token of your admiration.

10 CARNIVOROUS PLANTS

1. ALABAMA CANEBRAKE PITCHER PLANT.

2. BLADDERWORT.

3. BUTTERWORT.

4. COBRA LILY.

5. HOODED PITCHER.

6. HUNTSMAN'S HORN.

7. PINK FAN.

8. SUNDEW.

9. SWEET TRUMPET.

10. VENUS FLY TRAP.

The pitcher plant not only eats insects but is also capable of devouring small animals such as the rats and frogs which inhabit the Malaysian forests where it lives. The plant's leaves are shaped to form a pitcher, the inside of which has a slippery, waxy surface which reduces the chance of a creature's escape. The largest pitchers can be as much as 20in high and have special glands which secrete digestive juices. The plant acts as a stomach and can digest all the soft parts of the creature's body as well as absorbing its nutritional substances. It takes no more than a few days for the plant to devour completely a piece of meat thrown into the pitcher. Pitchers are also ideal for storing water and monkeys are often seen drinking from them, hence the plant's alternative name of 'monkey cup'.

THE TOP 20 DOG NAMES IN THE UNITED STATES

1. LADY.

2. KING.

3. DUKE.

4. PEPPY.

5. PRINCE.

6. PEPPER.

7. SNOOPY.

8. PRINCESS.

9. HEIDI.

10. = SAM.

    = COCO.

12. BUTCH.

13. PENNY.

14. RUSTY.

15. = SANDY.

    = SUSIE.

17. DUCHESS.

18. BLACKIE.

19. GINGER.

20. QUEENIE.

20 UNUSUAL U.S. DOG NAMES
(taken from dog licences)

1. ARF-ARF.

2. ASPHALT.

3. BIKINI.

4. BUGGER.

5. CAT.

6. CHIMNEY.

7. CUPCAKE.

8. DONUT.

9. FAG.

10. FLAKE.

11. HITLER.

12. IGLOO.

13. JELLY-BEAN.

14. LAMB CHOP.

15. LOLLIPOP.

16. LOVER BOY.

17. PUSSY.

18. REMBRANDT.

19. TWIT.

20. ZULU.

THE 10 MOST POPULAR UK CAT NAMES

1. SOOTY.

2. SMOKEY.

3. BRANDY.

4. FLUFFY.

5. TIGGER.

6. TOM.

7. GINGER.

8. SAM.

9. KITTY.

10. LUCKY.

10 UNUSUAL UK CAT NAMES

1. CHAIRMAN MIAOU.

2. CZUMCZUSZ.

3. APONICA TROGGS.

4. LYDIA LA POOSE.

5. PODGE.

6. SAUTE.

7. SCAMPI.

8. TEAPOT.

9. WOMBLE.

10. ZEBEDEE.

10 FREAK PETS

1. THE SPHINX CAT. Bred from a Canadian mutation, it is virtually hairless and has a damaged spine which results in a hopping walk coveted by connoisseurs of the breed.

2. The CROP PIGEON is bred with an over-sized crop and absurdly long feathers on its feet. The crop can't be cleaned naturally and the bird finds walking difficult.

3. POSITION CANARIES are bred to resemble the figures 1 and 7. Parts of their bodies are featherless and their over-stretched tendons mean they shift continually from foot to foot.

4. The MUNCHKIN CAT has short hind legs and three-inch front legs. It can hardly jump, can't groom itself and suffers from premature ageing of its long spine.

5. The CHINESE CRESTED DOG, once bred for the table, is almost hairless. As a result, it suffers from the cold.

6. The SHAR PEI, a dog designed in the US from a Chinese strain, is bred for its wrinkles.

7. A German breed of LOP-EARED RABBIT has ears as long as its body, rendering walking difficult.

8. PERSIAN CATS are bred to have 'piggy' faces. The nose is little more than a stump.

9. MUTANT GOLDFISH are deliberately bred with large growths on their faces.

10. TERRAPINS have been bred with two heads.

10 PETS WHICH CAME HOME

1. In October 1973, while truck driver Geoff Hancock stopped at a café near Darwin, Australia, his fox terrier Whisky jumped out of the cab and succeeded in getting lost. Nine months later, the resourceful Whisky arrived back at the Hancock family home in Melbourne after a solo journey of 1800 miles.

2. In 1953, a Persian cat called Sugar travelled 1,500 miles from Anderson, California, to Gage, Oklahoma, after her owners the Woods had moved there. They had left the cat with a neighbour in Anderson because she had a bad hip. Yet even with her injury, Sugar completed a mammoth 14-month trek across the Rockies to meet up with its former owners.

3. In the summer of 1977 Ken Phillips and his teenage son Shaun lost their cat Silky at Gin Gin, some 200 miles north of Brisbane, Australia. In March 1978 Silky suddenly appeared at the family home in Melbourne, nearly 1,500 miles away.

4. In 1983 Spot, a cross-bred sheepdog, jumped on board a London-bound National Express coach in Cardiff and refused to move. The dog got off at London's Victoria Coach Station; and then half an hour later, just as the coach was about to begin its return journey, Spot jumped back on, occupied the same seat and completed a 310-mile round trip.

5. In 1987, after she had killed two of his canaries, Vladimir Donsov banished his tortoiseshell cat Murka from his Moscow home and sent her to live with his mother 400 miles away in Voronezh. After just two days in Voronezh, Murka vanished. A year later she turned up at Mr. Donsov's Moscow apartment – dirty, hungry, pregnant and with the tip of her tail missing.

6. While holidaying in Cornwall with owner Louis Heston in 1976 Bede, an English setter, got lost. Six months later, the dog arrived home alone after a hazardous journey of over 300 miles.

7. In June 1985, Barbara Paule was driving a truck in Dayton, Ohio, when her cat, Muddy Water White, jumped out and vanished. Three years later, he returned to his home in Pennsylvania at the end of a 450-mile journey. He was so bedraggled after his ordeal that it was three days before Barbara recognised the cat as hers.

8. When the plane carrying its owner crashed in the wilds of Alaska, a white husky dog disappeared without trace. Despite being injured, it somehow

managed to find its way back to the spot where the plane had taken off – a journey of over 250 miles across frozen wasteland.

9.   When his farmer owner moved from Slapton in Devon to Payhembury, 50 miles away, Rusty the sheepdog naturally went too. But he soon grew homesick and within two weeks was back at his former abode in Slapton, having crossed numerous main roads ferrying holiday traffic.

10. In 1981 Mehmet Tunc, a Turk working in Germany and living on the island of Sylt in the north of the country, took his family and cat Minosch home for a short holiday. However, Minosch disappeared at the Turkish border and was not seen for another 61 days. That was when, back in Sylt, the Tunc family were roused by the sounds of scratching on their door. It was Minosch, damp and dejected following a journey of 1,500 miles.

10 ANIMAL RESCUES

1.   When Smudge the hamster toppled down a water pipe at his house in Swindon in 1995, his owners called out Wiltshire Fire Brigade who calculated that Smudge's journey would have taken him under the foundations of the house to a point below the front garden. Armed with spades, the firefighters began digging a trench until, 6ft down, they located the pipe. After removing a section of the piping they found Smudge, wet and bedraggled but otherwise remarkably healthy at the end of his great adventure.

2.   Nottinghamshire fire crews answered an emergency call to free a pet goldfish which had become stuck in an ornamental boot inside its bowl. After careful manipulation, the fish was freed to swim away.

3.   Worried that her kitten Oscar had muddy paws following a romp in the garden in 1994, four-year-old Stephanie Lefevre from Widnes decided that the only solution was to pop the pussy in the automatic washing machine. To ensure that the cat emerged in pristine condition, Stephanie put the machine on full cycle. As it rapidly began to fill with water, her mother ran to investigate the noise and saw Oscar's head peering through the glass door, surrounded by bubbles. After switching off the machine to stem the flow of water, she called the fire brigade and Oscar was released considerably fluffier and with the realisation that he only had eight lives left.

4.   Firefighters in Avon had to deal with a bull which had got its head stuck in a hole in the trunk of an oak tree. When tugging failed to achieve a result, they decided to hack out a hole in the tree around the bull's head and pull him out that way. It took some two hours to get the bull free. One of the crew commented: 'The bull was quite calm. More importantly, with its horns wedged in the tree, its dangerous end was out of action.'

5.   In 1994, fire crews in Gosport were called out to rescue Scatty the cat who was trapped inside the pool table of the Wych Way Inn public house. When the landlord had removed the money box, Scatty had climbed inside the table.

6.   Nottinghamshire firefighters were sent to free a pet python which had escaped from its tank and become trapped behind a radiator. To release the snake, they had to remove the radiator.

7.   In 1993, two weeks after disappearing while out for a walk in Clwyd, Mott

the border collie was found by a potholer at the foot of a 40ft-deep disused mineshaft. The potholer managed to climb down to the base of the shaft but the dog was heavier than he had anticipated and so he called out the local fire brigade who formed a human chain to bring Mott safely to the surface.

8.   Preparing to set off on the 15-mile journey from Newport Pagnell to Aylesbury, a woman loaded her suitcases on to the roof rack of her car. She then drove off, unaware that also attached to the roof-rack was her cat. It was only when she arrived in Aylesbury that she discovered the horrified cat hanging on for dear life. She tried to lift the cat down but it had been so terrified that it had dug its claws deep into the rack and could not be moved. Luckily, Buckinghamshire Fire Brigade were able to prise the poor thing from the rack. It has never watched an episode of Tom and Jerry since.

9.   Chasing a bird at its home in King's Lynn, an Alsatian puppy succeeded in getting its head stuck in a an ornamental garden wall. Norfolk fire crews managed to cut the dog free. The bird had simply flown out of the other side of the hole.

10. A cat in Peterborough travelled half a mile trapped in the suspension of a car. Hearing the miaowing, the car owner searched all over the car and even took a wheel off. Eventually admitting defeat, he called out the fire brigade who removed the front brake pipes to free the frightened ginger tom. One of his rescuers said: 'He was hissing and spitting, covered in dust, and was a bit bald on the head where he must have been dragged along the ground.'

10 CELEBRITY STEEDS

1. SILVER (The Lone Ranger).

2. SCOUT (Tonto).

3. TRIGGER (Roy Rogers).

4. BUTTERMILK (Dale Evans).

5. DIABLO (The Cisco Kid).

6. LOCO (Pancho).

7. RAWHIDE (The Range Rider).

8. LUCKY (Dick West).

9. TOPPER (Hopalong Cassidy).

10. MARSHAL (Matt Dillon)

Roy Rogers was so devoted to Trigger that when the horse died he had it stuffed and mounted. Hopalong Cassidy, known affectionately as Hoppy, was played on TV by the ageing William Boyd and had his own code of conduct for youngsters, emphasising the virtues of loyalty, honesty, kindness and ambition. And the Lone Ranger was considered such an epitome of American honesty and decency that Clayton Moore, who played the Masked Man, was later invited to the White House to meet that other pillar of American honesty and decency, Richard Nixon. Moore also made a good living out of opening supermarkets at $4,000 a time – it was extra if they wanted the horse.

10 ANIMALS WHICH HAD THEIR OWN TV SERIES

1. LASSIE, the collie bitch.

2. BLACK BEAUTY, the horse.

3. RIN TIN TIN, the Alsatian.

4. CHAMPION THE WONDER HORSE.

5. FLIPPER, the dolphin.

6. SALTY, the sea lion.

7. FURY, the black stallion.

8. SKIPPY, THE BUSH KANGAROO.

9. GENTLE BEN, the bear.

10. MY FRIEND FLICKA, the horse.

Lassie was treated like a Hollywood star. She lived in an air-conditioned kennel and was insured for $100,000. On the set, she rested on a mobile bed between takes. She needed to conserve her energy, for it was calculated that by 1960 she had brought 152 villains to justice, rescued 73 animals and birds, leapt through 47 windows, off 13 cliffs and on to 17 moving vehicles. Similarly, Rin Tin Tin had a valet, a personal chef, a limousine and a chauffeur for his exclusive use. He also had his own five-room dressing-room complex on the studio lot. Flipper, known originally as Susie, beat off 80 other dolphins to win the coveted role. No doubt there was some backstage bitching over the bucket of herrings that night! And one of Skippy's co-stars was a young Liza Goddard. It was an experience she will never forget. 'I was weed on by a wombat and I got lice either from an emu or a koala bear. I had to wash in DDT.'

10 HEROIC ANIMALS

1. **PRISCILLA THE PIG.** Owned by Victoria Herberta of Houston, Texas (with whom she sometimes shared a bed), Priscilla hit the headlines in 1984 when she rescued an 11-year-old boy from drowning. Paddling in Lake Somerville, Priscilla spotted that young Anthony Melton was in difficulties and swam to his assistance. She used her snout to keep the boy's head above water until he could hold on to her collar and then dragged him to the safety of the shore.

2. **NIPPER THE COLLIE.** When fire broke out at Ansty Farm, Sussex, in 1985, Nipper, the farm's five-year-old collie, saved calves and lambs by repeatedly venturing into the smoke and shepherding them to safety. As a result of the ordeal, the brave dog ended up with singed fur and blistered paws.

3. **CARLETTA THE COW.** At his Tuscany farm in 1986, Bruno Cipriano's pet cow, Carletta, saved him being gored by a boar when she charged at the beast and butted it with her horns.

4. **BRACKEN THE COLLIE.** In 1983 Ian Elliot was chopping down trees on his Canadian farm when a pine tree crashed on to him, breaking his back. His life was saved by his faithful sheepdog Bracken who lay across his stricken master to maintain his body temperature. Then when Bracken heard the sound of voices in the distance, he ran to the men and led them back to the injured Mr. Elliot.

5. **LEO THE POODLE.** In 1984 Leo, a four-year-old standard poodle, was out playing near his home in Hunt, Texas, with young brother and sister Sean and Erin Callahan when the trio encountered a rattlesnake. As the snake attacked, Leo leapt between it and 11-year-old Sean, enabling the boy to escape. Although receiving six potentially deadly bites to the head, Leo somehow survived.

6. **BRUCE THE LABRADOR/ALSATIAN.** When a four-year-old Dyfed boy got stuck in riverside mud and sank up to his armpits, Bruce cleverly lay on his side and gripped the boy's shoulder in his mouth to stop him sinking further into the mire. Fortunately, the boy's mother spotted their predicament and organised a rescue.

7. **BARRY THE ST. BERNARD.** During his 12-year career working in the Swiss Alps Barry rescued more than 40 people, among them a small boy trapped beneath an avalanche which had killed his mother. Barry spread himself across the boy's frozen body to keep him warm and licked his face until he woke up. To

complete the rescue, Barry carried the boy to the nearest house.

8. A SCHOOL OF DOLPHINS. In 1989 Adam Maguire was surfing near Sydney when he was attacked by a shark. As the shark moved in for the kill, it was distracted by a school of dolphins thrashing around in the water. To prevent the shark reaching its prey, the dolphins then swam around it in circles until Adam's friends had managed to rescue him.

9. WOODIE THE COLLIE CROSS. Ray Thomas of Cleveland, Ohio, and his fiancée Rae Anne Knitter were walking along a nature trail in the Rocky River Reservation one day in 1980 when Ray climbed to the top of a cliff to take some photographs. As he disappeared from sight, Rae Anne's collie cross, Woodie, began straining uncharacteristically on the lead. Eventually Woodie broke free and raced up the hill in Ray's footsteps. Rae Anne followed and spotted Ray lying unconscious in a stream at the foot of the 80ft cliff. With him was Woodie who had jumped off the cliff (breaking both hips in the process) and was nudging Ray's head to keep it above water. Both man and dog survived.

10. THE UNNAMED RABBIT. Hearing the family's pet rabbit scratching at its hutch, Tanya Birch woke up to find that her block of flats at Wisbech, Cambridgeshire, was on fire. She grabbed her two-year-old daughter, Heather, and fled to safety. Sadly, the rabbit died in the blaze.

10 BLUE PETER PETS

1. PETRA (mongrel dog).

2. HONEY (labrador retriever).

3. JASON (cat).

4. JOEY (parrot).

5. FRED/FREDA (tortoise).

6. PATCH (mongrel).

7. SHEP (collie).

8. WILLOW (cat)

9. GEORGE (tortoise).

10. BARNEY (parrot).

The first Blue Peter pet was Petra, the mongrel puppy who was introduced on the show in 1962 in a box wrapped in Christmas paper. Alas, two days later the puppy died of distemper and the producers had to hunt round frantically for a lookalike replacement. They found one in a pet shop in Lewisham, South London. Viewers were never told of the switch – as far as they were concerned, there was only ever one Petra. Although Petra II appeared gentle and loving on screen, in reality she was bad-tempered with poor eyesight and a shortage of teeth. She would gum presenters to death given half a chance. When she died in 1977, a sculpted bronze head of Petra was placed at the entrance to BBC Television Centre. Blue Peter's first tortoise appeared on the programme for two years as Fred before someone spotted that it was a girl and re-christened it Freda!

CHAPTER

MUSIC, FILM AND T.V.

JAILHOUSE ROCK – 10 ROCK STARS WHO HAVE SERVED TIME

1. KEITH RICHARDS (The Rolling Stones) – allowing a house to be used for the illegal smoking of cannabis (1967).

2. JIM MORRISON (The Doors) – drunk in public (1969).

3. MICK JAGGER (The Rolling Stones) – unlawful possession of four benzedrine tablets. He spent one night in Brixton Jail (1977).

4. SIOUXSIE SIOUX (Siouxsie and the Banshees) – obstruction (1977).

5. SID VICIOUS (The Sex Pistols) – charged with murdering his girlfriend, Nancy Spungen (1978).

6. CHUCK BERRY – tax evasion (1979).

7. HUGH CORNWELL (The Stranglers) – possession of drugs (1980).

8. DAVID CROSBY – possession of drugs and carrying a gun into a bar (1983).

9. JAMES BROWN – unlawful possession of a gun, drug possession and resisting arrest (1988).

10. MARK MORRISON – affray, threatening behaviour, firing a stun gun and getting an imposter to do his community service (1998).

20 UNRELEASED BEATLES TRACKS

1. ALL TOGETHER ON THE WIRELESS MACHINE.

2. CATCALL.

3. COMMONWEALTH SONG.

4. EVERY NIGHT.

5. GIMME SOME TRUTH.

6. HOT AS SUN.

7. I DON'T WANT TO SEE YOU AGAIN.

8. IF YOU'VE GOT TROUBLE.

9. JESSIE'S DREAM.

10. LEAVE MY KITTEN ALONE.

11. LOS PARANOIS.

12. NOT GUILTY.

13. PENINA.

14. SUZY PARKER.

15. TEDDY BOY.

16. THAT MEANS A LOT.

17. THINKING OF LINKING.

18. TIP OF MY TONGUE.

19. WATCHING RAINBOWS.

20. WHAT'S THE NEW MARY JANE?

Recorded during the White Album sessions, 'What's The New Mary Jane?' was supposed to have been the next Beatles single. But the split prevented its release.

20 BANDS AND THEIR ORIGINAL NAMES

1. BLUR (Seymour).

2. RADIOHEAD (On A Friday).

3. STATUS QUO (The Spectres).

4. THE BEACH BOYS (Carl and the Passions).

5. PROCUL HARUM (The Paramounts).

6. DAVE DEE, DOZY, BEAKY, MICK AND TICH (Dave Dee and the Bostons).

7. TALKING HEADS (The Artistics).

8. MARMALADE (Dean Ford and the Gaylords).

9. THE BYRDS (The Beefeaters).

10. THE WHO (The High Numbers).

11. MIDDLE OF THE ROAD (Los Caracas).

12. DEPECHE MODE (Composition of Sound).

13. SLADE (Ambrose Slade).

14. THE BAY CITY ROLLERS (The Saxons).

15. BLONDIE (The Stilettos).

16. CHICAGO (Chicago Transit Authority).

17. BLACK SABBATH (Earth).

18. MADNESS (The Invaders).

19. KAJAGOOGOO (Art Nouveau).

20. JOHNNY KIDD AND THE PIRATES (Freddie Heath and the Nutters).

HOW 10 BANDS GOT THEIR NAMES

1. DURAN DURAN took their name from the villain in Jane Fonda's 1968 film *Barbarella* since many of the early gigs were played at Barbarella's club in Birmingham.

2. LYNYRD SKYNYRD named themselves after Leonard Skinner, an unpopular gym teacher at their school.

3. LED ZEPPELIN were known as the New Yardbirds until they heard one of Keith Moon's favourite phrases: 'That went down like a lead Zeppelin'.

4. FRANKIE GOES TO HOLLYWOOD chose their name from an old newspaper story about Frank Sinatra moving into films.

5. T'PAU were named after Mr. Spock's Vulcan friend in *Star Trek*.

6. THIN LIZZY adopted their name from the robot Tin Lizzie who appeared in the Beano comic. They added the 'h' because they reckoned it wouldn't be sounded in Ireland.

7. BREAD came up with their name after being stuck in traffic behind a Wonder Bread lorry.

8. PROCUL HARUM were named after a friend's pedigree cat.

9. CROWDED HOUSE took their name from a cramped apartment they once shared.

10. TALKING HEADS saw a listing in a TV guide which referred to the 'talking heads' taking part in a TV debate.

According to Jonathan King, owner of their record label, 10CC got their name from the average amount of semen contained in male ejaculation.

10 SONGS WITH DISTRICTS OF LONDON IN THE TITLE

1. WATERLOO SUNSET – The Kinks, 1967.

2. FINCHLEY CENTRAL – The New Vaudeville Band, 1967.

3. LES BICYCLETTES DE BELSIZE – Engelbert Humperdinck, 1968.

4. LAST NIGHT IN SOHO – Dave Dee, Dozy, Beaky, Mick and Tich, 1968.

5. ANGEL – Rod Stewart, 1972.

6. BAKER STREET – Gerry Rafferty, 1978.

7. (I DON'T WANT TO GO TO) CHELSEA – Elvis Costello and The Attractions, 1978.

8. ELECTRIC AVENUE – Eddy Grant, 1983.

9. WEST END GIRLS – Pet Shop Boys, 1985.

10. CAMDEN TOWN – Suggs, 1995.

10 MUSICIANS WHO WERE MURDERED

1. SONNY BOY WILLIAMSON – U.S. harmonica player murdered in Chicago in 1948.

2. LITTLE WALTER – U.S. blues singer who suffered a fatal head injury following a fight in 1968.

3. JAMES SHEPPARD – the founder of U.S. group Shep and the Limelites, he was found dead in his car on the Long Island Expressway in 1970 after being attacked and robbed.

4. KING CURTIS – U.S. saxophonist stabbed to death in 1971.

5. AL JACKSON – the drummer with Booker T and The MGs was shot by burglars in 1975.

6. SAL MINEO – stabbed to death while walking home in Los Angeles in 1976.

7. JOHN LENNON – shot outside his New York home in 1980 by Mark Chapman, to whom he had given his autograph only a few hours earlier.

8. SAMUEL GEORGE – drummer with U.S. group The Capitols suffered fatal stab wounds in 1982.

9. MARVIN GAYE – shot dead by his father during a bitter row in 1984.

10. PETER TOSH – shot by burglars in 1987.

Sam Cooke was another to meet a violent end. Following a party in 1964, Cooke inadvertently stepped into the wrong motel room while in a state of undress. The manageress, who lived in that room, felt threatened by his presence and shot him dead.

10 WAYS IN WHICH THE NUMBER 9 AFFECTED JOHN LENNON'S LIFE

1. He and his son Sean were both born on 9 October.

2. His mother lived at 9 Newcastle Road, Wavertree, Liverpool.

3. As a student, he took the number 72 bus from his home to Liverpool Art College (7+2 = 9).

4. Future manager Brian Epstein first attended a Beatles concert at the Cavern in Liverpool on 9 November 1961 and clinched a record contract with EMI on 9 May 1962.

5. The group's first hit, 'Love Me Do', was on Parlophone disc 4949.

6. Lennon met Yoko Ono on 9 November 1966.

7. Their New York apartment was on West 72nd Street and their Dakota home was number 72 (7+2 = 9).

8. His fixation with the number 9 often manifested itself in his songs which included titles such as 'Number 9 Dream', 'Revolution 9' and 'One After 909'.

9. He was shot dead by Mark Chapman late on the evening of 8 December 1980 in New York but the five-hour time difference meant that it was 9 December in Liverpool.

10. His body was taken to the Roosevelt Hospital on New York's Ninth Avenue.

10 ROCK STARS BORN IN WALES

1. JULIAN COPE (The Teardrop Explodes).

2. DAVE EDMUNDS.

3. ANDY FAIRWEATHER-LOW (Amen Corner).

4. GREEN GARTSIDE (Scritti Politti).

5. ROGER GLOVER (Deep Purple).

6. PETE HAM (Badfinger).

7. MIKE PETERS (The Alarm).

8. RAMON PHILLIPS (The Nashville Teens).

9. ANDY SCOTT (Sweet).

10. STEVE UPTON (Wishbone Ash).

From Shirley Bassey through Tom Jones, Mary Hopkin, Shakin' Stevens and Bonnie Tyler to the Manic Street Preachers, Wales has always been proud of its musical roots. Tom Jones was born in Pontypridd as Thomas Woodward. In his younger days, he was frequently billed as 'The Twisting Vocalist from Pontypridd' but it was as Tommy Scott fronting The Senators that he was spotted by future manager Gordon Mills at the Top Hat Club, Merthyr Tydfil. Tom had worked in a glove factory and Gordon had been a bus conductor in Tonypandy. Even as a youngster, Tom attracted plenty of female attention and used to do his courting in the phone box at Pontypridd. Years later, when a new phone box was introduced, he arranged for the original to be shipped out to his home in Las Vegas to remind him of the many happy hours he spent in there.

20 BRITISH GROUPS OF THE SIXTIES WITH EXCEEDINGLY SILLY NAMES

1. BLODWYN PIG.

2. THE BONZO DOG DOO-DAH BAND.

3. DANTALIONS CHARIOT.

4. DEAD SEA FRUIT.

5. THE DOUGHNUT RING.

6. DR. MARIGOLD'S PRESCRIPTION.

7. ELMER GANTRY'S VELVET OPERA.

8. FARON'S FLAMINGOS.

9. THE FOURTEEN-HOUR TECHNICOLOUR DREAM.

10. THE FRUIT-EATING BEARS.

11. THE GIANT SUN TROLLEY.

12. HAPSASH AND THE COLOURED COAT.

13. HEDGEHOPPERS ANONYMOUS.

14. THE PINEAPPLE CHUNKS.

15. PINKERTON'S ASSORTED COLOURS.

16. PRINCIPAL EDWARDS' MAGIC THEATRE.

17. THE ST. VALENTINE'S DAY MASSACRE.

18. VAN DE GRAAF GENERATOR.

19. WAINWRIGHT'S GENTLEMEN.

20. WYNDER K. FROG.

10 PEOPLE WHO HAVE HAD A SONG WRITTEN ABOUT THEM

1. DON McLEAN – Killing Me Softly With His Song, Roberta Flack.

2. RITA COOLIDGE – Delta Lady, Joe Cocker.

3. WARREN BEATTY – You're So Vain, Carly Simon.

4. SYD BARRETT – Shine On You Crazy Diamond, Pink Floyd.

5. CAROLE KING – Oh Carol, Neil Sedaka.

6. ANGIE BOWIE – Angie, The Rolling Stones.

7. CHRISTIE BRINKLEY – Uptown Girl, Billy Joel.

8. PATTI BOYD – Layla, Derek and the Dominos.

9. BRIAN EPSTEIN – Baby You're A Rich Man, The Beatles.

10. BUDDY HOLLY – American Pie, Don McLean.

In addition to 'Baby You're A Rich Man', it is thought that John Lennon also wrote 'You've Got To Hide Your Love Away' for the Beatles' gay manager Brian Epstein after Epstein had made a pass at Lennon on holiday in Spain in spring 1963. Lennon penned the song on their return to England. Intense speculation surrounded the identity of the subject of 'You're So Vain' until Carly Simon finally admitted that 'There is nothing in the lyric which isn't true of Warren Beatty'. Pink Floyd dedicated 'Shine On You Crazy Diamond' to their erstwhile member, the reclusive Syd Barrett – it appeared on their album 'Wish You Were Here'. And after Neil Sedaka had written 'Oh Carol', Carole King replied with her own ditty, 'Oh Neil'...

20 SONGS WHERE THE TITLE IS NOT IN THE LYRICS

1. AFTER THE GOLD RUSH (Neil Young).

2. ALTERNATE TITLE (The Monkees).

3. AMOUREUSE (Kiki Dee).

4. ANNIE'S SONG (John Denver).

5. BLUE MONDAY (New Order).

6. BOHEMIAN RHAPSODY (Queen).

7. CREEQUE ALLEY (The Mamas and the Papas).

8. ELVIS IMPERSONATOR (The Manic Street Preachers).

9. GOLDFINGER (Ash).

10. THE LAST RESORT (The Eagles).

11. A LOVER'S CONCERTO (The Toys).

12. MARBLEHEAD JOHNSON (The Bluetones).

13. NEW YORK MINING DISASTER 1941 (The Bee Gees).

14. POSITIVELY FOURTH STREET (Bob Dylan).

15. THE RIDDLE (Nik Kershaw).

16. SLIGHT RETURN (The Bluetones).

17. SONG FOR WHOEVER (The Beautiful South).

18. A SORT OF HOMECOMING (U2).

19. SPACE ODDITY (David Bowie).

20. TUBTHUMPING (Chumbawamba).

10 CLASSIC SINGLES WHICH ONLY REACHED NUMBER 2 IN THE UK CHARTS

1. ALL RIGHT NOW (Free) 1970.

2. AMERICAN PIE (Don McLean) 1972.

3. BROWN SUGAR (The Rolling Stones) 1971.

4. HEARTBREAK HOTEL (Elvis Presley) 1956.

5. HOLDING BACK THE YEARS (Simply Red) 1986.

6. KAYLEIGH (Marillion) 1985.

7. LET IT BE (The Beatles) 1970.

8. LOLA (The Kinks) 1970.

9. MY GENERATION (The Who) 1965.

10. VIENNA (Ultravox) 1981.

Ultravox felt particularly aggrieved at being denied the Number One spot by Joe Dolce Music Theatre's novelty hit 'Shaddap You Face'.

10 SONG TITLES FEATURING UK PLACE NAMES

1. BELFAST CHILD (Simple Minds) 1989.

2. DAY TRIP TO BANGOR (DIDN'T WE HAVE A LOVELY TIME) (Fiddler's Dram) 1979.

3. DURHAM TOWN (THE LEAVIN') (Roger Whittaker) 1969.

4. GOING DOWN TO LIVERPOOL (The Bangles) 1986.

5. HERSHAM BOYS (Sham 69) 1979.

6. LUTON AIRPORT (Cats U.K.) 1979.

7. MARGATE (Chas and Dave) 1982.

8. PORTSMOUTH (Mike Oldfield) 1976.

9. ROCHDALE COWBOY (Mike Harding) 1975.

10. WINCHESTER CATHEDRAL (New Vaudeville Band) 1966.

10 MUSICIANS KILLED IN ROAD ACCIDENTS

1. EDDIE COCHRAN, 1960.

2. JOHNNY KIDD, 1966.

3. DUANE ALLMAN, 1971.

4. DICKIE VALENTINE, 1971.

5. CLARENCE WHITE (The Byrds), 1973.

6. MARC BOLAN, 1977.

7. HARRY CHAPIN, 1981.

8. DAVE PRATER (Sam and Dave), 1988.

9. PETE DE FREITAS (Echo and the Bunnymen), 1989.

10. COZY POWELL, 1998.

Eddie Cochran was killed at the age of 21 in a car crash at Chippenham, Wiltshire, on his way to London Airport and a flight back to the U.S. following a tour of England. Ironically, he had just recorded 'Three Steps To Heaven' which promptly became a posthumous Number One for him in the U.K. Duane Allman was killed in a motorbike accident in Macon, Georgia. By a macabre coincidence, fellow-Allman Brothers member Berry Oakley was killed in another motorbike crash just three blocks away a year later. The most famous rock shrine in the U.K. is the tree in Richmond, Surrey, into which the car carrying Marc Bolan crashed on 16 September 1977. Since then, the anniversary of his death has been marked by ribbons being tied to the tree and floral tributes laid at its base.

10 ROCK ECCENTRICS

1. IAN ANDERSON. The Jethro Tull singer with the wild eyes often used to walk around Luton with a lampshade on his head.

2. ROKY ERICKSON. Singer/guitarist with psychedelic Texan band The Thirteenth Floor Elevators. Erickson was convinced that he was an alien from Mars and consulted a lawyer to have this fact acknowledged officially.

3. KEITH MOON. Late drummer with The Who. Renowned for his wild behaviour, his speciality was dumping Rolls-Royces in swimming pools.

4. PRINCE. The diminutive popster has had more aliases than the Great Train Robbers – from 'Prince' to a squiggle, to 'The artist formerly known as Prince' to simply 'The artist'. Having changed his name to the squiggle, he proceeded to shout at London audiences: 'What's my name? What's my name?' Since nobody could pronounce the squiggle, his demand was greeted with total silence.

5. ARTHUR LEE. The frontman of Sixties band Love had a tendency to wander off stage during concerts to go to the supermarket.

6. SYD BARRETT. The creative force behind the early days of Pink Floyd has lived as a recluse for years. He has been known to use margarine as hair gel.

7. OZZY OSBOURNE. Wild-man of Black Sabbath, he once reputedly bit off a bat's head on stage.

8. MICHAEL JACKSON. The operations to have his skin made paler, the mask he wears around his face, the fact that his best friend is a chimpanzee... Enough said.

9. SKY SAXON. The singer with cult Californian band The Seeds would wander the streets of Los Angeles in a kaftan asking dogs: 'Pardon me, sir, could you tell me the time?' Also lived in a dustbin like his hero Top Cat.

10. VIV STANSHALL. Offstage, the leader of The Bonzo Dog Doo-Dah Band behaved like the archetypal eccentric English aristocrat. On stage, he once put raw meat into Ringo Starr's drum kit (while the Beatles were recording 'Revolver') in a bid to 'foil the Fabs' sound'.

10 SONGS WHICH HAVE TOPPED THE UK CHARTS WITH TWO DIFFERENT VERSIONS

1. WITH A LITTLE HELP FROM MY FRIENDS – Joe Cocker (1968) and Wet Wet Wet (1988).

2. SPIRIT IN THE SKY – Norman Greenbaum (1970) and Doctor and the Medics (1986).

3. EVERYTHING I OWN – Ken Boothe (1974) and Boy George (1987).

4. YOUNG LOVE – Tab Hunter (1957) and Donny Osmond (1973).

5. I GOT YOU BABE – Sonny and Cher (1965) and UB40 with Chrissie Hynde (1985).

6. MARY'S BOY CHILD – Harry Belafonte (1957) and Boney M (1978).

7. WITHOUT YOU – Nilsson (1972) and Mariah Carey (1994).

8. THIS OLE HOUSE – Rosemary Clooney (1954) and Shakin' Stevens (1981).

9. YOU'LL NEVER WALK ALONE – Gerry and the Pacemakers (1963) and The Crowd (1985).

10. LIVING DOLL – Cliff Richard and the Drifters (1959) and Cliff Richard and the Young Ones (1986).

Shakin' Stevens was only four when Rosemary Clooney reached Number One with 'This Ole House' and apparently had never even heard the song until the end of 1980. Three months later, he too enjoyed Number One status with the song. 'Everything I Own' was written by David Gates of Bread, yet when they released the song in the UK in 1972 it got no higher than Number 32. It took two cover versions – by Ken Boothe and Boy George – to reach Number One. Still, David Gates will have enjoyed the royalties.

20 ARTISTS WHO SANG ON 'WE ARE THE WORLD'

(U.S.A. For Africa were America's answer to Band Aid and this was their 1985 all-star charity single to help fight the famine in Ethiopia).

1. KIM CARNES.

2. RAY CHARLES.

3. BOB DYLAN.

4. DARYL HALL.

5. JAMES INGRAM.

6. MICHAEL JACKSON.

7. AL JARREAU.

8. BILLY JOEL.

9. CYNDI LAUPER.

10. HUEY LEWIS.

11. KENNY LOGGINS.

12. WILLIE NELSON.

13. LIONEL RICHIE.

14. KENNY ROGERS.

15. DIANA ROSS.

16. PAUL SIMON.

17. BRUCE SPRINGSTEEN.

18. TINA TURNER.

19. DIONNE WARWICK.

20. STEVIE WONDER.

10 ROCK SUICIDES

1. MICHAEL HOLLIDAY. The velvet-voiced British crooner shot himself in 1963, seemingly unable to cope with the pressures of fame.

2. JOE MEEK. Producer of The Tornados who shot himself on 3 February 1967, the anniversary of the death of his hero, Buddy Holly.

3. BOBBY BLOOM. Shot himself in a Hollywood motel room in 1974, although it may have been an accident.

4. PETE HAM. One half of Badfinger, he hanged himself in 1975. Tragically, his musical partner, Tom Evans, also committed suicide in 1983.

5. IAN CURTIS. The singer with Joy Division hanged himself in 1980.

6. THE SINGING NUN. Belgian nun Sister Luc-Gabrielle had a hit in 1963 with 'Dominique' under the name of 'The Singing Nun'. She left the convent in 1967 and reverted to her real name of Janine Deckers. In 1985, she and her companion of ten years Annie Pecher committed suicide, reportedly by downing a massive amount of barbiturates with alcohol.

7. RICHARD MANUEL. The pianist with The Band was found hanging in his Florida hotel room in 1986.

8. ROY BUCHANAN. The U.S. blues guitarist hanged himself in a prison cell in 1988 following his arrest for drunken behaviour.

9. DEL SHANNON was found shot dead in his Californian home in 1990, a .22 rifle by his side.

10. MICHAEL HUTCHENCE. The INXS singer was found hanging in a Sydney hotel room in 1997. The coroner's verdict was suicide although rumours were rife that his death was the result of a bizarre sex game which went wrong.

10 EUROVISION SONG CONTEST ROWS

1. The result of the 1969 contest, which ended in a four-way tie between France, Holland, Spain and the UK, caused such a furore that Norway, Sweden, Finland, Portugal and Austria refused to take part the following year.

2. Italy boycotted the 1981 contest, saying that it was too old-fashioned. And France backed out in 1982, French TV chiefs claiming: 'The cost is heavy for small and mediocre results.'

3. Luxembourg snubbed the 1995 contest because, as that year's European City of Culture, they considered it too tacky. Italy also shunned the 1995 event, claiming they couldn't fit it into their TV schedules. Cynics cited Italy's poor record in the contest as a more likely reason.

4. In 1978, Jordanian TV refused to show the Israeli entry on screen. Instead, while Izhar Cohen sang the victorious 'A-Bi-Ni-Bi', Jordanian viewers saw a bunch of flowers. When it seemed likely that Israel were going to win, Jordanian TV switched to an American detective series, Bronk. For the 1981 contest in Dublin, Jordan refused to acknowledge the presence of Israel at all, playing commercials and a brief musical interlude while Israel sang. And when voting began, Jordan cut transmission again because the scoreboard showed the name of Israel. Baffled viewers had to wait for another hour until a newsflash informed them that the United Kingdom had won.

5. A diplomatic row erupted in 1987 after BBC presenter Ray Moore light-heartedly referred to the Turkish group Locomotive as 'an ugly crowd'.

6. When Sweden and Norway finished second and third respectively in 1966, the Scandinavians were accused of being partial in their voting. And in 1968, Britain complained that Spain, who won, had deliberately not voted for the UK entry, Cliff Richard's 'Congratulations', in order to scupper its chances.

7. Dutch members of the audience booed the 1984 UK entry, 'Love Games' by Belle and the Devotions, after newspaper stories in Holland claimed that the song was similar to an old Supremes number.

8. In 1973, Irish singer Maxi threatened to walk out after a row about the arrangement of her song. A substitute singer flew to Luxembourg on stand-by

(rehearsing the song on the plane) but Maxi relented and sang on. She came nowhere.

9. Eurovision rules stated that an entry's melody and lyrics must be written by that country's nationals. So when Norway asked French linguistics lecturer Rene Herail to devise a song for the 1982 contest, he got round the loophole by not taking a writing credit for 'Adieu'. The nationality question surfaced again in 1985 when the Luxembourg entry was performed by a six-strong group comprising two Britons, a Canadian, one Dutch, one Belgian and a German.

10. Thirteen-year-old schoolgirl Sandra Kim became the youngest winner when she steered Belgium to victory in 1986. But as a result contestants started to get younger and there was widespread condemnation when, in 1989, France paraded 11-year-old Nathalie Paque and the Israeli singer was a 12-year-old boy called Gili.

The most remarkable story from the chequered 42-year history of the Eurovision Song Contest occurred in 1974 when plotters planning a military coup in Portugal used the playing of the country's Eurovision entry on radio as the signal for tanks to move in.

10 UNFORGETTABLE EUROVISION SONG CONTEST ENTRIES

1. Great titles have included 'Pump Pump' (Finland, 1976), 'Boum Badaboum' (Monaco, 1967), 'Bana Bana' (Turkey, 1989), 'A-Ba-Ni-Bi' (Israel, 1978) and Lulu's immortal 'Boom Bang-a-Bang' (UK, 1969). In protest at this banality, the 1977 Austrian entry was titled 'Boom Boom Boomerang'.

2. For sheer repetition, it is hard to beat Spain's triumphant 'La La La' of 1968. It contained no fewer than 138 la's.

3. One title which didn't exactly roll off the tongue was the 1964 German entry, 'Man Gewöhnt Sich So Schnell an das Schöne'.

4. In 1983, 16 years after Sandie Shaw's barefoot victory with 'Puppet on a String', Spain's Remedios Amaya tried the same shoeless gimmick. He came last with *nul points*.

5. The first nation to fail to receive a single vote was Norway in 1978, the pioneering song being 'Mil Etter Mil' (Mile After Mile) sung by Jahn Teigen. He called it the proudest moment of his life and predicted that it would make him a star. He was wrong.

6. Norway's 1980 song was about the construction of a hydro-electric power station. It came 16th out of 19. An earlier Norwegian entry, 'Voi-Voi' (1960) was an arrangement of a Lapp reindeer-herding call.

7. Neighbours Finland scored *nul points* in 1982 with a little number protesting about the building of a nuclear power station.

8. The 1973 Norwegian entry featured the lyrical rhyme: 'Come and join us! In the game of girl and boyness!'

9. The 1985 Luxembourg entry, 'Children, Kinder, Enfants', had previously been rejected by Germany.

10. Eurovision expert David Bridgeman rates the 1983 Turkish entry, 'Opera', as the worst entry to date. It simply consisted of the word 'opera' repeated over and over again.

10 UK EUROVISION FLOPS

1. RING-A-DING GIRL (Ronnie Carroll, 1962): 4th in the contest, reached no. 46 in the UK charts.

2. A MAN WITHOUT LOVE (Kenneth McKellar, 1966): 9th, no. 30 in charts.

3. MARY ANN (Black Lace, 1979): 7th, no. 42 in charts.

4. LOVE ENOUGH FOR TWO (Prima Donna, 1980): 3rd, no. 48 in charts.

5. LOVE IS... (Vikki, 1985): 4th, no. 49 in charts.

6. RUNNER IN THE NIGHT (Ryder, 1986): 7th, not in top 75 in charts.

7. ONLY THE LIGHT (Rikki, 1987): 13th, not in top 75 in charts.

8. LONELY SYMPHONY (Frances Ruffelle, 1994): 10th, no. 25 in charts.

9. GIVE A LITTLE LOVE BACK TO THE WORLD (Emma, 1990): 6th, no. 33 in charts.

10. A MESSAGE TO YOUR HEART (Samantha Janus, 1991): 10th, no. 30 in charts.

A good result in the Eurovision certainly doesn't guarantee chart success. Scott Fitzgerald's 1988 offering, 'Go', (which came second to Celine Dion) only reached Number 52 while Live Report's 'Why Do I Always Get It Wrong?' was runner-up in 1989 but got no higher than 73 in the UK charts.

10 SONGS WITH FRUIT IN THE TITLE

1. BLACKBERRY WAY (The Move) 1968.

2. BLUEBERRY HILL (Fats Domino) 1956.

3. CLEMENTINE (Bobby Darin) 1960.

4. CHERRY OH BABY (UB40) 1984.

5. LITTLE GREEN APPLES (Roger Miller) 1968.

6. ORANGE BLOSSOM SPECIAL (The Spotnicks) 1962.

7. PEACHES (The Stranglers) 1977.

8. PINEAPPLE HEAD (Crowded House) 1993.

9. RASPBERRY BERET (Prince and the Revolution) 1985.

10. STRAWBERRY FIELDS FOREVER (The Beatles) 1967.

10 BANDS IN FILMS

1. BILL HALEY AND THE COMETS: Rock Around The Clock.

2. GERRY AND THE PACEMAKERS: Ferry Across The Mersey.

3. THE DAVE CLARK FIVE: Catch Us If You Can.

4. THE WHO: The Kids Are Alright.

5. THE MONKEES: Head.

6. SLADE: Flame.

7. T REX: Born To Boogie.

8. LED ZEPPELIN: The Song Remains The Same.

9. THE SEX PISTOLS: The Great Rock 'n' Roll Swindle.

10. MADNESS: Take It Or Leave It.

10 RIDICULOUSLY LONG SONG TITLES

1. Calling Occupants of Interplanetary Craft (The Recognised Anthem of World Contact Day) – The Carpenters, 1977: 73 letters.

2. Rachmaninoff's Eighteenth Variation on a Theme by Paganini (The Story of Three Loves) – Winifred Atwell, 1954: 70 letters.

3. I'm In Love With The Girl On A Certain Manchester Megastore Checkout Desk – The Freshies, 1981: 60 letters.

4. Objects In The Rear View Mirror May Appear Closer Than They Are – Meat Loaf, 1994: 52 letters.

5. If I Said You Have a Beautiful Body Would You Hold It Against Me – Bellamy Brothers, 1979: 51 letters.

6. If I Love Ya Then I Need Ya, If I Need Ya Then I Want You Around – Eartha Kitt, 1994: 47 letters.

7. Gilly Gilly Oseenfeffer Katzenellen Bogen By The Sea – Max Bygraves, 1954: 45 letters.

8. San Francisco (Be Sure To Wear Some Flowers In Your Hair) – Scott McKenzie, 1967: 45 letters.

9. Have You Seen Your Mother Baby, Standing in the Shadow – The Rolling Stones, 1966: 44 letters.

10. There's a Guy Works Down the Chipshop Swears He's Elvis – Kirsty MacColl: 44 letters.

20 SONGS INSPIRED BY CHILDREN'S TV

1. BANANA SPLITS – The Dickies.

2. BATMAN THEME – The Kinks.

3. BLUE PETER – Mike Oldfield.

4. CAPTAIN SCARLET THEME – The Trudy.

5. DAVY CROCKETT – Humphrey Ocean.

6. DOCTORING THE TARDIS – The Timelords.

7. GET DOWN SHEP – The Barron Knights.

8. I TRUST VALERIE SINGLETON – The Cortinas.

9. THE LONE RANGER – Quantum Jump.

10. MAGIC ROUNDABOUT – Jasper Carrott.

11. POSTMAN PAT – Ken Barrie.

12. ROBIN HOOD – Gary Miller.

13. RUPERT – Jackie Lee.

14. THUNDERBIRDS THEME – The Shadows.

15. TOM BAKER – Human League.

16. TRUMPTON RIOTS – Half Man Half Biscuit.

17. TURTLE POWER – Partners in Kryme.

18. WHITE HORSES – Jacky.

19. THE WOMBLING SONG – The Wombles.

20. WORZEL'S SONG – Jon Pertwee.

10 MUSICIANS KILLED IN PLANE CRASHES

1. GLENN MILLER, 1944.

2. BUDDY HOLLY, 1959.

3. PATSY CLINE, 1963.

4. JIM REEVES, 1964.

5. OTIS REDDING, 1967.

6. JIM CROCE, 1973.

7. RONNIE VAN ZANT (Lynyrd Skynyrd), 1977.

8. RICKY NELSON, 1985.

9. KYU SAKAMOTO, 1985.

10. STEVIE RAY VAUGHAN, 1990.

Buddy Holly, Richie Valens and The Big Bopper all died on the same flight from Ohio to Minnesota, a flight they only made because Holly was in a hurry to get to the next gig and to organise clean laundry and get a good night's sleep. Patsy Cline's death was just one link in a chain of tragedy. Cline's plane crashed when she was on her way back to Nashville from Kansas City after giving a benefit concert for the widow of disc jockey Cactus Jack Call who had recently been killed in a car smash. Then, travelling to Cline's funeral, U.S. country star Jack Anglin was also killed in a car crash. Kyu Sakamoto was one of 520 victims when a Japan Airlines 747 crashed near Tokyo. Sakamoto achieved fleeting fame in 1963 with 'Sukiyaki', the only U.S. Number One to be sung entirely in Japanese.

10 UK NUMBER ONES WRITTEN BY PAUL McCARTNEY

1. BAD TO ME (Billy J. Kramer and the Dakotas) with John Lennon, 1963.

2. A WORLD WITHOUT LOVE (Peter and Gordon) with John Lennon, 1964.

3. MICHELLE (The Overlanders) with John Lennon, 1966.

4. MULL OF KINTYRE (Wings) with Denny Laine, 1977.

5. PIPES OF PEACE (Paul McCartney), 1983.

6. EBONY AND IVORY (Paul McCartney with Stevie Wonder), 1982.

7. OB-LA-DI OB LA-DA (Marmalade) with John Lennon, 1968.

8. WITH A LITTLE HELP FROM MY FRIENDS (Joe Cocker) with John Lennon, 1968.

9. WITH A LITTLE HELP FROM MY FRIENDS (Wet Wet Wet) with John Lennon, 1988.

10. GET BACK (The Beatles with Billy Preston) with John Lennon, 1969.
Just for the record, McCartney also co-wrote 16 Beatles Number Ones and produced Mary Hopkin's 1968 chart-topper, 'Those Were The Days'.

20 U.S. ONE-HIT WONDERS

(acts whose only hit reached Number One)

1. LAURIE LONDON – He's Got The Whole World In His Hands, 1958.

2. SHEB WOOLEY – Purple People Eater, 1958.

3. DOMENICO MODUGNO – Volare, 1958.

4. MARK DINNING – Teen Angel, 1960.

5. MAURICE WILLIAMS AND THE ZODIACS – Stay, 1960.

6. ERNIE K-DOE – Mother-in-Law, 1961.

7. BARRY McGUIRE – Eve of Destruction, 1965.

8. JOHN FRED AND HIS PLAYBOY BAND – Judy In Disguise (With Glasses), 1968.

9. THE LEMON PIPERS – Green Tambourine, 1968.

10. JEANNIE C. RILEY – Harper Valley P.T.A., 1968.

11. STEAM – Na Na Hey Hey Kiss Him Goodbye, 1969.

12. BILLY SWAN – I Can Help, 1974.

13. STARLAND VOCAL BAND – Afternoon Delight, 1976.

14. WILD CHERRY – Play That Funky Music, 1976.

15. RICK DEES AND HIS CAST OF IDIOTS – Disco Duck (Part 1), 1976.

16. ALAN O'DAY – Undercover Angel, 1977.

17. DEBBY BOONE – You Light Up My Life, 1977.

18. NICK GILDER – Hot Child In The City, 1978.

19. LIPPS, INC. – Funkytown, 1980.

20. TONY BASIL – Mickey, 1982

Sheb Wooley's sales technique was unusual. When playing the tune, he told MGM Records: 'It's nothing you wanna hear...it's the bottom of the barrel.' Nevertheless it sold over three million copies.

20 UK ONE-HIT WONDERS

(acts whose only hit reached Number One)

1. B. BUMBLE AND THE STINGERS – Nut Rocker, 1962.

2. THE OVERLANDERS – Michelle, 1966.

3. THE CRAZY WORLD OF ARTHUR BROWN – Fire, 1968.

4. ZAGER AND EVANS – In The Year 2525, 1969.

5. THE ARCHIES – Sugar Sugar, 1969.

6. NORMAN GREENBAUM – Spirit In The Sky, 1970.

7. MATTHEWS' SOUTHERN COMFORT – Woodstock, 1970.

8. TYPICALLY TROPICAL – Barbados, 1975.

9. J BARRIE – No Charge, 1976.

10. THE FLOATERS – Float On, 1977.

11. ALTHIA AND DONNA – Up Town Top Ranking, 1978.

12. BRIAN AND MICHAEL – Matchstalk Men And Matchstalk Cats And Dogs, 1978.

13. ANITA WARD – Ring My Bell, 1979.

14. LENA MARTELL – One Day At A Time, 1979.

15. FERN KINNEY – Together We Are Beautiful, 1980.

16. JOE DOLCE MUSIC THEATRE – Shaddup You Face, 1981.

17. CHARLENE – I've Never Been To Me, 1982.

18. M/A/R/R/S – Pump Up The Volume, 1987.

19. PARTNERS IN KRYME – Turtle Power, 1990.

20. DOOP – Doop, 1994

The backing singers on Brian and Michael's tribute to the artist L.S. Lowry were St. Winifred's School Choir, who themselves became one-hit wonders two years later with the excruciating 'There's No-One Quite Like Grandma'.

10 ARTISTS WHO MADE GUEST APPEARANCES ON OTHER PEOPLE'S RECORDS

1. RICK WAKEMAN played synthesizer on David Bowie's 'Space Oddity'.

2. MICK JAGGER sang backing vocals on Carly Simon's 'You're So Vain'.

3. ELTON JOHN played piano on the Hollies' 'He Ain't Heavy, He's My Brother'.

4. GEORGE HARRISON played guitar under the name of L'Angelo Mysterioso on Cream's 'Badge'.

5. KATE BUSH helped out with the vocals on Peter Gabriel's 'Games Without Frontiers'.

6. DAVE GILMOUR played guitar on Kate Bush's 'Wuthering Heights'.

7. PHIL COLLINS played drums on Adam Ant's 'Puss 'N Boots'.

8. MICHAEL JACKSON sang supporting vocals on Rockwell's 'Somebody's Watching You'.

9. MARK KING of Level 42 played bass on Midge Ure's 'If I Was'.

10. STEVIE WONDER played harmonica on Chaka Khan's 'I Feel For You'.

Other guest appearances include Eric Clapton playing guitar on the Beatles' 'While My Guitar Gently Weeps', Sting supplying high-pitched vocals on Dire Straits' 'Money For Nothing' and John Lennon, disguised as Dr. Winston O'Boogie, playing on Elton John's version of 'Lucy in the Sky With Diamonds'. But one of the most surprising assists was movie star Michael Douglas who sang backing vocals on Billy Ocean's 1986 hit 'When The Going Gets Tough (The Tough Get Going)'. The song featured in Douglas's movie The Jewel of the Nile.

20 SONG TITLES
FEATURING U.S. PLACES

1. EL PASO (Marty Robbins) 1960.

2. TWENTY-FOUR HOURS FROM TULSA (Gene Pitney) 1963.

3. VIVA LAS VEGAS (Elvis Presley) 1964.

4. LAST TRAIN TO CLARKSVILLE (The Monkees) 1967.

5. LET'S GO TO SAN FRANCISCO (The Flowerpot Men) 1967.

6. MASSACHUSETTS (The Bee Gees) 1967.

7. NASHVILLE CATS (The Lovin' Spoonful) 1967.

8. GALVESTON (Glen Campbell) 1969.

9. WICHITA LINEMAN (Glen Campbell) 1969.

10. SAN BERNADINO (Christie) 1970.

11. IS THIS THE WAY TO AMARILLO (Tony Christie) 1971.

12. INDIANA WANTS ME (R. Dean Taylor) 1971.

13. VENTURA HIGHWAY (America) 1972.

14. WHAT MADE MILWAUKEE FAMOUS (Has Made A Loser Out Of Me) (Rod Stewart) 1972.

15. ALL THE WAY FROM MEMPHIS (Mott the Hoople) 1973.

16. PHILADELPHIA FREEDOM (Elton John) 1975.

17. MISSISSIPPI (Pussycat) 1976.

18. THE BOSTON TEA PARTY (The Sensational Alex Harvey Band) 1976.

19. BOY FROM NEW YORK CITY (Darts) 1978.

20. RAINY NIGHT IN GEORGIA (Randy Crawford) 1981.

10 SINGLES BANNED BY THE BBC

1. TELL LAURA I LOVE HER – Ricky Valance (1960). In those days, the BBC banned any song about death.

2. JE T'AIME...MOI NON PLUS – Jane Birkin and Serge Gainsbourg (1969). Banned for its groaning, panting, heavy breathing and general sexual connotations. Fontana, who issued the record, were suddenly overcome by morality and deleted it when it reached Number Two in the UK charts. However, another label, Major Minor, had no such qualms, took over the master and were instantly rewarded with a Number One single.

3. WET DREAM – Max Romeo (1969). Too explicit.

4. GIVE IRELAND BACK TO THE IRISH – Paul McCartney (1972). Too political.

5. HI HI HI – Paul McCartney (1972). Too sexual.

6. BIG SIX – Judge Dread (1972). This and the follow-ups, 'Big Seven' and 'Big Eight', were considered too risqué.

7. MAGIC ROUNDABOUT – Jasper Carrott (1975). The B-side of 'Funky Moped' was banned for sexual innuendo.

8. GOD SAVE THE QUEEN – The Sex Pistols (1977). Too anarchic and disrespectful of Her Majesty.

9. RELAX – Frankie Goes To Hollywood (1983). This single was going nowhere until Radio 1 breakfast DJ Mike Read announced that he was going to refuse to play it because of its sexual content. Read's stand led to an all-out BBC ban and 'Relax' soaring to the top of the charts.

10. I WANT YOUR SEX (1987) – George Michael. Too raunchy.

The BBC also insisted to changes on The Kinks' 'Lola'. The offence was not caused by the song's transsexual lyrics, but by the line which mentioned Coca-Cola. Ever vigilant about advertising, the Corporation forced Ray Davies to change the words to 'Cherry-Cola' when performing on Top of the Pops.

10 ACTS WHOSE FIRST TWO HITS REACHED NUMBER ONE IN THE UK CHARTS

1. GERRY AND THE PACEMAKERS (How Do You Do It, 1963; I Like It, 1963).

2. MUNGO JERRY (In The Summertime, 1970; Baby Jump, 1971).

3. ROD STEWART (Maggie May, 1971; You Wear It Well, 1972).

4. ART GARFUNKEL (I Only Have Eyes For You, 1975; Bright Eyes, 1979).

5. FRANKIE GOES TO HOLLYWOOD (Relax, 1984; Two Tribes, 1984).

6. GEORGE MICHAEL (Careless Whisper, 1984; A Different Corner, 1986).

7. JIVE BUNNY AND THE MASTERMIXERS (Swing The Mood, 1989; That's What I Like, 1989).

8. NEW KIDS ON THE BLOCK (You Got It (The Right Stuff), 1989; Hangin' Tough, 1990).

9. ROBSON AND JEROME (Unchained Melody, 1995; I Believe, 1995).

10. THE SPICE GIRLS (Wannabe, 1996; Say You'll Be There, 1996).

10 MUSICIANS WHO DIED IN ACCIDENTS

1. JOHNNY ACE – U.S. R&B star shot himself while playing Russian roulette backstage, 1954.

2. BRIAN JONES – drowned in his swimming pool, 1969.

3. JOHN ROSTILL – the former Shadows member was electrocuted by his guitar, 1973.

4. 'MAMA' CASS ELLIOT – choked to death on a sandwich, 1974.

5. GRAHAM BOND – mysteriously fell to his death under a tube train at Finsbury Park Station, 1974.

6. KEITH RELF – the former singer with The Yardbirds was electrocuted while tuning his guitar, 1976.

7. SANDY DENNY – the lead singer with Fairport Convention died after falling downstairs, 1978.

8. TERRY KATH – the Chicago frontman was another to perish during a game of Russian roulette in 1978. His last words were: 'Don't worrry, it's not loaded.'

9. DENNIS WILSON – the Beach Boys drummer drowned in a boating accident off Southern California, 1983.

10. STEVE MARRIOTT – the former Small Faces singer died in a fire at his home in Arkesden, Essex, in 1991.

By a strange misfortune, when The Who drummer Keith Moon died from an accidental drug overdose in 1978, it was in the same London flat where 'Mama' Cass Elliot had died four years earlier.

10 BAND NAMES WHICH FEATURE U.S. PLACES

1. THE BAY CITY ROLLERS (after San Francisco).

2. BOSTON.

3. BUFFALO SPRINGFIELD.

4. CHICAGO.

5. COLORADO.

6. THE DETROIT SPINNERS (or EMERALDS).

7. MANHATTAN TRANSFER.

8. THE NASHVILLE TEENS.

9. THE NEW YORK DOLLS.

10. TEXAS.

10 SONGS WITH A DASH OF FRENCH

1. Michelle - THE OVERLANDERS.

2. Monsieur Dupont - SANDIE SHAW.

3. Jennifer Juniper - DONOVAN.

4. Lady Marmalade (Voulez-Vous Coucher Avec Moi Ce Soir?) - LABELLE.

5. Denis - BLONDIE.

6. Voulez-Vous - ABBA.

7. Ca Plane Pour Moi - PLASTIC BERTRAND.

8. Hold On Tight - ELECTRIC LIGHT ORCHESTRA.

9. Encore Une Fois - SASH!

10. To The End - BLUR.

20 ROCK STARS' REAL NAMES

1. ADAM ANT (Stuart Goddard).

2. ALICE COOPER (Vince Furnier).

3. DAVID ESSEX (David Cook).

4. ADAM FAITH (Terry Nelhams).

5. GEORGIE FAME (Clive Powell).

6. EMILE FORD (Emile Sweetman).

7. BILLY J. KRAMER (William Ashton).

8. CAPTAIN SENSIBLE (Ray Burns).

9. DEL SHANNON (Charles Westover).

10. FISH (Derekn Dick).

11. PAUL JONES (Paul Pond).

12. CHRIS DE BURGH (Christopher Davidson).

13. BONO (Paul Hewson).

14. BILLY OCEAN (Leslie Charles).

15. DR. JOHN (Malcolm Rebannack).

16. MEAT LOAF (Marvin Lee Aday).

17. SANDIE SHAW (Sandra Goodrich).

18. SUGGS (Graham McPherson).

19. NENA (Gabriela Kerner).

20. CONWAY TWITTY (Harold Jenkins).

Why anyone should want to change their name to Conway Twitty remains one of life's great mysteries.

20 BEAUTY QUEENS WHO BECAME FILM STARS

1. RAQUEL WELCH (Miss Photogenic 1953).

2. CYBILL SHEPHERD (Miss Teenage Memphis 1966).

3. MICHELLE PFEIFFER (Miss Orange County 1977).

4. YVONNE DE CARLO (Miss Venice Beach 1941).

5. DYAN CANNON (Miss West Seattle 1957).

6. KIM NOVAK (Miss Deepfreeze 1953).

7. JAYNE MANSFIELD (Miss Photoflash 1952).

8. SYLVIA KRISTEL (Miss Television Europe 1973).

9. LAUREN BACALL (Miss Greenwich Village 1942).

10. CLAUDIA CARDINALE (The Most Beautiful Italian Girl in Tunis 1956).

11. DEBBIE REYNOLDS (Miss Burbank 1948).

12. SHIRLEY JONES (Miss Pittsburgh 1951).

13. ANITA EKBERG (Miss Sweden 1951).

14. GINA LOLLOBRIGIDA (Miss Italy 1946).

15. ELKE SOMMER (Miss Viareggio 1959).

16. DOROTHY LAMOUR (Miss New Orleans 1931).

17. SOPHIA LOREN (Princess of the Sea 1948, Miss Elegance 1950).

18. VERONICA LAKE (Miss Florida 1937).

19. VERA MILES (Miss Kansas 1948).

20. ZSA ZSA GABOR (Miss Hungary 1936).

Michelle Pfeiffer was 18 and working as a supermarket check-out girl when her hairdresser suggested she try modelling. She was so bored she gave it a go and rang an agent who entered her in the Miss Orange County contest. She hasn't looked back since.

20 ACTORS WHO HAVE PLAYED SHERLOCK HOLMES

1. GEORGE TREVILLE (nine films 1912-13).

2. EILLE NORWOOD (47 films 1921-23).

3. JOHN BARRYMORE (film *Sherlock Holmes* 1922).

4. ARTHUR WONTNER (five films 1931-37).

5. RAYMOND MASSEY (film *The Speckled Band* 1931).

6. BASIL RATHBONE (15 films 1939-45).

7. ALAN WHEATLEY (TV series *Sherlock Holmes* 1951).

8. RONALD HOWARD (TV series *Sherlock Holmes* 1954).

9. JOHN GIELGUD (BBC radio series 1954).

10. CHRISTOPHER LEE (German film *Sherlock Holmes* and *The Deadly Necklace* 1962).

11. PETER CUSHING (film *The Hound of the Baskervilles* 1959, TV series *The Cases of Sherlock Holmes* 1968).

12. DOUGLAS WILMER (TV series *Sherlock Holmes* 1965).

13. STEWART GRANGER (TV movie *The Hound of the Baskervilles* 1972).

14. ROGER MOORE (TV movie *Sherlock Holmes in New York* 1976).

15. NICOL WILLIAMSON (film *The Seven-Per-Cent Solution* 1976).

16. PETER COOK (film The Hound of the Baskervilles 1978).

17. CHRISTOPHER PLUMMER (film *Murder By Decree* 1979).

18. TOM BAKER (TV film *The Hound of the Baskervilles* 1982).

19. IAN RICHARDSON (TV movies *The Sign of Four, The Hound of the Baskervilles* 1983).

20. JEREMY BRETT (TV series *The Adventures of Sherlock Holmes* 1986-93).

20 FILM WALK-ONS

1. CLIVE JAMES appeared as the most drunken of Bazza's mates in Barry Humphries' 1974 film *Barry McKenzie Holds His Own*. In the same movie, the then Australian Prime Minister Gough Whitlam played himself. Whitlam was no stranger to acting. He had played 'man in nightclub' in a 1938 movie, *The Broken Melody*.

2. Hollywood director STEVEN SPIELBERG made a cameo appearance as the clerk who receives Dan Aykroyd and John Belushi's money at the end of The *Blues Brothers*.

3. Artist PABLO PICASSO appeared in a crowd scene in Jean Cocteau's 1962 film *The Testament of Orpheus*.

4. Train robber RONNIE BIGGS played himself in the Sex Pistols' film *The Great Rock 'n' Roll Swindle*. A row broke out as to whether or not Biggs should be paid for the part – he had allegedly asked for a suitcase full of notes to be sent out to Brazil. In the end, he didn't receive a penny.

5. ED KOCH, the Mayor of New York in 1984, played himself in *The Muppets Take Manhattan*.

6. Jaws author PETER BENCHLEY had a walk-on part in the film, playing a reporter.

7. HUGH HEFNER, founder of the Playboy empire, was seen as a pipe-smoking ancient Roman in Mel Brooks' *History of the World – Part I*.

8. Sixties guru DR. TIMOTHY LEARY appeared as a diner at The Nouveau Woodstock vegetarian restaurant in the 1966 movie *Rude Awakening*.

9. DONALD TRUMP played Mr. Speculator in the 1989 movie *Ghosts Can't Do It*.

10. Singer BOB DYLAN guested as an *avant-garde* artist who used a buzz-saw as a brush in the 1990 movie *Catchfire*.

11. Thriller writer STEPHEN KING played a minister at a funeral in the 1989 film adaptation of his novel *Pet Sematary*.

12. American senator HUBERT HUMPHREY appeared as himself in Robert Redford's political movie *The Candidate*.

13. Discreetly wrapped in a towel, VISCOUNT ALTHORP, brother of the late Diana, Princess of Wales, made a fleeting appearance as a public schoolboy climbing out of the bath in the 1984 film *Another Country* which starred Colin Firth. Althorp was only on screen for three seconds and he wasn't allowed to speak because he didn't have an Equity card.

14. JONATHAN ROSS and MELVIN BRAGG played themselves in *The Tall Guy*.

15. Nobel Prize-winning author ERNEST HEMINGWAY had an uncredited bit part in the 1958 film *The Old Man and the Sea* which was based on his own novel.

16. American evangelist BILLY GRAHAM sponsored the 1967 film *Two a Penny* which starred Cliff Richard in the unlikely role of a drug-dealing art student. To underline his message, Graham himself made a cameo appearance.

17. HAROLD PINTER wrote the screenplay for *The Servant* (starring Dirk Bogarde) and played a 'society man' in one scene. In 1985, Pinter appeared as a bookshop customer in another of his films, *Turtle Diary*.

18. STING played a heroic officer and ROBIN WILLIAMS made a cameo appearance as the King of the Moon in Terry Gilliam's *The Adventures of Baron Munchausen*. Williams was listed in the credits as 'Ray D. Tutto'.

19. PETER SELLERS made a brief appearance in the 1962 film *The Road to Hong Kong* as a doctor examining Bob Hope for amnesia.

20. In his last-ever role, 80-year-old SIR RALPH RICHARDSON played the landlord of the Old Justice pub for one scene in Paul McCartney's *Give My Regards to Broad Street*. At the end of shooting, Richardson said to McCartney: 'Thank you, dear boy; not a comma out of place.' McCartney was delighted with this tribute to his screenwriting.

20 DISNEY VILLAINS

1. CRUELLA DE VIL (*101 Dalmatians*).

2. CAPTAIN HOOK (*Peter Pan*).

3. SHERE KHAN (*The Jungle Book*).

4. STEPMOTHER (*Cinderella*).

5. GASTON (*Beauty and the Beast*).

6. JAFAR (*Aladdin*).

7. MEDUSA (*The Rescuers*).

8. BEAR (*The Fox and the Hound*).

9. QUEEN (*Snow White and the Seven Dwarfs*).

10. STROMBOLI (*Pinocchio*).

11. CHERNOBOG (*Fantasia*).

12. QUEEN OF HEARTS (*Alice in Wonderland*).

13. RAT (*Lady and the Tramp*).

14. MALEFICENT (*Sleeping Beauty*).

15. MADAM MIM (*The Sword in the Stone*).

16. PRINCE JOHN (*Robin Hood*).

17. HORNED KING (*The Black Cauldron*).

18. RATIGAN (*The Great Mouse Detective*).

19. URSULA (*The Little Mermaid*).

20. SCAR (*The Lion King*).

10 CHILD STARS WHO HIT HARD TIMES

1. MARK LESTER. The star of the 1968 film *Oliver!* frittered away the money he had earned as a child and developed a drug habit. At one point, he was reduced to working in a Kensington pub.

2. JUSTIN HENRY. Nominated for an Oscar at eight, the child star of the 1979 tear-jerker *Kramer vs. Kramer* was working as a house-painter ten years later.

3. DREW BARRYMORE. The actress who made her name as an eight-year-old in *E.T.* is back in the big time but only after overcoming drug and alcohol problems and a reported attempted suicide.

4. TOMMY RETTIG. Lassie's human co-star was sentenced to five and a half years in a U.S. federal prison in 1976 for smuggling cocaine from Peru.

5. LENA ZAVARONI. The child singer from *Opportunity Knocks* had a long battle against the slimmers' disease anorexia nervosa.

6. LINDA BLAIR. The girl from *The Exorcist* is another child star who has had to overcome drug problems.

7. JACK WILD. The Artful Dodger in *Oliver!* became an alcoholic and a virtual recluse following the break-up of his first marriage. He has now beaten the booze.

8. BOBBY DRISCOLL played Jim Hawkins in the 1950 film version of Treasure Island but finished up in jail 11 years later for possession of drugs.

9. CARL SWITZER played Alfalfa in the *Our Gang* comedies of the 1920s but was killed in a gun battle in 1959.

10. RIVER PHOENIX died in 1993 at the age of 23 after collapsing outside a Los Angeles nightclub. The coroner said that drugs caused his death.

Many child stars struggle to cope with that dangerous phenomenon – the pushy parent. The mother of Allen Clayton Hoskins was so determined that he should land the part of Farina in the *Our Gang* series that she dressed him up as a girl for the auditions. The deception worked and thereafter Master Hoskins had to stay in drag and behave like a girl off-screen so that producer Hal Roach didn't suspect anything untoward.

20 HOLLYWOOD NICKNAMES

1. AMERICA'S SWEETHEART – Mary Pickford.

2. THE BLONDE BOMBSHELL – Betty Hutton.

3. THE BRAZILIAN BOMBSHELL – Carmen Miranda.

4. THE DUKE – John Wayne.

5. THE GIRL WITH THE MILLION DOLLAR LEGS – Betty Grable.

6. THE ITALIAN STALLION – Sylvester Stallone.

7. THE IT GIRL – Clara Bow.

8. THE LOOK – Lauren Bacall.

9. THE MAGNIFICENT WILDCAT – Pola Negri.

10. THE MAN OF A THOUSAND FACES – Lon Chaney snr.

11. THE MEANEST MAN IN THE WORLD – Jack Benny.

12. THE MEXICAN SPITFIRE – Lupe Velez.

13. THE MUSCLES FROM BRUSSELS – Jean-Claude Van Damme.

14. THE OOMPH GIRL – Ann Sheridan.

15. THE PLATINUM BLONDE – Jean Harlow.

16. THE PROFESSIONAL VIRGIN – Doris Day.

17. THE SEX KITTEN – Brigitte Bardot.

18. THE SEX THIMBLE – Dudley Moore.

19. THE SWEATER GIRL – Lana Turner.

20. THE VAGABOND LOVER – Rudy Vallee.

Apparently Lupe Velez, Mexican star of the 1940s, was blessed with the ability to rotate her left breast while the other remained motionless. She could also counter-rotate it, a feat which her Australian co-star Leon Erroll described as 'so supple and beautiful you couldn't believe your eyes'.

10 FILMS WITH ONE-LETTER TITLES

1. *A* (Italy, 1969). Sequels were, predictably, *B*, *C* and *D*.

2. *E* (Canada, 1982).

3. *G* (Great Britain, 1974).

4. *I* (Sweden, 1966).

5. *M* (U.S., 1951).

6. *W* (U.S., 1973).

7. *X* (Germany, 1928).

8. *Y* (Sweden, 1987).

9. *Z* (France/Italy, 1968).

10. *2* (U.S., 1983).

10 FILMS WHICH FEATURE PIGS

1. *Animal Farm* (1955).

2. *Babe* (1995).

3. *Big Top Pee Wee* (1988).

4. *Charlotte's Web* (1972).

5. *Doc Hollywood* (1991).

6. *Leon The Pig Farmer* (1992).

7. *Misery* (1990).

8. *Pigs* (1982).

9. *A Private Function* (1984).

10. *Razorback* (1984).

10 FILMS FEATURING DENTISTS

1. *THE GREAT MOMENT* (1944). About the invention of laughing gas.

2. *MARATHON MAN* (1976). Laurence Olivier as an evil dentist.

3. *CACTUS FLOWER* (1969). Walter Matthau played a dentist with a chaotic private life.

4. *THE PALEFACE* (1948). Bob Hope played the hapless man with the drill.

5. *THE MAN WHO KNEW TOO MUCH* (1934). Hitchcock spy thriller involved a sinister dentist.

6. *THE COUNTERFEIT TRAITOR* (1962). Featured a dentist who was a spy.

7. *EVERSMILE, NEW JERSEY* (1989). Daniel Day-Lewis played a travelling dentist.

8. *LEAVE 'EM LAUGHING* (1928). Laurel and Hardy dentistry caper where they were overcome by laughing gas.

9. *THE DENTIST* (1932). W.C. Fields as an impatient dentist.

10. *THE STRAWBERRY BLONDE* (1941). James Cagney as a turn-of-the-century Brooklyn dentist in a remake of *One Sunday Afternoon* which starred Gary Cooper.

10 'CARRY ON' GUEST STARS

1. BOB MONKHOUSE (*Carry On Sergeant*).

2. RICHARD O'SULLIVAN (*Carry On Teacher*).

3. AMANDA BARRIE (*Carry On Cabbie*).

4. BILL OWEN (*Carry On Nurse*).

5. WARREN MITCHELL (*Carry On Cleo*).

6. RICHARD O'BRIEN (*Carry On Cowboy*).

7. HARRY H. CORBETT (*Carry On Screaming*).

8. PENELOPE KEITH (*Carry On Doctor*).

9. JOHNNY BRIGGS (*Carry On Up The Khyber*).

10. WENDY RICHARD (*Carry On Matron*).

Richard O'Sullivan was still a child actor when he appeared in *Carry On Teacher* while Richard O'Brien was just an extra in *Carry On Cowboy*. The appearances of both Johnny Briggs and Amanda Barrie mean that both Mike and Alma Baldwin from *Coronation Street* have guested in *Carry On* films. David Essex, in his pre-singing days, had half a day's work as a page boy in the 1970 film *Carry On Henry* but his performance ended up on the cutting-room floor.

20 ACTORS WHO HAVE CHANGED THEIR NAMES

1. RED BUTTONS began life as Aaron Chwatt. The idea for his new identity came from his red hair and the 48 buttons on his bellboy uniform.

2. MICHAEL CAINE was born Maurice Micklewhite and took his stage name from a advertisement for the film *The Caine Mutiny*.

3. GARY COOPER started out as Frank Cooper but was persuaded to change his name to that of his agent's home town – Gary, Indiana.

4. MICHAEL CRAWFORD was known as Michael Dumble-Smith until he took his stage name from a passing Crawford's Biscuits lorry.

5. BETTE DAVIS was plain Ruth Davis until she decided to name herself after Balzac's Cousin Bette.

6. DORIS DAY scrapped Doris von Kapellof on the advice of bandleader Barney Rapp, for whom she had sung 'Day After Day'.

7. NICOLAS CAGE started life as Nicholas Coppola but changed it to distance himself from his uncle, director Francis Ford Coppola. He chose Cage from the comic book character, Luke Cage.

8. JUDY GARLAND wisely abandoned Frances Gumm in favour of something more romantic. She borrowed her first name from the Hoagy Carmichael song 'Judy' and took her surname from Chicago theatre critic Robert Garland. The necessity to change her name had been brought about by an early billing which called the 11-year-old 'Frances Glumm'.

9. CARY GRANT. The erstwhile Archibald Leach took the name 'Cary' from Cary Lockwood, the character he played in the stage comedy *Nikki*.

10. ROCK HUDSON was advised by his agent to change his name from Roy Scherer. The agent consulted an atlas to come up with a compound of the Rock of Gibraltar and New York State's Hudson River.

11. CAROLE LOMBARD, or Jane Peters as she was originally known, adopted her stage name from the Carroll, Lombardi Pharmacy on Lexington and 65th in New York.

12. ZEPPO MARX was christened Herbert Marx but was known as 'Zeppo' because his birth coincided with the first Zeppelin.

13. RAY MILLAND originally used his stepfather's surname, Mullane. Then he suggested 'Mill land' in honour of the beauty of his Welsh homeland.

14. ZERO MOSTEL was born Samuel Joel Mostel but was nicknamed 'Zero' on account of his appalling school grades.

15. LUKE PERRY started out as Coy Luther Perry III but chose Luke from his favourite movie, *Cool Hand Luke*, which he had first seen at the age of five.

16. OMAR SHARIF was Michael Shalhoub until he took 'Omar' from Second World War hero General Omar Bradley and 'Sharif' from the Arab word for nobility, *sherif*.

17. SIGOURNEY WEAVER was born Susan Weaver but chose her distinctive first name from a character in the novel *The Great Gatsby*.

18. OPRAH WINFREY was a mistake. Her name was supposed to be the Biblical 'Orpah' but the midwife spelt it wrongly on the birth certificate.

19. SHELLEY WINTERS was Shirley Schrift but took the name 'Shelley' from the poet.

20. MICHAEL YORK began as Michael Johnson until he took his stage name from York cigarettes.

10 FILMS WHERE A WOMAN KNEES A MAN WHERE IT HURTS

1. *BARB. WIRE* (Pamela Anderson).

2. *BLAZING SADDLES* (Madeline Kahn).

3. *CLUE* (Madeline Kahn).

4. *CUT-THROAT ISLAND* (Geena Davis).

5. *FOOL FOR LOVE* (Kim Basinger).

6. *THE FOUR MUSKETEERS* (Raquel Welch).

7. *GAUNTLET* (Sondra Locke).

8. *SCREAM* (Drew Barrymore).

9. *ROUBLE BOUND* (Patricia Arquette).

10. *WOLF* (Michelle Pfeiffer).

THE TOP 20 HOLLYWOOD DRAWS

(based on a survey conducted among film producers in February 1998)

1. TOM CRUISE.

2. HARRISON FORD.

3. MEL GIBSON.

4. TOM HANKS.

5. BRAD PITT.

6. ARNOLD SCHWARZENEGGER.

7. JIM CARREY.

8. JOHN TRAVOLTA.

9. BRUCE WILLIS.

10. JODIE FOSTER.

11. CLINT EASTWOOD.

12. JULIA ROBERTS.

13. ROBIN WILLIAMS.

14. JACK NICHOLSON.

15. KEVIN COSTNER.

16. SYLVESTER STALLONE.

17. NICOLAS CAGE.

18. SEAN CONNERY.

19. MICHAEL DOUGLAS.

20. LEONARDO DI CAPRIO.

10 BON MOTS FROM WOODY ALLEN

1. 'It's not that I'm afraid to die, I just don't want to be there when it happens' – Allen on death.

2. 'If only God would give me some clear sign! Like making a large deposit in my name at a Swiss bank' – Allen on God.

3. ' That was the most fun I've ever had without laughing' – Allen on sex (Annie Hall).

4. 'Hey, don't knock masturbation! It's sex with someone I love' – Allen on do-it-yourself sex (Annie Hall).

5. 'I don't want to achieve immortality through my work – I want to achieve it through not dying' – Allen on staying alive.

6. 'In Beverly Hills, they don't throw their garbage away. They make it into television shows' – Allen on Hollywood.

7. 'There is the fear that there is an afterlife but no one will know where it's being held' – Allen on life after death.

8. 'I was thrown out of N.Y.U. in my freshman year for cheating on my metaphysics final. You know, I looked within the soul of the boy sitting next to me' – Allen on metaphysics (Annie Hall).

9. 'Money's better than poverty, if only for financial reasons' – Allen on money.

10. 'I'm a practising heterosexual – but bisexuality immediately doubles your chances for a date on Saturday night' – Allen on sexuality.

10 ACTORS WHO HAVE SERVED TIME

1. BEBE DANIELS was jailed for ten days in 1921 for speeding. Her next movie, *The Speed Girl*, was about a movie star sent to prison for speeding.

2. ERROL FLYNN was imprisoned three times for assault. The final occasion was for hitting a New York cop whom Flynn reckoned had asked for his autograph in a threatening manner.

3. STACY KEACH served six months in Reading jail in 1984 for attempting to smuggle $4,500-worth of cocaine into Britain.

4. SOPHIA LOREN spent a month in prison in Rome in 1982 for income tax irregularities.

5. ROBERT MITCHUM served 59 days in a California jail in 1948 for possessing narcotics.

6. IVOR NOVELLO had a month's stay in Wormwood Scrubs after being convicted of obtaining petrol unlawfully during the Second World War.

7. DUNCAN RENALDO, the Romanian-born actor who went on to find fame as The Cisco Kid, served eight months in jail for illegal entry to the USA in 1932.

8. JANE RUSSELL went to prison in 1978 for drunken driving.

9. PHIL SILVERS was sent to reform school in Brooklyn for allegedly attacking his teacher. He claimed self-defence.

10. MAE WEST spent two days in jail in 1926 after her Broadway stage show *Sex* was ruled obscene. She received two days' remission for good behaviour.

10 FILMS ABOUT BASEBALL

1. *THE BABE RUTH STORY* (1948), starring William Bendix in the title role. Bendix played baseball for the New York Giants and the New York Yankees and, before turning to acting, played semi-professionally for two years.

2. *THE PRIDE OF THE YANKEES* (1942), starring Gary Cooper as Lou Gehrig.

3. *THE WINNING TEAM* (1952) with Ronald Reagan as Grover Cleveland Alexander.

4. *THE PRIDE OF ST. LOUIS* (1952), starring Dan Dailey as Dizzy Dean.

5. *FEAR STRIKES OUT* (1957), starring Anthony Perkins as Jim Piersall.

6. *ANGELS IN THE OUTFIELD* (1952) – a baseball manager gets help from above. Paul Douglas and Janet Leigh starred.

7. *TAKE ME OUT TO THE BALL GAME* (1949) – a Gene Kelly/Frank Sinatra musical.

8. *DAMN YANKEES* (1958) – musical starring Gwen Verdon and Tab Hunter.

9. *BULL DURHAM* (1988) – Kevin Costner (himself a former High School shortstop) starred with Tim Robbins and Susan Sarandon in the tale of minor league baseball team the Durham Bulls.

10. *A LEAGUE OF THEIR OWN* (1992) – Tom Hanks played the team coach in a film set in the 1940s.

10 HOLLYWOOD CONTRACTS

1. American actress MARGUERITE CLARK had a clause in her contract stating that she would not kiss on screen – on the orders of her husband, Harry Palmerston-Williams, whom she married in 1921. At the time, she was Mary Pickford's principal rival as 'America's sweetheart' but the no-kissing rule ruined her career and she retired in 1921.

2. CLARA BOW had it written into her contract with Paramount that none of the crew should use profane language in her presence. In return, Paramount insisted that she remain single and in 1926 offered her a $500,000 bonus on condition that she remained free of scandal during the tenure of the contract. She failed to collect.

3. EVELYN VENABLE was another star not permitted to kiss on screen. Her father had a clause to that effect inserted in her 1933 contract with Paramount.

4. JOAN CRAWFORD's 1930 contract with MGM went so far as to specify the hour by which she had to be in bed.

5. A 1931 Warner's contract ordered American actress and boxing fan VIVIENNE SEGAL not to yell at prize-fights in case she strained her voice.

6. The contract of JOE E. BROWN, the American comedian of the 1930s, forbade him to grow a moustache.

7. BUSTER KEATON's contract with MGM in the 1920s prevented him from smiling on screen.

8. JOHN BARRYMORE's contract said that he never had to be on set before 10.30am.

9. GEORGE ARLISS's contract at Warner in the early 1930s stated that he didn't have to remain on set any later than 4.30pm.

10. MAURICE CHEVALIER's contract with Paramount, signed as talkies were being introduced, was rendered invalid if he ever lost his French accent!

10 ACTORS AND THEIR INSURANCE

1. Boss-eyed BEN TURPIN was insured for $100,000 against the possibility of his eyes ever becoming normal again.

2. In the early 1930s, RKO insured ROSCOE ATES against losing his trademark stutter.

3. When child star SHIRLEY TEMPLE was first insured, her contract stipulated that no money would be paid if the youngster died or suffered injury while drunk.

4. JIMMY 'SCHNOZZLE' DURANTE knew that his bulbous nose was his fortune and accordingly had it insured for $100,000.

5. FRED ASTAIRE had his legs insured for $1,000,000.

6. CHARLIE CHAPLIN insured his famous feet for $150,000.

7. Hollywood heavyweight actor WALTER HIERS took out a $25,000 policy to insure against him losing weight.

8. Glamorous actress KATHLEEN KEY had her neck insured for $25,000.

9. When ANTHONY QUINN had his head shaved for his role as a magician in the 1968 film *The Magus*, he insured against the risk of his hair not growing again afterwards.

10. Irish actress SIOBHAN MCKENNA was not exactly renowned for her driving skills. The first time she sat behind the wheel she finished up in a ditch, the second time against a wall and the third time up a tree. Consequently, her insurance policy for the 1964 film *Of Human Bondage* precluded her from driving a car for the duration of the production.

10 HOLLYWOOD CANADIANS

1. YVONNE DE CARLO (born Vancouver).

2. DEANNA DURBIN (born Winnipeg).

3. GLENN FORD (born Quebec).

4. MICHAEL J. FOX (born Vancouver).

5. RAYMOND MASSEY (born Toronto).

6. BARBARA PARKINS (born Vancouver).

7. MARY PICKFORD (born Toronto).

8. WALTER PIDGEON (born New Brunswick).

9. WILLIAM SHATNER (born Montreal).

10. DONALD SUTHERLAND (born New Brunswick).

10 SEX CHANGE FILMS

1. *GLEN OR GLENDA?* (1953).

2. *THE CHRISTINE JORGENSEN STORY* (1970).

3. *MYRA BRECKINRIDGE* (1970) where surgeons transformed Rex Reed as movie critic Myron into Raquel Welch as Myra!

4. *DR. JEKYLL AND SISTER HYDE* (1971).

5. *DOG DAY AFTERNOON* (1975).

6. *LET ME DIE A WOMAN* (1979).

7. *THE WOMAN INSIDE* (1981).

8. *COME BACK TO THE 5 AND DIME, JIMMY DEAN, JIMMY DEAN* (1982).

9. *SOMETHING SPECIAL* (1986).

10. *CLEO/LEO* (1989).

10 FILMS SPAWNED BY CHILDREN'S TV PROGRAMMES

1. *THE FLINTSTONES.*

2. *DR. WHO AND THE DALEKS.*

3. *DOUGAL AND THE BLUE CAT.*

4. *THE GREAT MUPPET CAPER.*

5. *THE LONE RANGER AND THE LOST CITY OF GOLD.*

6. *THUNDERBIRDS ARE GO.*

7. *WOMBLING FREE.*

8. *TONS OF TROUBLE* (with Mr. Pastry).

9. *THE JETSONS.*

10. *BATMAN.*

10 HOLLYWOOD CHILDHOODS

1. CLARK GABLE is listed on his birth certificate as a girl.

2. JANE SEYMOUR was born with one green eye and one brown eye.

3. MARLON BRANDO used to wander so much on his way to kindergarten that his older sister Jocelyn had to take him to school on a leash.

4. As a child, ANN-MARGRET's family were so poor that they had to live in an Illinois funeral parlour. Every night she slept next to a casket.

5. DUDLEY MOORE was born with a club foot. As a result, his left leg is shorter than his right.

6. CANDICE BERGEN is the daughter of ventriloquist Edgar Bergen. When she was little, her father's dummy, the inimitable Charlie McCarthy, had a bigger bedroom and more clothes than her.

7. DEBBIE REYNOLDS was such a virtuous child that she earned 48 merit badges as a Girl Scout.

8. RITA HAYWORTH was born with one eye much larger than the other. She camouflaged it with specially constructed eyelashes.

9. Future Hollywood tough guy CHARLES BRONSON had a decidedly non-macho start to life. His family were so poor that he had to wear his sister's hand-me-down dresses to school.

10. DEMI MOORE was born cross-eyed.

10 BIG BREAKS

1. ROSCOE 'FATTY' ARBUCKLE owed his first break to a blocked drain. Working as a plumber's mate, he was summoned to unblock producer Mack Sennett's pipes one day in 1913 and Sennett immediately offered Arbuckle a role in his *Keystone Kops* comedies.

2. MICHAEL ELPHICK was working as an apprentice electrician at the newly-opened Chichester Theatre when he got chatting to the theatre director, Sir Laurence Olivier. Impressed by his enthusiasm, Olivier encouraged Elphick to audition for drama school.

3. CLARK GABLE landed his big break when, working as a telephone repair man, he came to mend the phone of drama coach Josephine Dillon. Gable broke off his engagement to another girl and married her, whereupon she took him under her wing and launched his acting career.

4. JUDY GARLAND won a contract at MGM by mistake. Louis B. Meyer saw 14-year-old Judy and 15-year-old Deanna Durbin in a 1936 short called Every Sunday and instructed an aide to 'Sign up that singer – the flat one'. He was referring to Durbin, who could sometimes sound a trifle flat, but the aide misheard and, thinking Mayer had said 'the fat one', signed dumpy little Judy Garland instead.

5. ROCK HUDSON was a postman whose round included agent Henry Willson. Hudson said he was bored with being a postman and so Willson, impressed by his looks and by the fact he had performed in school plays, arranged for him to meet director Raoul Walsh. It was Walsh who directed Hudson's movie debut, *Fighter Squadron*.

6. MARILYN MONROE used to work in an aircraft factory, inspecting parachutes and spraying fuselages. It was menial work until one day an army photographer called in to take propaganda pictures for the war effort and chose the young Norma Jean as a model. She revealed natural talent and the photographer recommended her to a modelling agency in Los Angeles. Soon her face was on the cover of a dozen different magazines. Marilyn Monroe had been born.

7. GEORGE RAFT started out as a small-time mobster with big ideas. One day, he was sent to demand protection money from night club queen Texas

Guinan but instead she talked him into appearing in her autobiopic *Queen of the Night Clubs*. It was his first step to stardom and a career playing mobsters.

8.   LANA TURNER was sales clerk Judy Turner in a Los Angeles lingerie store when she was 'discovered' by Warner Bros talent-spotter Solly Baiano. He liked what he saw, took her to the studio, tested her and renamed her after his daughter Lonnie.

9.   RAQUEL WELCH was working as the weather-girl on Sun Up, a San Diego breakfast show, when she was given the opportunity to do a spot of modelling on-air. She was only paid $7.50 a show but her appearances led to freelance modelling and a movie career.

10.   LORETTA YOUNG was 15 when she happened to answer the phone when director Mervyn Le Roy called to speak to her older sister, Polly Ann Young. Polly Ann was out but Loretta kept chatting and won a part in the 1927 movie *Naughty But Nice*.

10 FILMS FEATURING VENTRILOQUISTS

1. *THE GREAT GABBO* (1929) with Erich von Stroheim.

2. *THE UNHOLY THREE* (1930) with Lon Chaney.

3. *CHARLIE MCCARTHY, DETECTIVE* (1939) with Edgar Bergen.

4. *YOU CAN'T CHEAT AN HONEST MAN* (1939) with Edger Bergen and W.C. Fields.

5. *DEAD OF NIGHT* (1945) with Michael Redgrave.

6. *KNOCK ON WOOD* (1954) with Danny Kaye.

7. *HYPNOSIS* (1963).

8. *DEVIL DOLL* (1964) with Bryant Holliday.

9. *MAGIC* (1978) with Anthony Hopkins as a ventriloquist whose dummy drives him to murder.

10. *BROADWAY DANNY ROSE* (1984) with Woody Allen as an agent trying to find work for a vent with a stammer.

10 ACTORS WHO REJECTED STAR ROLES

1.   MICHAEL CAINE passed over the Oliver Reed role in the 1969 film *Women in Love* because of the nude wrestling scene with Alan Bates. 'I wouldn't have done it for $20 million,' said Caine.

2.   GARY COOPER turned down the role of Rhett Butler in the 1939 epic *Gone With The Wind* because he was convinced it would be a flop. Clark Gable was happy to prove him wrong.

3.   JOAN CRAWFORD backed out of the 1953 movie *From Here to Eternity* because she detested the costumes. Deborah Kerr took her place and won an Oscar nomination.

4.   HENRY FONDA turned down the role which earned Peter Finch a posthumous Oscar in the 1976 movie *Network* because he considered it to be 'too hysterical'.

5.   ANTHONY HOPKINS said 'No' to the part of *Gandhi* (1982) which won Ben Kingsley an Oscar.

6.   ANTHONY NEWLEY rejected the title role in the 1966 hit *Alfie* which made Michael Caine a major star.

7.   GEORGE RAFT turned down the lead in the 1941 classic *The Maltese Falcon*, allowing Humphrey Bogart to take over.

8.   ROBERT REDFORD turned down Dustin Hoffman's role in the 1967 hit *The Graduate*.

9.   GEORGE SEGAL quit the 1979 comedy *10* early in filming, enabling Dudley Moore to make his big Hollywood breakthrough.

10. SYLVESTER STALLONE walked out on the 1985 hit *Beverly Hills Cop* when his demand for more action scenes was rejected. Eddie Murphy took over.

10 CASES OF MOVIE CENSORSHIP

1. British censors refused to pass a scene in the 1928 American film *The Little Shepherd of Kingdom Come* featuring an elderly couple in a double bed. From then on, twin beds were used in Hollywood films to avoid problems with the lucrative British market. The British Board of Film Censors was described at the time as a collection of 'ex-colonels and maiden aunts in long flowered frocks.' They banned any form of screen relationship between coloured men and white women (but not between white men and coloured women) on the grounds that black men were considered then to be better-endowed than their white counterparts. So any form of contact between the two had strong sexual connotations.

2. In 1964, the Peking Cinema Institute banned an educational film entitled *Elementary Safety in Swimming in Rivers, Lakes and Seas.* The safety element was considered to be a bourgeois trait, calculated to undermine revolutionary daring.

3. The 12-year period that Josef Goebbels was Chief Censor for the Third Reich was an extremely liberal one for the German cinema...with one exception. For Hitler had ordered that any woman character in a film who broke up a marriage must die before the end credits.

4. In 1932, Japan cut a scene of Sylvia Sidney being embraced by Cary Grant in *Madame Butterfly* because her left elbow was exposed.

5. When the 1915 film *The Hypocrites* depicted a nude girl, the Mayor of Boston, Massachusetts, demanded that clothes be painted on to the woman's body frame by frame. During the 1920s, over-exposed legs and shoulders were forbidden on-screen in most U.S. states. Chicago cut a scene of a family man drawing the curtains of his house lest the idea should be conveyed that he was intending to kiss his own wife...or worse. Pennsylvania would not even permit scenes of women knitting baby garments.

6. In early Clarabelle Cow cartoons, the cow's udder was always discreetly draped by an apron for fear of upsetting the moral guardians.

7. Mickey Mouse was banned in Romania in 1935 because the authorities thought that he was likely to scare the nation's children.

8.   By 1934, censorship in the United States was so strict that British producer Herbert Wilcox found he could only get *Nell Gwynne* released in the U.S. by shooting a special scene, solely for America, in which Charles II married the orange-girl.

9.   In 1960, on the set of *Let's Make Love,* the censor was appalled to see Marilyn Monroe and Yves Montand writhing around during one scene. Monroe couldn't understand the fuss. 'What's wrong?' she asked. 'Well, it's horizontal,' replied the censor. 'It's as though you were getting ready for the sex act.' '*Oh, that*,' beamed Monroe: 'You can do that standing up.' The scene stayed in.

10.   The Mexican censor cut huge chunks from the 1983 movie *Silkwood* – all the scenes in which Cher was shown as a lesbian.

10 ACTORS WHO HAVE PLAYED MULTIPLE ROLES IN FILMS

1. ROLF LESLIE (27 parts in the 1913 life story of Queen Victoria, *Sixty Years a Queen*).

2. LUPINO LANE (24 parts in *Only Me*, 1929).

3. JOSEPH HENABERY (14 characters in *The Birth of a Nation*, 1915).

4. ROBERT HIRSCH (12 roles in *No Questions on Saturday*, 1964).

5. MICHAEL RIPPER (9 parts in *What a Crazy World*, 1963).

6. ALEC GUINNESS (8 roles in *Kind Hearts and Coronets*, 1949).

7. JERRY LEWIS (7 characters in *The Family Jewels*, 1965).

8. PETER SELLERS (3 roles in *The Mouse That Roared*, 1959).

9. TERRY-THOMAS (3 parts in *Arabella*, 1969).

10. RED SKELTON (3 characters in *Watch The Birdie*, 1950).

Peter Sellers revelled in tackling multiple roles. Alec Guinness was his hero and he played three characters in no fewer than three films – *The Mouse That Roared, Dr. Strangelove* and *Soft Beds, Hard Battles*. In Stanley Kubrick's *Dr. Strangelove, or How I Learned to Stop Worrying and Love the Bomb*, Sellers played U.S. President Merkin Muffley, RAF Group-Captain Lionel Mandrake and Strangelove himself – a mad Nazi-American inventor with an artificial arm. Kubrick wanted to achieve a 'satiric symmetry' in which 'everywhere you turn there is some version of Peter Sellers holding the fate of the world in his hands.' To this end, Kubrick also wanted Sellers to take on two other roles – Major 'King' Kong and General Buck Turgidson. But when Sellers broke an ankle, Slim Pickens took over as Kong. As for Turgidson, Sellers didn't like the role and thought it was too physically demanding to play yet another character. So George C. Scott stepped in. Incidentally, Sellers based Strangelove's curious little voice on a stills photographer called Weegee.

10 SEX SCENE CONFESSIONS

1. 'His idea of a romantic kiss was to go 'blaaah' and gag me with his tongue. He only improved once he married Demi Moore' – CYBILL SHEPHERD on BRUCE WILLIS.

2. 'On location it was really uncomfortable. He wasn't a good kisser. Then we came to London and had this great love scene. He was wonderful – I couldn't understand it. It turned out that his wife was with him in London. He was much looser when she was there' – CYBILL SHEPHERD on MICHAEL CAINE in *Silver Bears*.

3. VERONICA LAKE got on so badly with FREDRIC MARCH during *I Married A Witch* that she kneed him in the groin during their love scene.

4. 'I have never considered myself to be a sex symbol. Nobody asked me to do sex scenes – it would only have depressed people' – LAUREN BACALL.

5. 'It was really sexy. I enjoyed bumping up against it even though it had black stuff all over it so that by the end of shooting my face was covered in black goo' – KIM BASINGER being turned on by MICHAEL KEATON's Batman costume.

6. KENNETH WILLIAMS' moment of unbridled passion with JOAN SIMS in *Carry On Up The Khyber* was somewhat marred by Williams' persistent flatulence.

7. 'When I read there was a scene where I had to moon, I thought it was a joke. When I realised it wasn't, I made all the crew moon too so I could look at their ugly bottoms' – EMILY LLOYD on *Wish You Were Here*.

8. LANA TURNER used to chew gum to keep her mouth fresh for screen clinches. CLARK GABLE kissed her so forcibly during *Homecoming* that when they drew back, the pair were attached by a ribbon of sticky gum! From then on, she gargled.

9. 'It's a little too sick, real or feigned, to do it in front of your mother' – JENNIFER JASON LEIGH discussing a sex scene in her 1996 movie *Georgia*, the screenplay for which had been written by her mother, BARBARA TURNER. Leigh asked Turner to leave the set at the crucial moment.

10. 'God, I miss my husband' – PATSY KENSIT's whispered words to MEL GIBSON during their naked romp in *Lethal Weapon 2*.

20 HOLLYWOOD INSULTS

1. JULIE ANDREWS. 'Working with her is like being hit over the head with a Valentine's card' – CHRISTOPHER PLUMMER.

2. MARLON BRANDO. 'He has preserved the mentality of an adolescent. When he doesn't try and someone's speaking to him, it's like a blank wall. In fact it's even less interesting because behind a blank wall you can always suppose that there's something interesting there' – BURT REYNOLDS.

3. RICHARD CHAMBERLAIN. 'You're doing it the wrong way round, my boy. You're a star and you don't know how to act' – SIR CEDRIC HARDWICKE.

4. JOAN COLLINS. 'She's common, she can't act – yet she's the hottest female property around these days. If that doesn't tell you something about the state of our industry today, what does?' – STEWART GRANGER, 1984.

5. JOAN CRAWFORD. 'The best time I ever had with Joan Crawford was when I pushed her down the stairs in *Whatever Happened to Baby Jane?*' – BETTE DAVIS.

6. GRETA GARBO. 'Co-starring with Garbo hardly constituted an introduction' – FREDRIC MARCH.

7. RICHARD GERE. 'I'm always trying to find diplomatic ways to talk about Richard and the movie *An Officer and a Gentleman*. I liked him before we started but that is the last time I can remember talking to him' – DEBRA WINGER.

8. REX HARRISON. 'The most brilliant actor that I have ever worked with. I've liked others very much more' – ANNA NEAGLE.

9. JERRY LEWIS. 'Lewis used to be one of my heroes. When I was a kid, I did pantomimes to his records. He was an enormously talented, phenomenally energetic man who used vulnerability very well. But through the years, I've seen him turn into this arrogant, sour, ceremonial, piously chauvinistic egomaniac' – ELLIOTT GOULD.

10. SHELLEY LONG. 'Then there was the question of Shelley's hair (on *Hello Again*). We had to re-shoot the first ten days because it was wrong. All I can say about Shelley is that she is a perfectionist' – GABRIEL BYRNE.

11. SOPHIA LOREN. 'I do not talk about Sophia. I do not wish to make for her publicity. She has a talent, but it is not such a big talent' – GINA LOLLOBRIGIDA.

12. JAYNE MANSFIELD. 'Dramatic art in her opinion is knowing how to fill a sweater' – BETTE DAVIS.

13. SARAH MILES. 'She's a monster. If you think she's not strong, you'd better pay attention' – ROBERT MITCHUM.

14. STEVE McQUEEN. 'A Steve McQueen performance just naturally lends itself to monotony. Steve doesn't bring much to the party' – ROBERT MITCHUM.

15. MARILYN MONROE. 'It's like kissing Hitler' – TONY CURTIS.

16. MARGARET O'BRIEN. 'If that child had been born in the Middle Ages, she'd have been burned as a witch' – LIONEL BARRYMORE.

17. BARBRA STREISAND. 'Filming with Streisand is an experience which may have cured me of movies' – KRIS KRISTOFFERSON.

18. ESTHER WILLIAMS. 'Wet she's a star. Dry, she ain't' – FANNY BRICE.

19. MICHAEL WINNER. 'To say that Michael Winner is his own worst enemy is to provoke a ragged chorus from odd corners of the film industry of "Not while I'm alive"' – BARRY NORMAN.

20. LORETTA YOUNG. 'She was and is the only actress I really dislike. She was sickeningly sweet, a pure phoney. Her two faces sent me home angry and crying several times' – VIRGINIA FIELD.

10 MOVIE BLUNDERS

1. Television aerials can be seen on the roofs of Victorian London in the 1966 comedy *The Wrong Box*.

2. During a scene in *The Sound of Music*, an orange-box is clearly visible stamped with the words 'Produce of Israel'. Yet the film was set in 1938 – ten years before Israel was founded.

3. The heroine of the Swedish film *Adalen 31*, set in 1931, strips off in one scene to reveal bikini marks. The bikini wasn't invented until 1946.

4. Some of the chariot racers in *Ben Hur* sported wristwatches.

5. Richard Harris appeared as King Arthur in *Camelot* with a piece of Elastoplast visible on his neck.

6. Tyre tracks can be spotted on the ground in the western *Stagecoach*.

7. When the citizens of Amity celebrate 4 July in *Jaws*, there are no leaves on the trees. This was because the scene was actually shot in May.

8. The Portman Square flat where the hero lives in the 1956 movie *Twenty-Three Paces to Baker Street* boasts a balcony overlooking the Thames. It must have been a big balcony since Portman Square is more than two miles from the river.

9. The reflection of the camera can be seen in a mirror in the 1985 movie *Falling in Love*, starring Robert De Niro and Meryl Streep.

10. Edward G. Robinson's character gets sent to Alcatraz in 1927 during the movie *The Last Gangster*. Yet Alcatraz first became a prison in 1934.

10 CHARACTERS FROM CAMBERWICK GREEN

1. PETER, the postman.

2. MRS. DINGLE, the postmistress.

3. DR. MOPP.

4. MRS. HONEYMAN, the chemist's wife.

5. MICKEY MURPHY, the baker.

6. MR. CARRAWAY, the fishmonger.

7. WINDY MILLER.

8. MR. CROCKETT, the garage-owner.

9. THOMAS TRIPP, the milkman.

10. ROGER VARLEY, the chimney-sweep.

10 WACKY RACERS

1. DICK DASTARDLY AND MUTTLEY IN THE MEAN MACHINE.

2. THE SLAG BROTHERS IN THE BOULDERMOBILE.

3. THE GRUESOME TWOSOME IN THE CREEPY COUPE.

4. PROFESSOR PAT PENDING IN THE CONVERT-A-CAR.

5. PENELOPE PITSTOP IN THE COMPACT PUSSYCAT.

6. SARGE AND MEEKLEY IN THE ARMY SURPLUS SPECIAL.

7. THE ANT HILL MOB IN THE ROARING PLENTY.

8. RED MAX IN THE CRIMSON HAYBAILER.

9. PETER PERFECT IN THE VAROOM ROADSTER.

10. RUFUS RUFFCUT AND SAWTOOTH IN THE BUZZ WAGON.

20 STARS WHO BEGAN IN SOAPS

1.   TOM BERENGER. Nominated for an Academy Award for his role in Platoon, Berenger had lousy luck in the American soap *One Life to Live*. His character Tim Siegel fell in love with a nun and died after falling down a flight of stairs.

2.   MICHAEL CRAWFORD. One of Crawford's first roles was as a patient bandaged from head to toe in the British medical soap *Emergency – Ward 10* where he managed to forget his only line. He had written it on the bedsheet which he then lifted up and uttered the immortal words: 'Have you seen this, nurse?'

3.   TED DANSON. The star of *Cheers* and *Three Men and a Baby* had a shady past as crooked attorney Tom Conway in the U.S. daytime soap *Somerset*.

4.   PATTY DUKE won an Oscar for her role as Helen Keller in *The Miracle Worker* but got an early break as a child actress on the American soap *The Brighter Day*.

5.   CHARLES DURNING. Twice nominated for Academy Awards and best remembered as the man who fell for Dustin Hoffman in *Tootsie*, Durning earlier had equally bad luck when being killed off as loving husband Gil McGowan in the U.S. soap *Another World*.

6.   MIA FARROW first shot to fame as virginal Allison Mackenzie in the 1960s tear-jerker *Peyton Place*.

7.   ALBERT FINNEY was another budding star who played a patient on *Emergency – Ward 10*.

8.   FIONA FULLERTON made her name as a nurse on the BBC's *Angels* in the 1970s.

9.   DAVID HASSELHOFF. The star of *Knight Rider* and *Baywatch* had earlier taken over the role of Snapper Foster in the popular American daytime soap *The Young and the Restless*.

10. TOMMY LEE JONES spent four years on *One Life to Live* in which time his character Mark Toland had an extra-marital affair, was involved in blackmail and was wanted for murder. So it was appropriate that his first major role outside of soaps was as Gary Gilmore in *The Executioner's Song*.

11. KEVIN KLINE. One of his early jobs was as Woody Reed in the American soap *Search For Tomorrow*.

12. MALCOLM McDOWELL. The future *Clockwork Orange* star had an unlikely role as PR man Crispin Ryder in *Crossroads*.

13. RUE McCLANAHAN, man-hungry Blanche from *The Golden Girls*, was once a regular in *Another World* playing super-bitch Caroline Johnson.

14. RYAN O'NEAL played hot-head Rodney Harrington in *Peyton Place*.

15. ELAINE PAIGE was another who escaped from *Crossroads*. She had a small part as Caroline Winthrop back in the late 1960s.

16. CHRISTOPHER REEVE was the first person to be called a bastard on American daytime TV when he played two-timing rat Ben Harper in *Love of Life*.

17. SUSAN SARANDON played the hapless Patrice Kahlman on *A World Apart* and the evil Sarah Fairbanks in *Search For Tomorrow*.

18. TOM SELLECK. Before hitting the big time, Selleck played some steamy scenes as Jed Andrews in *The Young and the Restless*.

19. KATHLEEN TURNER. Before earning her big break as greedy seductress Matty Walker in the movie *Body Heat*, Turner had practised being nasty in the American soap *The Doctors* where she played Nola Aldrich, a scheming bitch who specialised in wrecking men's lives.

20. SIGOURNEY WEAVER played the demure Avis Ryan in *Somerset*.

10 STARS WHO APPEARED IN CORONATION STREET

1. RICHARD BECKINSALE was PC Wilcox of Tile Street Police Station, sent to arrest Ena Sharples in 1969 for staging a sit-in.

2. DAVY JONES. The future Monkee played Ena Sharples' grandson Colin Lomax in one episode of *Coronation Street* back in 1961. After giving him a biscuit, Ena sent him on an errand to buy a form for her will, and he was never seen again.

3. GORDEN KAYE appeared as hairdresser Bernard Butler, Elsie Tanner's nephew, in 1969.

4. BEN KINGSLEY. The star of *Gandhi* played Ron Jenkins who chatted up Irma Barlow in the early 1970s.

5. ARTHUR LOWE made his name in the 1960s as the Street's pompous lay-preacher Leonard Swindley, jilted at the altar by Emily Nugent, before his classic portrayal of Captain Mainwaring in *Dad's Army*.

6. JOANNA LUMLEY played graduate Elaine Perkins who was wooed by Ken Barlow in 1973.

7. PETER NOONE. Prior to achieving pop stardom as Herman of Herman's Hermits, Noone played Len Fairclough's son, Stanley, in the early 1960s.

8. PRUNELLA SCALES appeared in the Street in 1961 as bus conductress Eileen Hughes.

9. PAUL SHANE owes his success to a walk-on part in the Street as Alf Roberts' boss. While waiting for the kettle to boil, comedy writer Jimmy Perry spotted Shane's 45-second appearance in the 1979 episode and knew immediately that he was the man to play Ted Bovis in *Hi-De-Hi*.

10. MARTIN SHAW played hippie commune leader Robert Croft who took over an empty house on the Street in 1968.

20 SOAP-HOPPERS

The following have all appeared in more than one soap

1. TONY ADAMS (Dr. Neville Bywaters, *General Hospital;* Adam Chance, *Crossroads*).

2. JOHNNY BRIGGS (Cliff Layton, *Crossroads;* Mike Baldwin, *Coronation Street*).

3. MALANDRA BURROWS (Damon Grant's girlfriend Lisa, *Brookside;* Kathy Glover, *Emmerdale*).

4. EDWARD CLAYTON (Stan Harvey, *Crossroads;* Arthur Parkinson, *Brookside*).

5. DIANA DAVIES (Norma Ford, *Coronation Street;* Caroline Bates, *Emmerdale*).

6. PETER DEAN (Fangio Bateman, *Coronation Street;* Pete Beale, *EastEnders*).

7. DAVID EASTER (Pat Hancock, *Brookside;* Pete Callan, *Family Affairs*).

8. LARRY HAGMAN (Ed Gibson, *The Edge of the Night;* J.R. Ewing, *Dallas*).

9. SUE JENKINS (Gloria Todd, *Coronation Street;* Jackie Corkhill, *Brookside*).

10. ROBERTA KERR (Wendy Crozier, *Coronation Street;* Jan Glover, *Emmerdale*).

11. ANNIE MILES (Sue Sullivan, *Brookside;* Maria Simons, *Family Affairs*).

12. SUE NICHOLLS (Marilyn Gates, *Crossroads;* Audrey Roberts, *Coronation Street*).

13. RICHARD NORTON (Ryan McLachlan, *Neighbours;* Shane Cochran, *Brookside*).

14. STEVEN PINDER (Roy Lambert, *Crossroads;* Max Farnham, *Brookside*).

15. WENDY RICHARD (Joyce Harker, *The Newcomers;* Pauline Fowler, *EastEnders*).

16. PAM ST. CLEMENT (Mrs. Eckersley, *Emmerdale;* Pat Butcher, *EastEnders*).

17. ALYSON SPIRO (Alison Gregory, *Brookside;* Sarah Sugden, *Emmerdale*).

18. STAN STENNETT (Norman Crabtree, *Coronation Street;* Sid Hooper, *Crossroads*).

19. RICHARD THORP (Dr. Rennie, *Emergency – Ward 10;* Alan Turner, *Emmerdale*).

20. BILL TREACHER (Sidney the milkman, *Mrs. Dale's Diary;* Arthur Fowler, *EastEnders*).

20 SOAP CHARACTERS WHO HAVE ACQUIRED NEW HEADS

1. Scott Robinson, *Neighbours* (DARIUS PERKINS to JASON DONOVAN).

2. Miss Ellie Ewing, *Dallas* (BARBARA BEL GEDDES to DONNA REED).

3. Steven Carrington, *Dynasty* (AL CORLEY to JACK COLEMAN).

4. Patricia Dunne, *Sons And Daughters* (ROWENA WALLACE to BELINDA GIBLIN).

5. Fallon Colby, *Dynasty* (PAMELA SUE MARTIN to EMMA SAMMS).

6. Tracy Barlow, *Coronation Street* (CHRISTABEL FINCH to HOLLY CHAMARETTE to DAWN ACTON).

7. Nicky Tilsley, *Coronation Street* (WARREN JACKSON to ADAM RICKETTS).

8. Mark Fowler, *EastEnders* (DAVID SCARBORO to TODD CARTY).

9. Martin Fowler, *EastEnders* (JON PEYTON PRICE to JAMES ALEXANDROU).

10. Gordon Collins, *Brookside* (NIGEL CROWLEY to MARK BURGESS).

11. Lucy Collins, *Brookside* (KATRIN CARTLIDGE to MAGGIE SAUNDERS to KATRIN CARTLIDGE again).

12. Geoff Rogers, *Brookside* (KEVIN CARSON to STEPHEN WALTERS).

13. Katie Rogers, *Brookside* (DEBBIE REYNOLDS to DIANE BURKE).

14. Tony Dixon, *Brookside* (GERARD BOSTOCK to MARK LENNOCK).

15. Leo Johnson, *Brookside* (LEEON SAWYER to STEVEN COLE).

16. Jack Sugden, *Emmerdale* (ANDREW BURT to CLIVE HORNBY).

17. Toby Mangel, *Neighbours* (FINN GREENTREE KEENE to BEN GEURENS).

18. Marilyn Gates, *Crossroads* (SUE NICHOLLS to NADINE HANWELL).

19. Dolly Skilbeck, *Emmerdale* (KATHERINE BARKER to JEAN ROGERS).

20. C.C. Capwell, *Santa Barbara* (PETER MARK RICHMAN to LLOYD BOCHNER to PAUL BURKE to CHARLES BATEMAN).

THE FIRST 10 CORONATION STREET WEDDINGS

1. March 1961. Joan Walker and Gordon Davies.

2. October 1961. Harry Hewitt and Concepta Riley (honeymoon Ireland).

3. August 1962. Ken Barlow and Valerie Tatlock (honeymoon London).

4. October 1963. Jerry Booth and Myra Dickinson.

5. December 1965. David Barlow and Irma Ogden.

6. September 1967. Steve Tanner and Elsie Tanner (honeymoon Lisbon).

7. May 1968. Dennis Tanner and Jenny Sutton.

8. July 1970. Elsie Tanner and Alan Howard (honeymoon Paris).

9. April 1972. Ernest Bishop and Emily Nugent (honeymoon Edale).

10. October 1973. Ken Barlow and Janet Reid.

Sometimes life mirrors soap. Two years after their *Coronation Street* wedding, PAT PHOENIX and ALAN BROWNING (who played Elsie Tanner and Alan Howard) tied the knot for real in a lavish showbiz ceremony complete with top hats and tails and horse-drawn carriages. Neither marriage lasted long. Phoenix and Browning had drifted apart by the time Browning died of liver disease in 1978 while on-screen Alan Howard went off with another woman. Few of the other early Street weddings fared much better. Harry Hewitt was killed in 1967 when a jack collapsed and a van fell on him; Valerie Barlow was electrocuted by a faulty hair-dryer plug in 1971; Jerry and Myra Booth were divorced in 1967; David Barlow was killed in a car crash in Australia in 1970; Steve Tanner was killed after falling downstairs during a fight in 1968; Ernest Bishop was shot dead in a wages snatch in 1978; and Janet Reid committed suicide after her divorce from Ken Barlow. Clearly in soaps, staying single is the best way to a healthy life.

10 SCARCELY-REMEMBERED U.K. SOAPS

1. ALBION MARKET (1985-86). Much-hyped tale of Manchester market-folk that was axed after just 100 episodes. Guest stars included Sixties pop star Helen Shapiro as hairdresser Viv and Tony Booth (Tony Blair's father-in-law) as Ted Pilkington, landlord of the Waterman's Arms pub.

2. THE APPLEYARDS (1952-57). The BBC's idea of an 'ordinary, workaday family living in a little house'. Starred Constance Fraser and Frederick Piper.

3. THE DOCTORS (1969-71). Set among a group of doctors, nurses and health visitors in a North London practice. Starred John Barrie as crusty Dr. John Somers and Justine Lord as sexy Dr. Liz McNeal.

4. GEMS (1985—89). Daytime soap about the Covent Garden rag trade. The central characters were the Stone brothers, Stephen and Alan.

5. MIRACLES TAKE LONGER (1984). Set against the unglamorous backdrop of a Community Advice office, this daytime soap starred Patsy Byrne as organiser Betty Hackforth but lasted barely four months.

6. ROOMS (1974-77). Afternoon serial, the location for which was a house converted into bedsits at 35 Mafeking Terrace, London W14. Sylvia Kay played landlady Dorothy.

7. STARR AND COMPANY (1958). The fictional town of Sullbridge, 50 miles south of London, was the setting for the tales of a family buoy-making firm founded by retired naval engineer Joseph Starr. Ran aground after four months.

8. TAFF ACRE (1981). A twice-weekly saga of the Johnson family living in a fictional South Wales village, some 12 miles from Cardiff. Starred Richard Davies as unemployed Max Johnson and Rhoda Lewis as his breadwinner wife Beth.

9. UNITED! (1965-67). The adventures of struggling Brentwich United Football Club, managed by Gerry Barford (David Lodge). After Barford's sacking, Ronald Allen (later of Crossroads fame) came in to play the new manager.

10. WEAVERS GREEN (1966). A twice-weekly story of two country vets practising in an East Anglian village. Starred Grant Taylor and Megs Jenkins.

10 THINGS YOU NEVER KNEW ABOUT SOOTY

1. Amateur magician HARRY CORBETT bought the original Sooty glove puppet for 7s 6d in 1948 to keep his family amused on a wet holiday in Blackpool. Sooty has had his own TV series since 1952.

2. One year when the Corbett family went on holiday, Harry had driven a few miles when he suddenly stopped the car. Realising he had forgotten Sooty, he insisted on driving back to collect him.

3. Sooty used to travel everywhere in a cardboard box with air holes so that he could breathe.

4. MARJORIE CORBETT used to puzzle butchers by buying sausages by the yard instead of the pound. 'They're for Sweep's Christmas decorations,' she would explain.

5. A storm broke out in 1964 when Harry planned to introduce Soo, a panda girlfriend for Sooty. The BBC decreed that such a move would be to bring sex into children's television. The Corporation backed down after a newspaper campaign and allowed Soo to join the show, but only on condition that she and Sooty never touched.

6. Harry's brother LESLIE used to operate Sweep. When he had to give Sweep up owing to work commitments, Leslie was so upset that he had to be treated for depression.

7. Harry's son MATTHEW took over Sooty in 1975 after Harry suffered a near-fatal heart attack.

8. In 1980, Sooty landed in bother after an innocuous scene in which he put Sweep in a tranquilising booth. The story escalated to the point where the tabloids accused Sooty of peddling hard drugs!

9. Famous Sooty fans have included the children of GEORGE HARRISON, MICK JAGGER and JOHN CLEESE and grown-ups CLIFF RICHARD, TOMMY STEELE and Iron Maiden drummer NICKO MCBRAIN.

10. Among those who have been squirted by Sooty's water-pistol are PRINCE PHILIP, TERRY WOGAN, JERRY HALL and JOAN COLLINS. The only person to have taken offence was dog-handler BARBARA WOODHOUSE.

20 ON-AIR TV BLUNDERS

1. On a live edition of *Top of the Pops* in 1964, ALAN 'FLUFF' FREEMAN introduced the Sounds Orchestral hit 'Cast Your Fate to the Wind' as 'Cast Your Wind to the Fate'.

2. PATRICK MOORE, presenter of the long-running astronomy programme *The Sky at Night*, swallowed a fly during an early show. He said: 'I had just opened my mouth to make some world-shattering pronouncement when in it flew. The producer said he saw a look of glazed horror come into my eyes, after which I gave a strangled gulp and went on.'

3. For a 1950s BBC production of *Robin Hood*, the back-projection plate was inserted incorrectly so that all of the trees in Sherwood Forest appeared on screen upside-down.

4. In his 1961 comedy series *Bingo Madness*, the diminutive CHARLIE DRAKE was rendered unconscious after a stunt in which he was hurled through a bookcase went wrong. The screen was blacked out, the rest of the series cancelled and Drake lay in a coma for several days before recovering.

5. At the end of an interview with Duran Duran on *The Tube*, PAULA YATES discovered that she had been sitting on the microphone and nobody had heard a word.

6. A hairdresser's error on the detective series *Randall & Hopkirk (Deceased)* meant that KENNETH COPE, who played Marty Hopkirk, wore his wig the wrong way round for two episodes before anyone spotted the mistake.

7. With British Summer Time about to end, JIMMY HILL concluded an edition of *Match of the Day* with the reminder: 'Good night. And don't forget tonight to put your cocks back.'

8. In 1956, PAUL SCOFIELD's closing speech in a live TV production of *Hamlet* was cut short to make way for an advert for Kia Ora orange juice. Furious ATV boss Lew Grade rang up. 'What happened?' he boomed. The young transmission controller replied: 'Oh, they all died in the end.'

9. When the wrong track was played on *Top of the Pops*, JIMI HENDRIX found himself miming to an Alan Price hit. Hendrix said: 'I like the voice, man, but I don't know the words...'

10. Bringing his pet mouse and pet eagle into the studio for the 1950s children's series *All Your Own* and explaining how well they got on together, a schoolboy could only watch in horror as the eagle's natural instincts got the better of him and he swooped from his perch and ate the mouse.

11. On *The Antiques Roadshow*, ARTHUR NEGUS once dropped someone's prized clock, causing it to shatter into a hundred pieces. 'Never mind,' said the forgiving owner, 'It will give me something to do in the evenings putting it together.'

12. FRANKIE HOWERD sparked protests by walking on stage for *Sunday Night at the London Palladium* carrying a Union Jack upside-down.

13. During an exhibition of marrow-dangling on *Blue Peter*, the intrepid JOHN NOAKES was knocked out by a five-pound imitation marrow and taken to hospital for an X-ray.

14. In 1985, the last episode of JACKIE COLLINS' mini-series *Hollywood Wives* was accidentally screened in Britain with 15 crucial minutes missing. None of the 10 million viewers rang in to complain.

15. MRS. SYBIL DICKINSON of Strood in Kent wrote in to the 1954 wish-granting series *Ask Pickles*, requesting to stroke a lion. She was anticipating a cub but was instead faced with a half-grown, ten-month-old monster which promptly snapped at the studio manager's legs and then savaged the sleeve of Mrs. Dickinson's dress.

16. An edition of *Tomorrow's World* featured a lady demonstrating a portable bath. In the finest BBC tradition, she was suitably concealed with bubbles — until the heat from the studio lights began to melt the foam.

17. A misheard instruction to the *Top of the Pops* crew meant that DEXY'S MIDNIGHT RUNNERS ended up performing their soul tribute 'Jackie Wilson Said' in front of a huge blow-up of darts player Jocky Wilson.

18. Introducing Sir Stafford Cripps at a 1951 political broadcast, BBC announcer MCDONALD HOBLEY declared: 'And now, the moment you have been waiting for — the Chancellor of the Exchequer, Sir Stifford Crapps.'

19. On a live edition of the children's series *Zoo Time*, DESMOND MORRIS found that every lion the camera was pointed at immediately mounted the female and started mating frantically...in front of millions of bemused youngsters.

20. ANDREW SACHS went through agony as the hapless Spanish waiter Manuel in *Fawlty Towers*. Once John Cleese (as Basil) whacked him so hard over the head with a frying-pan that he almost knocked him out.

10 GUEST VOICES ON THE SIMPSONS

1. LIZ TAYLOR (who gurgled baby Maggie Simpson's first words).

2. MERYL STREEP.

3. MICHELLE PFEIFFER.

4. BOB HOPE.

5. DUSTIN HOFFMAN.

6. MICHAEL JACKSON (as a weirdo).

7. DAVID DUCHOVNY.

8. GILLIAN ANDERSON.

9. PAUL MCCARTNEY.

10. AEROSMITH.

10 FORGOTTEN SUPERHEROES

1. BIFF BANNON. A U.S. Marine, big, dumb and strong, who appeared in *Speed Comics* in 1939.

2. BOMBER BURNS. American stunt flier Jack 'Bomber' Burns was attached to the RAF during the Second World War. Shot down by the Germans, he hid in the Scottish Highlands and customised his plane with machine guns, a cannon and a flame-thrower. Featured in *Victory Comics* 1941.

3. ADMIRAL FUDGE. This young, bespectacled adventurer dressed as Napoleon in a comic strip in the *New York World* newspaper, 1908.

4. DR. GRAVES. A pipe-smoking supernaturalist who travelled the world investigating strange phenomena. Appeared in *Charlton Comics*, 1966.

5. HAIRBREADTH HARRY. Teenager Harry (real name Harold Hollingsworth) fought crime in the shape of the moustachioed Rudolph Rassendale. Harry's girlfriend was Belinda Blinks. Appeared as a comic strip in *The Philadelphia Press* in 1906, graduating to six silent films in the 1920s.

6. LANCE O'CASEY. A swashbuckling sailor accompanied everywhere by his first mate, a monkey named Mister Hogan. Featured in *Whizz Comics*, 1940.

7. LARIAT SAM. Violence-hating cowboy with a talking horse, Tippytoes. His sworn enemy was Badlands Meeney. Sam's voice came courtesy of Dayton Allen. Appeared on *The Captain Kangaroo Show* on U.S. TV from 1962.

8. DR. THIRTEEN. Ghost-buster Dr. Terrence Thirteen, a non-believer in the supernatural, made his debut in *DC Comics* in 1951.

9. AGENT KEN THURSTON. A government agent with the code name X, he fought Communists, spies and assorted enemies of the state in *The Man Called X*, a U.S. radio show from 1952 and on TV, 1956-58.

10. TIM TYLER. Orphan Tim and his buddy Spud Slavins set off for Africa in search of adventure and joined a police force known as the Ivory Patrol. A U.S. comic strip from 1928.

20 TV CAMEO ROLES

1. Wearing a commissionaire's uniform and top hat, JOHN LENNON appeared as a lavatory attendant in a 1966 sketch on *Not Only...But Also* with PETER COOK and DUDLEY MOORE. The scene was filmed outside the men's toilet in Broadwick Street in London's Soho. Lennon became involved in the show through his friendship with Cook.

2. Two years earlier, THE BEATLES had dressed up as dustmen for a sketch on *Blackpool Night Out* with comedians MIKE and BERNIE WINTERS. In another sketch on the same show, RINGO played a hospital patient.

3. Running for U.S. President in 1968, RICHARD NIXON went on *Rowan and Martin's Laugh-In* just to say the show's catchphrase 'Sock it to me'. He needed six takes to get it right. Nixon's opponent, HUBERT HUMPHREY, declined an offer to appear on the show. In the end, Nixon won by just a million votes. Dick Martin later remarked: 'A lot of people have accused us...'

4. John Wayne also did a *Laugh-In* walk-on, uttering the solitary line: 'Well, I don't think that is funny.' And SAMMY DAVIS JR. featured in a running gag where every time he started to sing, he was dropped through a trap-door.

5. DENIS HEALEY was the only human to appear on *Spitting Image*. He pretended to be hurt that people mistook him for a puppet.

6. THE BEACH BOYS and JERRY LEE LEWIS had walk-ons in *T.J. Hooker*.

7. BOY GEORGE reportedly paid £42,000 to play himself as a kidnap victim in an episode of *The A-Team*.

8. Among guests seen peering from windows as *Batman* scaled buildings in the TV series were EDWARD G. ROBINSON, GEORGE RAFT and SAMMY DAVIS JR.

9. THE DUCHESS OF YORK made a cameo appearance in *Friends*. The story had Joey bumping into her on a sightseeing tour of London.

10. RICHARD BRANSON also popped up in *Friends* as street-seller Tricky Dicky. Although it took over two hours to film his scene as Branson stumbled over his lines, the Virgin boss said afterwards: 'I've definitely gone up in my children's estimation. I have finally got their respect.' Other *Friends* guests have included JULIA ROBERTS, JEAN-CLAUDE VAN DAMME and BROOKE SHIELDS.

11. PHIL COLLINS played a British conman in an episode of *Miami Vice*. Other guest spots on the show went to LITTLE RICHARD and JAMES BROWN but GEORGE MICHAEL turned down the chance to play a waiter.

12. CLIVE JAMES played a postman in *Neighbours*.

13. MICHAEL PALIN appeared as a surfer in *Home and Away*.

14. BOB HOPE, BURT REYNOLDS, MICKEY ROONEY, DICK VAN DYKE and JULIO IGLESIAS all had cameo roles in episodes of *The Golden Girls*.

15. Former U.S. President GERALD FORD and Secretary of State HENRY KISSINGER both guested on *Dynasty*.

16. JOHN CLEESE played an art gallery visitor in a 1979 episode of *Dr. Who*. 'It only took an hour and a half to do and was great fun,' remembers Cleese, who only lived six minutes from BBC Television Centre.

17. DAVID CROSBY once guested on *Ellen*.

18. Supermodel KATE MOSS appeared on *French and Saunders* as the love interest in their send-up of Mel Gibson's *Braveheart*.

19. FRANK SINATRA made a guest appearance on an episode of *Magnum P.I.* as a New York cop. He was said to be a big fan of the show.

20. In THE RUTLES' 1978 spoof Beatles documentary *All You Need Is Cash*, a heavily-disguised GEORGE HARRISON played a TV interviewer. Harrison admitted to being a big fan of the Rutles concept. MICK JAGGER and PAUL SIMON also had walk-on parts as themselves.

10 DR. WHO VILLAINS

1. BRAGEN (Bernard Archard).

2. ELEK (Philip Madoc).

3. THEODORE MAXTIBLE (Marius Goring).

4. MONARCH (Stratford Johns).

5. THE RANI (Kate O'Mara).

6. COUNT SCARLIONI (Julian Glover).

7. TEGANA (Derren Nesbitt).

8. THE VALEYARD (Michael Jayston).

9. CAPTAIN VARGA (Bernard Bresslaw).

10. KING YRCANOS (Brian Blessed).

10 DR. WHO ASSISTANTS

1. SUSAN FOREMAN (Carole Ann Ford — the first Doctor).

2. STEVEN TAYLOR (Peter Purves — the first Doctor).

3. ZOE HERRIOT (Wendy Padbury — the second Doctor).

4. LIZ SHAW (Caroline John — the third Doctor).

5. JO GRANT (Katy Manning — the third Doctor).

6. SARAH JANE SMITH (Elisabeth Sladen — the third and fourth Doctors).

7. NYSSA (Sarah Sutton — the fourth and fifth Doctors).

8. TEGAN JOVANKA (Janet Fielding — the fifth Doctor).

9. PERI BROWN (Nicola Bryant — the fifth and sixth Doctors).

10. MELANIE BUSH (Bonnie Langford — the sixth and seventh Doctors).

10 STARS WHO MADE EARLY APPEARANCES ON CHILDREN'S TV

1. STEPHANIE BEACHAM (*Rainbow*).

2. MICHAEL CAINE (*The Adventures of William Tell*).

3. DAVID CASSIDY (*The Partridge Family*).

4. RONNIE CORBETT (*Crackerjack*).

5. MICHAEL CRAWFORD (*Billy Bunter of Greyfriars School*).

6. JUDI DENCH (*Rainbow*).

7. ANITA DOBSON (*Play Away*).

8. MICKEY BRADDOCK (later Monkee MICHAEL DOLENZ) (*Circus Boy*).

9. DAVID HEMMINGS (*Billy Bunter of Greyfriars School*).

10. JEREMY IRONS (*Play Away*).

11. MICK JAGGER (*Seeing Sport*).

12. DAVID JASON (*Do Not Adjust Your Set*).

13. PATRICK MCGOOHAN (*The Adventures of Sir Lancelot*).

14. ROGER MOORE (*Ivanhoe*).

15. RICHARD O'SULLIVAN (*The Adventures of Robin Hood*).

16. JIMMY PAGE (*All Your Own*).

17. PRUNELLA SCALES (*The Secret Garden*).

18. JOHN SCHLESINGER (*Ivanhoe*).

19. ROBERT SHAW (*The Buccaneers*).

20. DENNIS WATERMAN (*Just William*).

20 CASES OF TV CENSORSHIP

1. The American network banned the words 'breasts' and 'virgin' from *M*A*S*H*. Writer LARRY GELBART got round the ban by inventing a soldier from the Virgin Islands.

2. ELVIS PRESLEY's act was considered so overtly sexual that on America's *Ed Sullivan Show*, he was only filmed from the waist up.

3. In 1966, the BBC tried to postpone an episode of *Pinky and Perky*, entitled 'You Too Can Be a Prime Minister', until after the forthcoming general election lest the programme should contain political bias. There was such an outcry that it was reinstated.

4. 13 episodes of *Upstairs, Downstairs* were banned in the U.S. for 17 years because they dealt with homosexuality and adultery.

5. In the 1950s the BBC banned any jokes about honeymoon couples, chambermaids, fig leaves, lodgers and commercial travellers. Ladies' underwear was another taboo topic. The line 'Winter draws on' was strictly forbidden.

6. The Australian soap *Number 96* contained such risqué bedroom scenes that, for transmission in moralistic Melbourne, a thick black band was superimposed on the bottom half of the screen.

7. Although made in 1978, Roy Minton's Borstal play *Scum*, which contains a vicious rape, was banned from British television until 1991.

8. Dennis Potter's *Brimstone and Treacle*, made in 1976, was not screened in Britain for another 11 years because it dealt with the rape of a handicapped girl.

9. The 1969 drama *Big Breadwinner Hog* (starring PETER EGAN) became the first British programme to be axed in mid-series owing to its violence.

10. For fear of upsetting watchdogs, DICK VAN DYKE and his TV wife MARY TYLER MOORE had to sleep in separate beds on *The Dick Van Dyke Show*.

11. SYLVIA PETERS, the BBC's celebrated announcer of the 1950s, was ordered to wear plastic flowers on the front of her dresses to conceal any hint of cleavage. One evening, after wearing a fashionable strapless evening gown, she was reprimanded by puritanical programme chief Cecil McGivern: 'You looked as if you were appearing in the bath. Please wear a stole in future.'

12. BBC founder LORD REITH once demanded that the statue of Prospero and

Ariel, which graces the entrance of Broadcasting House, be taken down so that the size of their genitals could be reduced.

13. LUCILLE BALL was never allowed to say 'pregnant' on *I Love Lucy*. It had to be 'expecting'.

14. An episode of MICHAEL BENTINE's *It's a Square World*, in which a Chinese junk sank the House of Commons, was banned by the BBC until after an approaching general election. A baffled Bentine commented: 'Apparently, there is a BBC edict that you must show parity to the parties at election time. I would have imagined that if you sank the Commons you were showing parity to everybody!'

15. Produced in 1966, PETER WATKINS' drama *The War Game*, about a hypothetical nuclear attack on Britain, was banned until 1985 because it was thought that it would frighten elderly people to death.

16. In 1997, Channel 4's *The Big Breakfast* banned All Saints' singer MELANIE BLATT from appearing live on the programme for six months after she swore on-air.

17. Dancer KERRY MARTIN was sacked from the BBC's Fifties pop show *Six-Five Special* for wiggling too much during a routine.

18. A full-frontal male nude and actress GEMMA CRAVEN's nipples were censored from Dennis Potter's *Pennies From Heaven*.

19. American network ABC refused to let a fully-dressed Jeff Colby kiss wife Fallon's foot in *The Colbys* for fear of encouraging foot-fetishists.

20. In 1961, Granada prepared a documentary on television censorship. It was banned.

10 EXAMPLES OF THE POWER OF TELEVISION

1. Worried that *Steptoe and Son* might keep Labour voters away from the polling-booths at the 1964 general election, HAROLD WILSON persuaded the BBC to postpone transmission until 9pm on election night. Wilson estimated that the move might be worth a dozen seats to him. Labour won the election by just four seats.

2. Labour had voiced similar fears about the transmission of *Wagon Train* on the night of the 1959 election. The programme was not moved and Labour lost.

3. Convicts on a chain-gang in America's Deep South threatened to riot when a warden said he'd stop them watching *The Fugitive*.

4. In an early episode of *Coronation Street*, Ena Sharples said she didn't like chocolate eclairs. Eight years later, she ate two on the show and the letters poured in!

5. When *The Magic Roundabout* was taken off in June 1968, the fiercest petition for its return came from an army camp.

6. The times of Sunday evening Church services in Britain were changed to avoid clashing with the 1967 adaptation of John Galsworthy's *The Forsyte Saga*. Early-closing day in a Dutch city was also altered because no one stayed to shop. And militant students in Prague postponed a rally to watch the programme.

7. *Star Trek*'s WILLIAM SHATNER was holidaying in a deserted village in a remote wilderness by the Caspian Sea when a waiter, who spoke no English, came up to him and said: 'Captain Kirk?'

8. To the concern of their superiors, Merseyside police officers imitated *Starsky and Hutch* by adopting sunglasses on patrol and wearing their gloves with the cuffs turned down.

9. *A Family at War*, a dour 52-parter set in wartime Liverpool, became Denmark's most popular programme in the 1970s. The rush home to see it brought traffic in Copenhagen to a standstill.

10. A *Candid Camera* stunt showed presenter PETER DULAY appearing to eat a goldfish (it was really a slice of carrot) from a tank in a dry cleaner's shop. A woman rang the programme to say that after watching it, her small son had gone into the next room and eaten their pet goldfish.

10 DEFECTIVE DETECTIVES

1. MARK SABER — one arm.

2. COLONEL MARCH — one eye.

3. MIKE LONGSTREET — blind.

4. CHIEF ROBERT T. IRONSIDE — wheelchair-bound.

5. COLUMBO — no dress sense.

6. FRANK CANNON — obese.

7. THEO KOJAK — bald.

8. JIM BERGERAC — ex-alcoholic with dodgy leg.

9. JIM ROCKFORD — ex-con.

10. EDDIE SHOESTRING — ex-nervous breakdown.

10 U.S. DETECTIVE SHOWS NOT SET IN LOS ANGELES

1. HOMICIDE — LIFE ON THE STREET (Baltimore).

2. THE STREETS OF SAN FRANCISCO (San Francisco).

3. N.Y.P.D. BLUE (New York).

4. MIAMI VICE (Miami).

5. FATHER DOWLING INVESTIGATES (Chicago).

6. BANACEK (Boston).

7. HAWAII FIVE-O (Hawaii).

8. McCLOUD (New York).

9. VEGA$ (Las Vegas).

10. McMILLAN AND WIFE (San Francisco).

10 TV SCANDALS

1. After CLIFF RICHARD appeared on the ITV pop show *Oh Boy!* in 1958, newspapers attacked his 'crude exhibitionism' and accused him of 'smouldering on screen'. One warned: 'Don't let your daughter go out with people like this.'

2. Diplomatic relations between Britain and Saudi Arabia were broken off in 1980 following the screening of the dramatised documentary *Death of a Princess*. The British ambassador in Jeddah was sent home, King Khaled cancelled a planned trip to Britain and £200 million in exports were lost.

3. A storm of protest broke in 1965 after critic KENNETH TYNAN became the first person to say 'fuck' on British television during an interview on the late-night satire show *BBC3*.

4. In 1954, the BBC received over 1,200 complaints in two weeks about the amorous behaviour of Australian RON RANDALL, temporary chairman on *What's My Line?* He blew a kiss to viewers at the end of one show, kissed a challenger on another and even promised to kiss panellist Barbara Kelly.

5. BLUE PETER was censured in 1964 over a ginger-pop recipe described by the Temperance Union as 'a dangerously alcoholic brew'.

6. An irate singer tipped a bowl of sugar over the head of *New Faces* panellist ALAN A. FREEMAN who had called him 'too camp'.

7. The 1954 adaptation of George Orwell's *1984* prompted nearly a thousand calls to the BBC complaining about a horror programme being shown on a Sunday. And four motions were tabled in Parliament accusing the BBC of unnecessarily frightening the audience.

8. A major row broke out in 1971 after HAROLD WILSON stopped an interview with DAVID DIMBLEBY during the programme *Yesterday's Men*. Wilson moaned about the BBC's political bias against the Labour Party.

9. Interviewer BILL GRUNDY was suspended for two weeks after appearing to goad the Sex Pistols into swearing on a 1976 edition of *Today*.

10. After cameras showed only the shoulders of actress LISA GASTONI when she stood up in a low-cut dress at the end of *Juke Box Jury*, callers besieged the BBC complaining that she appeared to be naked.

CHAPTER

THE WORLD ABOUT US

20 IRISH PROVERBS

1. Bare walls make giddy housekeepers.

2. Never burn a penny candle looking for a halfpenny.

3. The second boiled broth is always the best.

4. Marry a woman from Truagh and you marry all Truagh.

5. The shoemaker's wife and the blacksmith's horse often go unshod.

6. A coat twice turned is not worth sleeving.

7. Never say die when there is meat on the shin of a wren.

8. It is all the same to the man with the brogues where he puts his foot.

9. When it is raining porridge, the beggars have no spoons.

10. Though the carpenter is bad, the splinter is good.

11. Hills far away are green but they often have sour bottoms. (sour = boggy)

12. It is hard to hunt the hare out of the bush it is not in.

13. A trout in the ashes is better than a salmon in the water.

14. The more you tramp the dunghill the more the dirt rises.

15. Put a mud turf on a dish and it will be a mud turf still.

16. If the cat was churning it is often she would have her paws in it.

17. It's hard to make a choice between two blind dogs.

18. Don't go putting wool on the sheep's back.

19. Never bolt your door with a boiled carrot.

20. You can't make a piano out of a bacon box.

20 DREAMS AND THEIR SEXUAL CONNOTATIONS

1. AEROPLANE (penis).

2. BOTTLE (vagina).

3. DART (sexual penetration).

4. DOME (woman's breast).

5. FAIRIES (the feminine side of a man's personality).

6. FIG (testicles).

7. FROG (male genitals).

8. GOAT (male sexuality).

9. GUN (penis).

10. HARBOUR (womb).

11. LOCOMOTIVE GOING INTO TUNNEL (sexual intercourse).

12. MERMAID (fear of frigidity in a woman).

13. MOUNTING A HORSE (sex act).

14. NOSEBLEED (female genitalia).

15. ROLLER-COASTER (sex act).

16. SWEETS (sexual pleasures).

17. SWINGS (desire).

18. VALLEY (hollow in woman's body between breasts or thighs).

19. WATER-LILY (vagina).

20. WOLF (repressed sexual urges).

Apparently the wolf in 'Little Red Riding Hood' represents an inexperienced woman's fear of sexual contact with a man. In its earliest forms, the story is thought to have acted as a warning to young girls against sleeping with men.

10 NATIONAL SUPERSTITIONS

1. CHINA: Sweeping out a house removes all the good luck, especially on Chinese New Year.

2. HOLLAND: People with red hair bring bad luck.

3. IBIZA: It is bad luck to allow a priest on a fishing boat.

4. ICELAND: An unmarried person who sits at the corner of a table won't marry for seven years. A pregnant woman who drinks from a cracked cup risks having a baby with a hare-lip.

5. IRELAND: It is unlucky to use broken tombstones for the walls of a cottage. It is lucky to spill drink on the ground.

6. JAPAN: Picking up a comb with its teeth facing your body brings bad luck.

7. MALTA: Churches with two towers are fitted with a clock face in each but the two clocks always tell different times to confuse the Devil about the time of the service.

8. NIGERIA: A man hit with a broom becomes impotent unless he retaliates seven times with the same broom. Sweeping a house at night brings misfortune to the occupants.

9. POLAND: Bringing lilac into the house is a sure sign of impending death.

10. SCOTLAND: Red and green should never be worn together. It is unlucky to throw vegetables on to the fire and to carry a spade through the house. This means that a grave will soon be dug. And three swans flying together means a national disaster is imminent.

20 UNUSUAL SOCIETIES

1. ALAN WHICKER APPRECIATION SOCIETY.

2. ANCIENT ASTRONAUT SOCIETY.

3. BAGPIPE SOCIETY.

4. BOOMERANG SOCIETY.

5. BUS ENTHUSIASTS SOCIETY.

6. CELTIC RE-ENACTMENT SOCIETY.

7. CHEESE CLUB.

8. CHEIROLOGICAL SOCIETY (open to devotees of handwriting).

9. DENTAL HISTORY SOCIETY.

10. EUROVISION SONG CONTEST FAN CLUB.

11. FLAT EARTH SOCIETY.

12. FLOTATION TANK ASSOCIATION.

13. GEORGE FORMBY SOCIETY.

14. LAND OF THE GIANTS APPRECIATION SOCIETY.

15. MALEDICTA SOCIETY (for those who like swearing).

16. POLICE HISTORY SOCIETY.

17. RICHARD III APPRECIATION SOCIETY.

18. SAUSAGE APPRECIATION SOCIETY.

19. TEST-CARD CIRCLE.

20. WALLPAPER HISTORY SOCIETY.

THOMAS COOK'S FIRST 10 OVERSEAS TOURS

1. PARIS (1855).

2. SWITZERLAND (1863).

3. ITALY (1864).

4. U.S.A (1866).

    = CANADA (1866).

6. EGYPT (1869).

7. JAPAN (1872).

    = CHINA (1872).

    = INDIA (1872).

10. SCANDINAVIA (1875).

As secretary of the Leicester Temperance Society, Thomas Cook organised his very first tour in 1841 to take friends of temperance by train from Leicester to nearby Loughborough in support of the cause. The charter was so successful that Cook expanded his horizons to more exotic climes and arranged a trip to the Paris Exhibition in 1855, at £10 a head. Unfortunately the Brighton and South Coast Railway refused to co-operate so it was necessary to make a detour via Harwich, Antwerp, Brussels, Cologne and Strasbourg before reaching the French capital. Thus passengers were able to see half of Europe for their money. No wonder they came home satisfied. By 1863, Cook had won over the Brighton and South Coast, thereby securing his gateway to the Continent. That year, he announced a trip to Switzerland and Mont Blanc via Paris, an offer taken up by over 500 eager customers. The price for the 21-day tour was £19 17s 6d. Thomas Cook had hit upon a goldmine.

THE 10 LARGEST ENGLISH COUNTIES (area in sq. km.)

1. NORTH YORKSHIRE (8,320).

2. CUMBRIA (6,810).

3. DEVON (6,720).

4. LINCOLNSHIRE (5,890).

5. NORFOLK (5,360).

6. NORTHUMBERLAND (5,030).

7. HEREFORD AND WORCESTER (3,930).

8. SUFFOLK (3,800).

9. HAMPSHIRE (3,770).

10. KENT (3,730).

THE 10 SMALLEST ENGLISH COUNTIES (area in sq. km.)

1. ISLE OF WIGHT (380).

2. RUTLAND (394).

3. TYNE & WEAR (540).

4. CLEVELAND (580).

5. GREATER MERSEYSIDE (650).

6. WEST MIDLANDS (900).

7. BEDFORDSHIRE (1,240).

8. BERKSHIRE (1,260).

9. GREATER MANCHESTER (1,290).

10. AVON (1,340).

10 UNUSUAL FESTIVALS

1. CHEESE-ROLLING (U.K., May). Cheese-rolling has taken place on the 1 in 2 slopes of Cooper's Hill, near Birdlip in Gloucestershire, since the 15th Century. At 6pm on Spring Bank Holiday Monday, local youths line up at the top of the hill alongside a 7lb circular Double Gloucester cheese. When the cheese is released, the competitors hurtle down the hill in an attempt to catch it before it reaches the bottom. Eight people were injured during the 1992 event and further accidents caused the 1998 event to be cancelled amidst much controversy.

2. DAY OF THE DEAD (Mexico, 2 November). According to Indian folklore, this is the day when the deceased return to life. Families conduct macabre graveside picnics, offering food to the dead, and then tuck into a feast of their own, eating chocolate coffins, sugar wreaths and fancy breads adorned with skulls and crossbones.

3. DOO DAH PARADE (U.S., Thanksgiving). A spoof version of the glittering Rose Parade held each year in Pasadena, California, the Doo Dah Parade has deliberately become a byword in tackiness with badly-decorated floats, inept drill teams and a routine where businessmen in suits perform with their briefcases.

4. GOTMAAR FESTIVAL (India, September). On the day following the September full moon, the 45,000 inhabitants of Pandhura divide themselves into two groups and start hurling rocks at each other until sunset when the fighting ends. The festivities can get out of hand. In 1989 there were 616 casualties, including four deaths.

5. GRANDMOTHERS' FESTIVAL (Norway, July). First held at Bodo in 1992, the festival sees grannies riding motorbikes, racehorses, skydiving and scuba-diving. The star of the inaugural event was 79-year-old Elida Anderson who became the world's oldest bungee-jumper.

6. KING OF THE MOUNTAIN FESTIVAL (Australia, October). With a summit just 140ft above the surrounding plains, Mount Wycheproof in Victoria is registered as the lowest mountain in the world. This fact is celebrated annually with a foot-race up the mountain with each contestant carrying a sack of wheat weighing 140 lb.

7. LA TOMATINA (Spain). This festival dates back to 1944 when the fair at

Buñol was ruined by hooligans hurling tomatoes at the procession. Now each year the town stages a 90-minute mass fight with 190,000lb of ripe tomatoes, an event which has relegated the annual fair to the status of a mere sideshow.

8. MOOSE-DROPPING FESTIVAL (Alaska, July). The town of Talkeetna plays host to an annual celebration of moose-droppings. Stalls sell jewellery and assorted knick-knacks made from moose-droppings but pride of place goes to the moose-dropping-throwing competition where competitors toss gold-painted moose-droppings into a target area, the winner being the one who lands his dropping closest to the centre target.

9. RUNNING OF THE SHEEP (U.S., September). Reedpoint, Montana, stages a gentle alternative to Spain's famous Running of the Bulls. Each September hundreds of sheep charge down Main Street for six blocks. Contests are held for the ugliest sheep and prettiest ewe while shepherds assemble to recite poetry.

10. SWINGING THE FIREBALLS (Scotland, New Year's Eve). Residents of Stonehaven march through the town swinging great balls of fire made from wire netting and filled with driftwood, pine cones, twigs and oil-soaked rags. The balls are then thrown into the harbour to herald the New Year. The ceremony is thought to date back to the Middle Ages when the townsfolk tried to charm the sun from the heavens during the long, cold winter months.

10 MISHAPS ON FRIDAY THE 13TH

1.   1930. SIR HENRY SEGRAVE was killed on Friday, 13 June on Lake Windermere attempting to break the world water speed record.

2.   1972. A plane crash in Chile left survivors stranded in the Andes without food supplies. They were forced to turn to cannibalism in order to survive.

3.   1979. PRINCE CHARLES walked into scaffolding poles at Exeter Cathedral.

4.   1981. The British Museum had to cancel a lecture entitled 'Good and Bad Luck in the Ancient World', scheduled for Friday, 13 November, after the lecturer was taken ill.

5.   1984. TERENCE TALBOT was due in court on Friday 13, January to face a drink-driving charge. On the way to court, he was involved in a car crash.

6.   1984. A hurricane ripped across Britain on Friday, 13 January, killing nine people.

7.   1986. Dentist GIL WILLETTS arrived at his surgery to find it flooded. Then his drill packed up.

8.   1987. Gravedigger JOHN GIBLIN ended up in hospital on Friday, 13 March after falling into an open grave and breaking his leg on the coffin.

9.   1989. Share prices collapsed on Friday, 13 October.

10. 1992. An earthquake in eastern Turkey killed over 1,000 people on Friday, 13 March.

Some people suffer repeated misfortune on Friday the 13th. DAVID WARREN's plane was struck by lightning on the fateful day in 1967 and the following year his car caught fire. To guard against further disaster, he took out a £25,000 insurance policy in 1969 and managed to get through the day unscathed. A fellow-Briton, retired bus driver BOB RENPHREY, took to spending every Friday the 13th in bed following a chain of doomsday accidents which included writing off four cars, falling into a river and walking through a plate-glass door.

20 AGE-OLD CURES

1. Binding the temples with a rope with which a man has been hanged relieves a headache.

2. Urinating in an open grave cures incontinence.

3. Passing a child three times under the belly of a donkey cures whooping cough.

4. Taking the tooth of a live mole and wearing it cures toothache,

5. Wrap a child suffering from mumps in a blanket, take it to a pig sty, rub the child's head against the pig's back and the mumps will pass from the child to the pig.

6. Touching a corpse's hand cures a sore throat.

7. Washing in a corpse's washing water cures epileptic fits.

8. Stick an elder twig in your ear and wear it night and day to cure deafness.

9. Carry a child through a flock of sheep to cure respiratory problems.

10. Carry a dead shrew in your pocket to ward off rheumatism.

11. Reading the Eighth Psalm three times, three days in the week for three weeks over the heads of children will cure mouth ulcers.

12. Driving three nails into your skull eases a headache.

13. To cure fever, place the patient on a sandy shore when the tide is coming in. The waves will carry away the disease.

14. The eye of a frog suspended from the neck cures ophthalmia.

15. Cut off the head of an eel and rub its blood on your skin to cure warts.

16. A cork under your pillow at night cures cramp.

17. Rubbing the grease off church bells into your body cures shingles.

18. Tying a hairy caterpillar in a bag around a child's neck cures whooping-cough.

19. Throwing a dung beetle over your shoulder cures stomach ache.

20. After a cow has been slaughtered and while its body is still steaming, shove your head into the carcass, draw the folds of flesh around your neck and inhale. Apparently, this is a sure-fire cure for tuberculosis.

20 UNUSUAL PHOBIAS

1. ALEKTOROPHOBIA — fear of chickens.

2. AULOPHOBIA — fear of the flute.

3. CLINOPHOBIA — fear of going to bed.

4. ECCLESIAPHOBIA — fear of churches.

5. EISOPTROPHOBIA — fear of mirrors.

6. GENIOPHOBIA — fear of chins.

7. GENUPHOBIA — fear of knees.

8. GYMNOTOPHOBIA — fear of nudity.

9. ICHTHYOPHOBIA — fear of fish.

10. LEVOPHOBIA — fear of the left side.

11. LINONOPHOBIA — fear of string.

12. METEOROPHOBIA — fear of being hit by a meteor.

13. NEPHELOPHOBIA — fear of clouds.

14. ODONTOPHOBIA — fear of teeth.

15. OURANOPHOBIA — fear of heaven.

16. PEDIOPHOBIA —fear of dolls.

17. POGONOPHOBIA — fear of beards.

18. SIDEROPHOBIA — fear of the stars.

19. STYGIOPHOBIA — fear of hell.

20. TRISKAIDEKAPHOBIA — fear of the number 13.

German physicist Philipp Lenard suffered from onomatophobia, the fear of certain names, in his case that of Sir Isaac Newton. Even though Newton had died 135 years before Professor Lenard was born, Lenard couldn't bear to speak, hear or see Newton's name. At lectures, he would turn his back on the students if Newton's name had to be mentioned. Lenard's phobia stemmed from a hatred of all British scientists whom he accused of stealing German ideas.

THE NICKNAMES OF 20 U.S. STATES

1. ALABAMA — Cotton State.

2. ARKANSAS — Bear State.

3. CONNECTICUT — Nutmeg State.

4. DELAWARE — Diamond State.

5. FLORIDA — Sunshine State.

6. INDIANA — Hoosier State.

7. IOWA — Hawkeye State.

8. KENTUCKY — Bluegrass State.

9. LOUISIANA — Pelican State (a pelican features on the coat of arms)..

10. MICHIGAN — Wolverine State.

11. MINNESOTA — Gopher State.

12. MISSISSIPPI — Magnolia State.

13. MISSOURI — Show Me State.

14. NEW HAMPSHIRE — Granite State.

15. NORTH CAROLINA — Tar Heel State.

16. NORTH DAKOTA — Flickertail State (for its large population of squirrels).

17. OHIO — Buckeye State (for the trees that grow there).

18. OREGON — Beaver State.

19. UTAH — Beehive State.

20. WISCONSIN — Badger State (because Wisconsin miners are believed to have made homes by burrowing underground).

THE 20 LARGEST AMERICAN STATES

(Area in sq km)

1. ALASKA (1,531,100).

2. TEXAS (691,200).

3. CALIFORNIA (411,100).

4. MONTANA (381,200).

5. NEW MEXICO (315,000).

6. ARIZONA (294,100).

7. NEVADA (286,400).

8. COLORADO (269,700).

9. WYOMING (253,400).

10. OREGON (251,500).

11. UTAH (219,900).

12. MINNESOTA (218,700).

13. IDAHO (216,500).

14. KANSAS (213,200).

15. NEBRASKA (200,400).

16. SOUTH DAKOTA (199,800).

17. NORTH DAKOTA (183,100).

18. OKLAHOMA (181,100).

19. MISSOURI (180,600).

20. WASHINGTON (176,700).

THE 20 SMALLEST AMERICAN STATES

(Area in sq km)

1. DISTRICT OF COLUMBIA (180).

2. RHODE ISLAND (3,100).

3. DELAWARE (5,300).

4. CONNECTICUT (13,000).

5. HAWAII (16,800).

6. NEW JERSEY (20,200).

7. MASSACHUSETTS (21,500).

8. NEW HAMPSHIRE (24,000).

9. VERMONT (24,900).

10. MARYLAND (31,600).

11. WEST VIRGINIA (62,900).

12. SOUTH CAROLINA (80,600).

13. MAINE (86,200).

14. INDIANA (93,700).

15. KENTUCKY (104,700).

16. VIRGINIA (105,600).

17. OHIO (107,100).

18. TENNESSEE (109,200).

19. PENNSYLVANIA (117,400).

20. MISSISSIPPI (123,600).

10 BIZARRE AMERICAN LOCAL LAWS

1. In ALASKA, it is illegal to look at a moose from the window of an aircraft or any other flying vehicle.

2. In OKLAHOMA, it is illegal to catch whales or to get a fish drunk. Oklahoma is an inland state.

3. In MILWAUKEE, residents must keep pet elephants on a leash while walking them on public streets.

4. In MUNCIE, INDIANA, it is illegal to carry fishing tackle in a cemetery.

5. A law at KIRKLAND, ILLINOIS, forbids bees from flying over the town.

6. An OHIO law states that pets have to carry lights on their tails at night.

7. At GREENE, NEW YORK STATE, it is against the law to walk backwards while eating peanuts during a concert.

8. In WATERLOO, NEBRASKA, barbers are prohibited from eating onions between the hours of 7am and 7pm.

9. At INTERNATIONAL FALLS, MINNESOTA, it is illegal for a dog to chase a cat up a telegraph pole. Owners are liable to be fined.

10. It is illegal to carry an ice-cream cone in your pocket in LEXINGTON, KENTUCKY.

United States legislature allows for a wide variety of strange laws from states, counties and towns eager to preserve their identity. Some appear more than a little superfluous, such as the edict from the City Council of CHICO, CALIFORNIA, banning nuclear weapons. Anyone caught detonating a nuclear device within the city limits could face a fine of up to $500.

20 FOREIGN CURRENCIES YOU MAY NOT HAVE COME ACROSS

1. Aht (THAILAND).

2. Colón (COSTA RICA).

3. Dalasi (GAMBIA).

4. Dong (VIETNAM).

5. Goude (HAITI).

6. Guarani (PARAGUAY).

7. Kina (PAPUA NEW GUINEA).

8. Kwanza (ANGOLA).

9. Lempira (HONDURAS).

10. Lilangeni (SWAZILAND).

11. New Kip (LAOS).

12. Ngultrum (BHUTAN).

13. Ougiya (MAURETANIA).

14. Pataca (MACAO).

15. Pula (BOTSWANA).

16. Quetzal (GUATEMALA).

17. Riel (CAMBODIA).

18. Taka (BANGLADESH).

19. Tugrik (MONGOLIA).

20. Won (NORTH KOREA).

Cheese was once a form of currency in some European countries. In 16th-century Denmark it was used to pay church taxes.

10 PLACES WHERE UFOS HAVE BEEN REPORTED

1. ASHLAND, NEBRASKA. Police patrolman Herbert Schirmer said he was on patrol in the early hours of 3 December 1967 when he came across a flying saucer. He went on to state under hypnosis that he had been abducted by the alien occupants whom he described as being just under 5ft tall with big chests, thin heads, cat-like eyes and 'funny-looking' lips. They were dressed in one-piece silver suits with no zips. He said that he asked the aliens whether they had kidnapped people and was told that there was 'a breeding analysis programme' involving some humans. He didn't pursue this line of questioning in case he too was kidnapped.

2. BLACKFORD COUNTY, INDIANA. De Wayne Donathan and his wife were driving home early on evening in October 1973 when they spotted a tractor-like vehicle parked by the side of the road. As they got nearer, they saw two silver-suited figures dancing. The Donathans drove past and when they turned round the figures had disappeared, but two separate bright lights were flickering in the sky.

3. DRAKENSBERG MOUNTAINS, SOUTH AFRICA. In the spring of 1951, a driver was stopped late at night by a short man with a domed, bald head and a strange voice who said he needed water. The witness took the water to a disc-shaped craft and was invited inside where he met a second alien. When asked where they came from, the entities pointed at the sky and said: 'From there'.

4. KAIKOURA, NEW ZEALAND. On 21 December 1978, Captains Verne Powell and John Randle were flying from Blenheim to Christchurch when they saw several radar and visual sightings of UFOs. At one point, there were five strong radar targets where none should have been. Ten days later, Channel O from Melbourne retraced the flight and filmed a mysterious object with a flashing light. Its identity remains a mystery.

5. LIVINGSTON, SCOTLAND. On 9 November 1979, forester Robert Taylor was confronted by a large, globe-shaped craft hovering above the ground. Suddenly, two spherical, mine-like objects rushed towards him, grabbed him by the legs and dragged him towards the craft. The choking smell caused him to pass out. When he awoke, his trousers were torn and the craft had gone. He

couldn't walk or talk properly and had a raging thirst for two days.

6. NEW YORK STATE. After watching UFOs on the evening of 2 May 1968, Shane Kurz fell asleep. When she woke, muddy footprints led into the house from outside. Years later under regression hypnosis she recalled being drawn to the window by a telepathic voice calling to her. She then went to a UFO in a muddy field where she was taken inside the craft and raped by the alien leader.

7. PALOMOR GARDENS, CALIFORNIA. George Adamski claimed he regularly spoke to aliens, his first encounter being in the Californian desert on 20 November 1952. Apparently the two communicated in sign language and telepathy, the alien indicating that he came from Venus. Adamski went on to claim that he had often travelled in flying saucers, in the course of which he also met Martians and Saturnians.

8. VALENSOLE, FRANCE. On 1 July 1965, farmer Maurice Masse saw a six-legged, egg-shaped UFO in his lavender field. Two entities emerged, wearing green ski suits. They were 4ft tall with large bald heads, big eyes and no lips and they made strange gutteral sounds. One pointed a rod at Masse, immobilising him. After the close encounter, no lavender plants would grow on the landing site for ten years.

9. VILVORDE, BELGIUM. On 19 December 1973, a man went into his kitchen in the middle of the night and saw a 3ft-tall green humanoid glowing in his garden. It had pointed ears and big yellow oval eyes. After a few moments, it made a V-sign before walking up and over the garden wall. The witness calmly went on to make a snack.

10. WEXFORD, REPUBLIC OF IRELAND. Two teenage boys were out walking one evening in September 1924 when they encountered a solid beam of light, several feet long, travelling through the air a few feet off the ground. It climbed over a hedge and across a field until it met a railway line and moved off, following the track. The boys maintained that they saw the object for a good five minutes.

THE MEANINGS BEHIND 20 CAPITAL CITIES

1. **ADDIS ABABA** (Ethiopia) — new flower.

2. **ALGIERS** (Algeria) — the islands.

3. **BAGHDAD** (Iraq) — God's gift.

4. **BANGKOK** (Thailand) — wild plum village.

5. **BEIJING** (China) — northern capital.

6. **BRUSSELS** (Belgium) — buildings on a marsh.

7. **BUENOS AIRES** (Argentina) — good winds.

8. **CAIRO** (Egypt) — victorious.

9. **CANBERRA** (Australia) — meeting-place.

10. **COPENHAGEN** (Denmark) — merchants' harbour.

11. **DELHI** (India) — threshold.

12. **DUBLIN** (Republic of Ireland) — black pool or lake.

13. **JAKARTA** (Indonesia) — place of victory.

14. **KHARTOUM** (Sudan) — elephant's trunk.

15. **KUALA LUMPUR** (Malaysia) — mud-yellow estuary.

16. **KUWAIT CITY** (Kuwait) — enclosed.

17. **MONTEVIDEO** (Uruguay) — I saw the mountain.

18. **RANGOON** (Myanmar) — end of strife.

19. **SAN SALVADOR** (Salvador) — holy saviour.

20. **TEHRAN** (Iran) — warm place.

10 COUNTRIES' FORMER NAMES

1. BELIZE (British Honduras).

2. BOTSWANA (Bechuanaland).

3. BURKINA FASO (Upper Volta).

4. CAMBODIA (Kampuchea).

5. ETHIOPIA (Abyssinia).

6. IRAN (Persia).

7. MALAWI (Nyasaland).

8. SRI LANKA (Ceylon).

9. TANZANIA (Tanganyika).

10. ZAIRE (Belgian Congo).

THE WORLD'S 10 LARGEST ISLANDS (area in sq km)

1. AUSTRALIA (7,892,300).

2. GREENLAND (2,131,600).

3. NEW GUINEA (790,000).

4. BORNEO (737,000).

5. MADAGASCAR (587,000).

6. BAFFIN (507,000).

7. SUMATRA (425,000).

8. HONSHU (Hondo) (228,000).

9. GREAT BRITAIN (219,000).

10. VICTORIA, Canada (217,300).

THE WORLD'S 10 HIGHEST WATERFALLS (in metres)

1. ANGEL (upper fall), Venezuela (807).

2. ITATINGA, Brazil (628).

3. CUQUENAN, Guyana/Venezuela (610).

4. ORMELI, Norway (563).

5. TYSEE, Norway (533).

6. PILAO, Brazil (524).

7. RIBBON, U.S.A. (491).

8. VESTRE MARDOLA, Norway (468).

9. RORAIMA, Guyana (457).

10. CLEVE-GARTH, New Zealand (450).

THE WORLD'S 10 LONGEST RIVERS (length in km)

1. NILE (North-East Africa) (6,695).

2. AMAZON (South America) (6,516).

3. CHANG JIANG (China) (6,380).

4. MISSISSIPPI-MISSOURI (U.S.A) (6,019).

5. OB-IRTYSH (Russia) (5,570).

6. YENISEI-ANGARA (Russia) (5,550).

7. YELLOW RIVER (Huang He) (China) (5,464).

8. ZAIRE (Congo) (4667).

9. MEKONG (Asia) (4425).

10. AMUR (Russia) (4416).

20 LOST DISTILLERIES OF SCOTLAND

1. ARDGOWAN, Greenock (1896-1952).

2. ARDLUSSA, Campbeltown (1879-1923).

3. AUCHINBLAE, Kincardineshire (1896-1926).

4. BON ACCORD, Aberdeen (1855-1910).

5. BONNINGTON, Edinburgh (1798-1853).

6. DALARUAN, Campbeltown (1824-1922).

7. DEAN, Edinburgh (1881-1922).

8. DRUMCALDIE, Windygates, Fife (1896-1903).

9. LEN ALBYN, Inverness (1846-1986).

10. GLEN CAWDOR, Nairn (1898-1927).

11. GLENCOULL, Angus (1897-1929).

12. GLENMAVIS, Bathgate (1795-1910).

13. GLENSKIACH, Easter Ross (1896-1926).

14. GLENUGIE, near Peterhead (1821-1983).

15. GRANGE, Burntisland (1795-1925).

16. LANGHOLM, Dumfriesshire (1765-1921).

17. LOCHINDAAL, island of Islay (1829-1929).

18. MAN O'HOY, Stromness, Orkney (1817-1928).

19. RIECLACHAN, Campbeltown (1825-1934).

20. YOKER, Glasgow (1770-1928).

The isolated settlement of Campbeltown near the Mull of Kintyre used to be the whisky capital of Scotland. No fewer than 33 distilleries were founded in the town and major customers included the German army. Now there are just two distilleries — Glen Scotia and Springbank.

10 BUILDINGS WITH A DIFFERENCE

1.   The CROCODILE HOTEL near Ayers Rock in the heart of the Australian outback is a building complex in the shape of a crocodile. The 'eyes' protrude from the reception area, the rooms run along the 'body' to the 'tail' and the hotel swimming pool is located in the creature's 'alimentary canal'.

2.   The PINEAPPLE LODGE stands in Dunmore Park, Central Scotland. The lower part of the building is an ordinary octagonal tower but from the tops of the columns sprout stone, spiky leaves, transforming it into a 53ft-high pineapple. It was built in 1761 at the request of the Fourth Earl of Dunmore for reasons known only to himself.

3.   JULES' UNDERSEA LODGE is an underwater hotel, five fathoms down in Bora Lagoon in the Florida Keys. A converted underwater research station, it has a restaurant and two rooms, both with private baths, and can accommodate six guests at a time. Each room has a giant porthole to enable guests to observe passing fish.

4.   Overlooking the town of Oban in Scotland is a replica of the Colosseum, known locally as MCCAIG'S FOLLY. It was the brainchild of banker and self-styled art critic JOHN STEWART MCCAIG who, after a trip to Italy, sought to re-create the glory of Rome in his own backyard. It was intended as a museum and art gallery, but when McCaig died with only the shell built everybody lost interest. It now exists as a vast blackened cylinder and encloses a public garden.

5.   The ICE HOTEL at Jukkasjarvi, Swedish Lapland, offers the ultimate in cold comfort — a building constructed out of ice where the average room temperature is minus four degrees centigrade. The beds are made from packed snow topped with spruce boughs and reindeer skins. The hotel melts every April and has to be rebuilt the following winter.

6.   In 1919, American newspaper magnate WILLIAM RANDOLPH HEARST decided to build a simple bungalow for himself and movie-star girlfriend MARION DAVIES. The result, nearly twenty years and $8 million later, was an exotic fantasy castle, THE ENCHANTED HILL, at San Simeon, California. The home was modelled on a Spanish Renaissance cathedral and Hearst was known to dismantle entire suites from Spanish palaces and reconstruct them at San

Simeon. The main dining-hall was furnished with 500-year-old choir stalls from Catalonia.

7. The six-storey ELEPHANT HOTEL at Margate, New Jersey, is in the shape of a huge elephant, complete with trunk and tusks. It was built in 1881 by JAMES V. LAFFERTY as a real-estate promotion. The 65ft- high concrete elephant, named Lucy, was used as a tavern before being converted into a hotel. The reception area is in her hind legs and a staircase in each leg leads up to the main rooms.

8. SIR THOMAS TRESHAM was obsessed with the power of numbers and in 1597 ordered the building of a TRIANGULAR LODGE at Rushton, Northamptonshire, in which everything relates to the number three — a homage to the Trinity. It has three sides, each of which measures 33ft, three gables on each side, three storeys and triangular or hexagonal rooms decorated with trefoils or triangles in groups of three. All of the Latin inscriptions have 33 letters.

9. As an industrialist flew into Durban, South Africa, in 1971, he looked down and saw what appeared to be a crashed plane on the ground. In fact it was DOOKIE RAMDARIE's new AEROPLANE HOUSE, a home built in the shape of an aircraft, the bedrooms being housed in the wings. Buoyed by his success, Ramdarie went on to create a bus factory in the shape of a bus and, in 1981, he designed the SHIP HOUSE, a house in the form of a ship, complete with funnel and lifeboats.

10. An otherwise ordinary terraced house at HEADINGTON, Oxford, is adorned with a 25ft-long glassfibre shark buried nose-down in the roof. The sculpture was erected by the house-owner BILL HEINE as a protest against man's inhumanity.

20 UNUSUAL BRITISH PUB NAMES

1. A BIT ON THE SIDE (Chippenham).

2. THE BULLNOSE MORRIS (Cowley, Oxford). Named after a car once built at the nearby car plant.

3. THE CAT AND CUSTARD POT (Paddlesworth, Kent).

4. THE CLOG AND BILLYCOCK (Pleasington, near Blackburn) named after a previous landlord who used to wear clogs and a type of bowler hat known as a billycock.

5. THE COW AND SNUFFERS (Llandaff North, near Cardiff).

6. THE FROG AND NIGHTGOWN (London SE1).

7. HELP ME THROUGH THIS WORLD (Bury).

8. THE HOUSE WITHOUT A NAME (Colchester).

9. I AM THE ONLY RUNNING FOOTMAN (London W1).

10. INN OF THE SIXTH HAPPINESS (Ilford) after the Ingrid Bergman film of the same name.

11. THE KICKING CUDDY (Coxhoe, Durham). A 'cuddy' is a donkey.

12. THE NOBODY INN (Doddiscombsleigh, Devon).

13. THE OLDE TIPPLING PHILOSOPHER (Caldicot, near Chepstow).

14. PORT OUT AND STARBOARD HOME (Peterborough) or 'posh' for short, the nickname of the local football team, Peterborough United.

15. THE SHREW BESHREWED (Hersden, near Canterbury).

16. THE SLUG AND LETTUCE (Stratford upon Avon).

17. THE THIRSTY KIPPER (Port Erin, Isle of Man). 'Kipper' was naval slang for a stoker.

18. THE VULTURE'S PERCH (Hamilton).

19. THE WORLD TURNED UPSIDE DOWN (London SE1).

20. THE YUTICK'S NEST (Blackburn). A 'yutick' is a whinchat.

10 BRITISH PUBS NAMED AFTER OCCUPATIONS

1. THE BRUSHMAKER'S ARMS (Upham, near Southampton).

2. THE COALHEAVER'S ARMS (Peterborough).

3. THE FLAX DRESSERS (Ashby-de-la-Zouch, Leicestershire).

4. THE FLESHER'S ARMS (Dumfries). In some parts of Scotland, butchers were known as 'fleshers'.

5. THE FLINT KNAPPERS (Brandon, Suffolk). Flint knappers had the job of breaking up flintstones.

6. THE HUFFLER'S ARMS (Dartford). Hufflers used to ferry goods to ships anchored offshore.

7. THE LATHCLEAVER'S ARMS (Brighton). Lathcleavers worked in the timber trade.

8. THE PUDDLER'S ARMS (Briton Ferry, near Neath). Puddlers stirred the molten iron in a furnace.

9. THE PYROTECHNIST'S ARMS (London SE15).

10. THE SNAKE CATCHER (Brockenhurst, Hampshire).

10 FOREIGN NAMES FOR COLONEL MUSTARD

1. COLONEL MOUTARDE (Belgium, France).

2. KOLONEL MUSTARD (Netherlands).

3. OBERST VON GATOW (Germany).

4. MADAME CURRY (Switzerland).

5. MARQUÉS DE MARINA (Spain).

6. CORONEL MONTEIRO (Portugal).

7. SI. MUSTARDAS (Greece).

8. ÖVERSTE SENAP (Sweden, Finland, Denmark).

9. OBERST GULIN (Norway).

10. COLONELLO MUSTARD (Italy).

The thought of Colonel Mustard swapping his tweeds and army boots for a floral dress and stilettos every time he ventures to Switzerland is mind-boggling. But he is not the only Cluedo participant to use an alias when travelling abroad. In France, the Rev. Green is known as Dr. Olive; Miss Scarlett calls herself Fröken Röd in Scandinavia; Mrs. Peacock becomes the romantic Dona Violeta in Brazil; and in the same country the chameleon-like Professor Plum changes to Professor Black. Meanwhile in the United States, the perpetual victim, Dr. Black, is known as Mr. Boddy. Cluedo was devised by English solicitor's clerk ANTHONY E. PRATT in 1944. Mr. Pratt, who described himself as 'an introvert full of ruminations, speculations and imaginative notions', teamed up with his wife, an amateur artist. She did the drawings and it is on the board which she designed that the game is still played today. With six characters, six weapons and nine rooms, there are a potential 324 different murder combinations. Cluedo went on sale in 1949 and has since been sold in some 75 countries. It has been calculated that enough rope has been included in these sets to encircle the world.

20 TRADE NAMES WHICH ARE ABBREVIATIONS

1. ALCAN (Aluminium of Canada).

2. BABYCHAM (Baby champ — the infant perry drink won first prize at every agricultural show. The name had the added advantage of suggesting champagne).

3. BRITAX (British Accessories, the manufacturer).

4. BRITVIC (British Vitamin Products).

5. BRYLCREEM (brilliantine and cream).

6. CASTROL (castor oil).

7. DISPRIN (dissolvable aspirin).

8. DRAMBUIE (the Gaelic *dram* (drink) and *buidh* (pleasing).

9. DUREX (durability, reliability, excellence — its three prime requisites).

10. ELASTOPLAST (elastic plaster).

11. ETAM (Établissement Meilleur, the French hosiery company. It means 'best company').

12. FINDUS (Fruit Industries, name of Swedish company).

13. FLYMO (Flying mower).

14. HOVIS (from the Latin *hominis vis*, meaning 'strength of man').

15. LEGO (from the Danish *leg godt*, meaning 'play well').

16. NESCAFÉ (Nestlé and *café*, the French for coffee).

17. QUINK (quick-drying ink).

18. RADOX (radiated oxygen, something the original foot bath was claimed to do).

19. TEFLON (polytetrafluoroethylene).

20. VELCRO (from the French *velours* (velvet) and *croché* (hooked)).

10 ACCIDENTAL INVENTIONS

1. FISH FINGERS. Birds Eye had planned to launch frozen herring sticks to capitalise on the plentiful supplies of cheap British herring. The Herring Savoury, as it was called, went on sale in South Wales but had too many bones for most customers. As very much a second choice, Birds Eye simultaneously test-marketed frozen cod sticks in Southampton. These proved infinitely more popular and so in 1955 cod fish fingers were launched at the expense of the herring.

2. ICE-CREAM CONE. At the 1904 St. Louis World's Fair CHARLES E. MENCHES, a young ice-cream salesman, apparently presented his girlfriend with an ice-cream sandwich and a bunch of flowers. Since she had no vase for the flowers, the resourceful lady is said to have rolled the layers of the sandwich into the shape of a cone to act as a vase.

3. LIQUORICE ALLSORTS. Selling liquorice sweets individually, Bassett's travelling salesman CHARLIE THOMPSON met with little enthusiasm from wholesalers until, one day at Leicester in 1899, he accidentally dropped his bags of sweets, mixing them all up. The wholesaler suddenly expressed interest in the new mixture and Thompson realised he had inadvertently hit upon a winner.

4. MICROWAVE OVEN. PERCY SPENCER, a physicist and engineer with American radar equipment manufacturers Raytheon, was employed during the Second World War to make the magnetrons used in radar systems. He had noticed that the magnetrons gave off as much heat as a large lightbulb and used them to warm his hands on cold days. But it wasn't until he discovered a melted sweet in his pocket and realised the cause that the possibility occurred to him of cooking food with microwaves.

5. NON-STICK SAUCEPAN. In 1938 ROY PLUNKETT of the American company Du Pont was working on refrigerants when he stumbled across a polymer called polytetrafluoroethylene, or Teflon for short. Du Pont began producing Teflon commercially ten years later but it needed another fortuitous encounter for it to be considered for kitchenware. In 1954, French fishing-rod manufacturer MARC GRÉGOIRE chanced upon a process which would enable a Teflon coating to be applied to metal. It occurred to him that the non-stick properties would be ideal for kitchen utensils and he founded the Tefal company to make frying pans and saucepans.

6.   NYLON. Three years into his study of polymerisation DR. WALLACE CAROTHERS, a research chemist with Du Pont, discovered that a fibre of extreme tensile strength could be drawn from a mass of polymers. His task hadn't even been to create a specific product but the fibre, known as nylon, was launched in 1938, by which time Carothers, a depressive, had committed suicide.

7.   PAPER TISSUE. In 1924, Kimberly-Clark brought out paper Celluwipes, up-market make-up removers. Sales were slow until the company began to take note of customers' letters which reported that the tissues were perfect for nose-blowing. So they were relaunched as Kleenex.

8.   POST-IT NOTE. A research chemist with the American 3M Corporation, SPENCER SILVER was told to create the strongest glue on the market. Instead he came up with a temporary glue which wouldn't stick to anything for long. Its only benefits were that it could be reused and left no residue on the material to which it was applied. Silver's glue lay idle for ten years until in 1980 a colleague, ARTHUR FRY, who sang in a church choir, noted that a little of the glue on a strip of paper made a bookmark which did not fall from the pages of the hymn-book nor soil the pages. The Post-it note was marketed by 3M the following year.

9.   SUPERGLUE. While studying ethyl cyanoacrylate in the 1950s scientists with photographic company Eastman Kodak accidentally stuck together the glass prisms of a refractometer. This alerted them to the unique bonding properties of cyanoacrylates, or superglues as they became known.

10. TCP. In 1917 COUNT CALLIMACHI, a Romanian biochemist working in London, invented what he hoped would be a cure for venereal disease. He named the liquid TCP (he thought it contained trichlorophenol) but it proved ineffective against VD. However, its antibacterial properties were quickly recognised and it was marketed to relieve sore throats, cuts and bites.

THE 20 GREATEST INVENTIONS IN HISTORY

1. THE TOILET SYSTEM.

2. THE COMPUTER.

3. THE PRINTING PRESS.

4. FIRE.

5. THE WHEEL.

6. RADIO.

7. ANTIBIOTICS.

8. THE INTERNET.

9. TRANSISTOR.

10. THE LASER.

11. ANTISEPTICS.

12. CONTRACEPTION.

13. ANTIVIRAL THERAPY.

14. PLASTICS.

15. FLIGHT.

16. THE LEVER.

17. TRANSGENIC ANIMALS.

18. ELECTRIC LIGHT.

19. ARTIFICIAL DYES.

20. THE BALL.

These were the results of a 1998 magazine survey. Some doubt as to its worth must be drawn from the fact that the widget (a device used for canned draught beer) was named the 30th most important invention in history, ahead of the telephone (no. 34), the parachute (46), the compass (52) and the screw (54).

10 INVENTIONS WHICH ARE OLDER THAN YOU MIGHT THINK

1. BRA. In ancient Rome, female gymnasts wore a scarf called a *strophium* over the breasts to provide support. The modern bra was created in 1913 by MARY PHELPS JACOB, an American socialite living in Paris, her prototype model being two handkerchiefs tied to a length of ribbon.

2. COMB. The comb dates back to Scandinavia around 8000 BC.

3. COOKERY BOOK. The first volume of recipes was published in AD 62 by the Roman APICIUS. Titled *De re coquinaria,* it described the feasts enjoyed by the Emperor Claudius.

4. DENTURES. The first sets of dentures were in use around the 16th century.

5. DICTIONARY. The first known dictionary appeared in Mesopotamia around 600 BC.

6. MIRROR. The mirror dates back to ancient Egypt.

7. PLASTIC SURGERY. In the third century BC, AMYNTHAS OF ALEXANDRIA is believed to have carried out the first nose-job.

8. SLEEPING PILL. The sleeping pill was invented in the first century BC by CELSUS, a Roman medical writer. He gave patients suffering from insomnia a pill made from mandrake and henbane.

9. TOOTHBRUSH. Although the first nylon toothbrush didn't appear until 1938, a form of toothbrush was first seen in a Chinese painting at the end of the 15th century. Toothpaste goes back even further, to the first century AD — a Roman mix of vinegar, honey, salt and glass frit.

10. UMBRELLA. The umbrella was a Chinese invention in the second century BC.

20 LITTLE-KNOWN INVENTORS

1. GEORGE C. BEIDLER, American inventor of the photocopier, 1903.

2. HARRY BREARLEY, English inventor of stainless steel, 1913.

3. WILLIS CARRIER, American inventor of air-conditioning, 1902.

4. GEORGES CLAUDE, French inventor of neon lighting, 1910.

5. MRS. W.A. COCHRAN, American inventor of the automatic dishwasher, 1889.

6. ADOLPH E. FICK, German inventor of contact lenses, 1887.

7. DR. R.N. HARGER, American inventor of the breathalyser (or 'drunkometer' as it was then known), 1938.

8. EDWIN T. HOLMES, American inventor of the burglar alarm, 1858.

9. MILLER REESE HUTCHINSON, American inventor of the hearing-aid, 1901.

10. WHITCOMB L. JUDSON, American inventor of the zip, 1893.

11. CARLTON C. MAGEE, American inventor of the parking meter, 1935.

12. JACK MARKS, English inventor of the boxer's gumshield, 1902.

13. KARL LUDWIG NESSLER, German inventor of the hair perm, 1906. He only became a hairdresser because his eyesight was too poor for shoemaking.

14. JAMES RANSOME, English inventor of the motor mower, 1902.

15. ERIK ROTHEIM, Norwegian inventor of the aerosol, 1926.

16. LUCIEN B. SMITH, American inventor of barbed wire, 1874.

17. CHARLES STRITE, American inventor of the pop-up toaster, 1927.

18. JOHANN VAALER, Norwegian inventor of the paper clip, 1900.

19. ARTHUR WYNNE, English inventor of the crossword, 1913.

20. JOSEPH L. ZIMMERMAN, American inventor of the telephone answering machine, 1949. His first device was called the Electronic Secretary.

10 TRADE NAMES THAT HAVE ENTERED THE ENGLISH LANGUAGE

1. BIRO.

2. ESCALATOR.

3. HOOVER.

4. JACUZZI.

5. LINOLEUM.

6. PLASTICINE.

7. SELLOTAPE.

8. THERMOS.

9. VASELINE.

10. XEROX.

The biro was the brainchild of Hungarian hypnotist, sculptor and journalist LASZLO BIRO. In 1938 he was editing a government-sponsored magazine and, on a trip to the printers in Budapest, began considering the virtues of transferring the printers' quick-drying ink to pens. Biro produced a patent for his pen, which featured a rotating steel ball-point, in 1943 around which time he met Englishman Henry Martin, a government employee who recognised the potential of the new pen in wartime. It didn't leak at any altitude (making it ideal for aircrew), it was able to write on damp paper and at awkward angles and could write 200,000 words without refilling. Martin acquired the U.K. rights from Biro and in 1944 began producing ball-point pens for the RAF. Biro not only lost out in Britain but he also forgot to patent his invention in the United States. It was a costly lapse since Gimkel's of New York sold 10,000 at $12.50 apiece on the first day of sale in 1945.

10 CONDOM BRAND NAMES

1. BILLY BOY (Germany).

2. ENORMEX (U.K.).

3. EUROGLIDER (Netherlands).

4. HAPPY FACE (New Zealand).

5. HONEYMOON SUPER STIMULATION (Germany).

6. JIFFI EXCITER (U.K.).

7. LICKS (U.S.A.) .

8. MAMBA (Sweden).

9. POWER PLAY (U.S.A.).

10. SKIN LESS SKIN (Japan).

Italian anatomist GABRIELLE FALLOPIUS published the first known description of a condom in 1564. It was made from linen but most early condoms were of animal intestines, soaked before use. Since they were porous, people were advised to wear two at a time — one on top of the other. Casanova used condoms made from the dried gut of a sheep while the Japanese preferred condoms made from tortoiseshell, presumably to slow things down. The vulcanisation of rubber brought about a new material and the brand Durex, much to the confusion of Australians to whom sellotape is known as Durex. Japan uses more condoms than any other country — they are sold door-to-door by 'skin ladies' — and the Tokyo head office of manufacturer Fuji Latex is built in the shape of a condom. Sweden has its own official penis character, Proud Pete, to encourage the use of condoms while some Danish restaurants began serving after-dinner condoms instead of mints. Flavours include banana, lemon, liquorice, mint, strawberry, Caribbean coconut and peach punch. There are condoms that glow in the dark and musical condoms. Italian physics student Lino Missio has patented a condom with a microchip which warns of any tear during sex by playing a Beethoven theme.

20 CARS WHICH ARE NAMED AFTER PEOPLE

1. ALFA-ROMEO (Nicola Romeo — the 'Alfa' stood for *Anonima Lombarda Fabbrica Automobili,* or Lombardy Automobile Works Company).

2. ASTON MARTIN (Lionel Martin who won races on Aston Clinton hill, near Aylesbury).

3. BUGATTI (Ettore Bugatti).

4. CHEVROLET (Louis Chevrolet).

5. CHRYSLER (Walter Percy Chrysler).

6. CITRÖEN (André-Gustave Citröen).

7. DAIMLER (Gottfried Daimler).

8. FERRARI (Enzo Ferrari).

9. HILLMAN (William Hillman).

10. HONDA (Soichiro Honda).

11. LANCIA (Vincenzo Lancia).

12. MASERATI (the Maserati brothers — Carlo, Bindo, Alfieri, Ettore and Ernesto).

13. MERCEDES (Mercedes Jellinek, the ten-year-old daughter of Austrian financier and motor-racing enthusiast Emil Jellinek).

14. OPEL (Adam Opel).

15. PEUGEOT (Armand Peugeot).

16. PORSCHE (Ferdinand Porsche).

17. ROLLS-ROYCE (Charles Rolls and Henry Royce).

18. SKODA (Emil Skoda).

19. TOYOTA (Sakichi Toyoda — the family changed the name to Toyota since 'Toyoda' needs ten characters in Japanese but 'Toyota' only eight. And eight is the Japanese lucky number).

20. VANWALL (Tony Vandervell).

20 FAMOUS OWNERS OF LAND ROVERS

1. BRYAN ADAMS.

2. JIM CARREY.

3. FIDEL CASTRO.

4. SEAN CONNERY.

5. KEVIN COSTNER.

6. TOM CRUISE.

7. MICHAEL DOUGLAS.

8. JANE FONDA.

9. MICHAEL J. FOX.

10. MEL GIBSON.

11. JANET JACKSON.

12. MICHAEL JORDAN.

13. BILL MURRAY.

14. JACK NICHOLSON.

15. ROSS PEROT.

16. MEG RYAN.

17. STING.

18. PATRICK SWAYZE.

19. ROBIN WILLIAMS.

20. OPRAH WINFREY.

20 FAMOUS HARLEY-DAVIDSON OWNERS

1.   MUHAMMAD ALI.

2.   ANN-MARGRET.

3.   CHER.

4.   ERIC CLAPTON.

5.   DAVID COPPERFIELD.

6.   JACK DEMPSEY.

7.   NEIL DIAMOND.

8.   CLINT EASTWOOD.

9.   CLARK GABLE.

10. GOLDIE HAWN.

11. BILLY JOEL.

12. DON JOHNSON.

13. CHARLES LINDBERGH.

14. GEORGE MICHAEL.

15. CROWN PRINCE OLAF OF NORWAY.

16. OLIVIA NEWTON-JOHN.

17. PRISCILLA PRESLEY.

18. LOU REED.

19. BARBRA STREISAND.

10. LIZ TAYLOR.

Created by WILLIAM S. HARLEY and ARTHUR DAVIDSON in a small shed in Milwaukee in 1903, the Harley-Davidson has become a celebrity status symbol, its popularity confirmed by films such as *Easy Rider*. Dan Aykroyd, star of *The Blues Brothers*, is another celebrated HD owner and led John Belushi's funeral procession on a Harley.

10 EARLY ATTEMPTS TO FLY

1.   Man's attempts at flight date back to around 1020 when OLIVER OF
MALMESBURY, an English Benedictine monk, strapped a huge pair of wings to
his body and endeavoured to soar into the air from Malmesbury Abbey. He
broke both legs.

2.   In 1742, fearless French nobleman the MARQUIS DE BACQUEVILLE
launched an ambitious attempt to fly across the River Seine in Paris with paddles
strapped to his arms and legs. With a huge crowd assembled below, he leaped
from a window ledge on the top floor of his house and began flapping vigorously.
He dropped like a stone but had the good fortune to land on a pile of old
clothes in a washerwoman's boat which had been moored on the riverbank to
witness the flight. As a result, he sustained nothing worse than a broken leg.

3.   CANON DESFORGES of the Collegiate Church of Saint Croix d'Etampes in
France devised an intricate flying machine, comprising a wickerwork basket, a
huge canopy and manually-operated wings. The Canon was supremely confident
of success and, in 1772, announced his intention to fly from Etampes to Paris.
Alas, launched from a high building in Etampes, it plummeted straight to the
ground. The Canon broke several bones.

4.   In 1783, JACQUES CHARLES released a large unmanned balloon from Paris.
It landed in Gonesse where it was attacked and destroyed by villagers who
thought it was a monster.

5.   In 1785, Frenchman JEAN-PIERRE BLANCHARD set out to become the first
balloonist to fly across the English Channel. With a wealthy American, JOHN
JEFFRIES, as his sponsor and passenger, Blanchard took off from Dover but the
balloon began to sink perilously close to the sea. To lighten the load, they
jettisoned the flapping wings and rudder which were attached to the basket and
then their own coats. As the balloon continued to drop, they were forced to
discard their trousers! This emergency action saved the day and they landed
safely on French soil.

6.   An anonymous American designer wrote to a science magazine in 1865
suggesting that manned flight could be achieved with a contraption powered by
ten eagles. He envisaged the birds being tethered to the rim of a circular frame
with the passenger seated in the centre. The eagles would be steered by sets of
reins.

7.   Belgian shoemaker VINCENT DE GROOF came up with a device which was part flapper, part parachute. It had 'bat-like wings' controlled by three wooden levers which were worked by the arms and legs. The idea was that he was to be taken by balloon to an altitude of 1,000ft above London and would then fly over the capital. His maiden flight was his last. The wing frame failed and de Groof plunged to his death in a street in Chelsea.

8.   The aerial velocipede was the brainchild of Monsieur A. GOUPIL in the 1870s. Resembling a unicycle beneath a Zeppelin, it proved spectacularly unsuccessful despite an optimistic write-up in the French trade press.

9.   In 1885, DR. W.O. AYRES of New Haven, Connecticut, designed a flying bedstead driven by seven propellers — six for lift and one for propulsion. Two of the lifting propellers were worked by foot pedals while compressed-air motors drove the other four. It never threatened to take off.

10. In the early years of this century the Parisian COUNT DE GUISEUX is said to have achieved modest hops with his Aeroplane Bicycle. The device featured large wings fixed to a bicycle with a propeller linked to the drive chain of the back wheel. To have any hope of elevation, the Count had to pedal furiously, making any form of sustained flight an exhausting prospect.

20 LONDON UNDERGROUND STATIONS WHICH HAVE CHANGED THEIR NAMES

1. ACTON TOWN (Mill Hill Park until 1910).

2. ALDWYCH (Strand until 1915).

3. ARSENAL (Gillespie Road until 1932).

4. BARBICAN (Aldersgate until 1968).

5. BECONTREE (Gale Street until 1932).

6. DEBDEN (Chigwell Lane until 1949).

7. EUSTON SQUARE (Gower Street until 1909).

8. FULHAM BROADWAY (Walham Green until 1952).

9. GREEN PARK (Dover Street until 1933).

10. HOUNSLOW WEST (Hounslow Barracks until 1925).

11. KENSINGTON (OLYMPIA) (Kensington (Addison Road) until 1946).

12. LAMBETH NORTH (Westminster Bridge Road until 1917).

13. MARYLEBONE (Great Central until 1917).

14. MONUMENT (Eastcheap until 1884).

15. MOOR PARK (Sandy Lodge until 1923).

16. OAKWOOD (Enfield West until 1934).

17. RAVENSCOURT PARK (Shaftesbury Road until 1888).

18. SURREY DOCKS (Deptford Road until 1911).

19. WARREN STREET (Euston Road until 1908).

20. WEST KENSINGTON (North End (Fulham) until 1877).

20 APHRODISIAC FOODS

1. ALLIGATOR.

2. APRICOTS.

3. BEAR'S PAWS.

4. CELERY.

5. CUTTLEFISH (fried).

6. DUCK BEAK.

7. FROG'S LEGS.

8. FRUIT BAT (curried).

9. GARLIC.

10. GINGER.

11. MACARONI.

12. OYSTERS.

13. PARSNIPS (young).

14. PIG'S TROTTERS.

15. PRUNES.

16. RATTLESNAKE.

17. SNAILS.

18. SPINACH.

19. TERMITES.

20. TRUFFLES.

In the unlikely event of being able to lay our hands on bear's paws or rattlesnake most of us peak at oysters. They contain dopamine, a chemical said to stimulate desire. The tomato was once considered such an aphrodisiac that the Puritans declared it to be poisonous. It became known as the 'love apple' because the English thought the French called it *pomme d'amour*. In fact, it was really known as *pomme du Moor*, having come to France from South America via North Africa.

10 FOODS WHICH ORIGINATE FROM SOUTH AMERICA

1. BUTTER BEAN.

2. GOURD.

3. PEPPER.

4. PINEAPPLE.

5. POTATO.

6. PUMPKIN.

7. RUNNER BEAN.

8. STRAWBERRY.

9. SWEET CORN.

10. TOMATO.

10 FOODS WHICH ORIGINATE FROM ASIA

1. APRICOT.

2. BANANA.

3. CUCUMBER.

4. EGGPLANT.

5. LEMON.

6. LIME.

7. ONION.

8. ORANGE.

9. PEACH.

10. TANGERINE.

10 FASCINATING FACTS ABOUT SPAM

1. Spam stands for Shoulder Pork and hAM.

2. It was launched by the Geo. A. Hormel Company of Austin, Minnesota, in 1937 and became a great favourite of military cooks during World War Two because it contained protein, was easy to digest and convenient.

3. Former Russian President NIKITA KHRUSHCHEV admitted that during the war 'without Spam we wouldn't have been able to feed our army.'

4. At the end of the war, PRESIDENT EISENHOWER wrote to Hormel: 'I ate my share of Spam along with millions of other soldiers. I'll even confess to a few unkind words about it — uttered during the strain of battle, you understand. But as the former commander-in-chief of the allied forces, I believe I can still officially forgive you your only sin: sending us so much of it.'

5. Spam came to Britain as part of the Lend-Lease Act whereby food given to the U.K. would be paid for when the war was over. Often the only meat available, it became indispensible until rationing ended in 1954.

6. A six-year-old Dorset boy became addicted to Spam and ate his way through six tins of the stuff every week for three years. He had to be sent to a child psychiatrist to get him back on a normal diet.

7. Over four billion cans of Spam have been sold worldwide.

8. The Hormel plant at Austin measures the size of 19 football pitches and contains an oven that cooks 450 cans of Spam a minute.

9. But Spam was not part of the G.I.s' diet in the Gulf War. At the request of the Saudi authorities it was taken off the military menu, pork being a forbidden food there.

10. Monty Python's Spam song was warmly greeted by the manufacturers. Michael Palin recalled: 'The Spam people were very keen and promised they would send us several free tins of Spam. We said: "No, that's all right. Thanks anyway..."'

10 HAUNTED ROYAL HOMES

1. ALTHORP PARK, Northamptonshire. The home of the Spencer family since 1508, Althorp boasts a number of ghosts including a groom, a child and the seventh Earl. The groom, who served the second Earl, manifested himself at the foot of a clergyman guest's bed in the early 1830s, while the ghost of a Victorian girl appeared before one of the Spencer daughters in the picture gallery just before the First World War. The seventh Earl, known as Jack, died in 1975 but several witnesses saw him some months later among the crowd at the wedding of his son Johnnie (Diana's father) to Raine. Since then the butler's wife has twice seen her late employer on the stairs, both sightings being preceded by a sudden blast of hot air. She was so startled the first time that she said, 'How nice to see you, my lord!' without remembering that he'd been dead for years.

2. BUCKINGHAM PALACE, London. The ghost of a monk has been seen walking along the terrace overlooking the Palace gardens on Christmas Day and the sound of a gunshot has been heard in a first-floor office where Major John Gwynne, private secretary to Edward VII, shot himself after becoming involved in a divorce scandal.

3. CLARENCE HOUSE, London. The ballroom at Clarence House is reputed to be haunted by the ghost of Arthur, Duke of Connaught.

4. GLAMIS CASTLE, Angus, Scotland. The ghost of Janet, Lady Glamis, burnt at the stake in the 16th century on trumped-up charges of witchcraft and of trying to poison James V of Scotland, has been seen floating above the castle clock-tower. Her 'body' is surrounded by a lurid glow, depicting her tragic death.

5. HAMPTON COURT PALACE, London. Anne Boleyn, who once lived there, has been seen gliding along corridors in the blue dress she wore for the portrait which still hangs in the Palace. The screams of Catherine Howard, another of Henry VIII's executed wives, have been heard and she has been spotted hurrying along the Long Gallery, a re-enactment of her final plea for mercy. Henry's third wife, Jane Seymour, is also said to haunt the Palace, dressed in white and carrying a burning candle. Additionally, two cavaliers are said to haunt the Fountain Court and a ghostly dog has been glimpsed on the King's Staircase.

6. KENSINGTON PALACE, London. The ghost of the dying George II has been seen looking anxiously from one of the Palace windows towards the

weather-vane, hoping for a fair wind which would bring ships with news of his troops engaged in foreign fields.

7. THE ROYAL PAVILION, Brighton. A passage beneath the building is thought to be haunted by the Prince Regent, for whom it was built, while the ghost of Martha Gunn, known as 'The Brighton Bather' (she is believed to have bathed with the Prince in his youth), was identified at a pre-war banquet at the Pavilion.

8. ST. JAMES'S PALACE, London. On 31 May 1810 the body of Sellis, valet to the loathed Duke of Cumberland, son of George III, was found at St. James's Palace, his head almost severed from his body. Remarkably, the verdict was suicide but the finger of suspicion pointed at the Duke who was rumoured to have been enjoying an affair with Sellis's daughter, wife or both. Thereafter Sellis's ghost appeared in the Palace with his throat cut, accompanied by the smell of fresh blood.

9. SANDRINGHAM HOUSE, Norfolk. The ghost of a mysterious page-boy was spotted some 20 years ago by a lady guest. The boy came into her room in the middle of the night, brandishing a pole, and proceeded either to light or snuff non-existent candles. Those who give credence to such matters believe that the boy could have been galvanised into action by renovations which were being carried out at Sandringham at the time.

10. WINDSOR CASTLE, Berkshire. George III is said to haunt the Castle Library and the spectre of a young guardsman is thought to patrol the Long Walk.

10 COCA-COLA SLOGANS

1. DELICIOUS! REFRESHING! EXHILARATING! INVIGORATING! (1886).

2. THE PAUSE THAT REFRESHES (1929).

3. IT'S THE REFRESHING THING TO DO (1936).

4. IT'S THE REAL THING (1942, revived in 1969).

5. GLOBAL HIGH SIGN (1944).

6. THINGS GO BETTER WITH COKE (1963).

7. HAVE A COKE AND A SMILE (1979).

8. COKE IS IT (1982).

9. YOU CAN'T BEAT THE FEELING (1987).

10. ALWAYS (1993).

Originally concocted by Atlanta pharmacist JOHN STYTH PEMBERTON as a headache cure, Coca-Cola proved a popular thirst-quencher with the addition of soda. Unfortunately Pemberton was a poor salesman, and shortly before his death in 1888 he sold the secret formula plus his share in Coca-Cola to businessman ASA G. CANDLER for $1,200. Thirty years later, Candler too sold the company...for $25 million. The formula remains a closely-guarded secret, but in 1985 Coca-Cola announced that after 99 years it was abandoning the Pemberton formula in favour of a supposedly new improved taste called 'New Coke'. 'The best has been made even better' proclaimed company chairman ROBERTO GOIZUETA. Before taking this momentous decision, Coca-Cola spent $4 million and two years of market research. Yet within three months public pressure forced the company to admit that it had made a mistake and was bringing back the old Coke under the name 'Coca-Cola Classic'.

THE 20 MOST POPULAR U.K. HOUSE NAMES

1. THE BUNGALOW.

2. THE COTTAGE.

3. ROSE COTTAGE.

4. THE SCHOOL HOUSE.

5. HILLCREST.

6. THE LODGE.

7. WOODLANDS.

8. THE COACH HOUSE.

9. HILLSIDE.

10. THE GABLES.

11. THE OLD SCHOOL HOUSE.

12. THE VICARAGE.

13. SUNNYSIDE.

14. THE CROFT.

15. TREETOPS.

16. IVY COTTAGE.

17. GREENACRES.

18. FAIR VIEW.

19. THE WILLOWS.

20. THE FIRS.

One enterprising home-owner called his abode 'House at Pooh Corner' because it was near a sewage farm. Similarly, when Walsall FC were looking for a name for their new stadium in 1990, someone suggested that since the ground was being built on the site of an old sewage works, it should be called W.C. Fields.

RAINING SPRATS AND FROGS — 10 CASES OF ODD WEATHER

1. In October 1947 marine biologist Alan Bajikov observed a downpour of fish while breakfasting with his wife at MARKSVILLE, LOUISIANA. Sunfish, minnows and black bass plummeted from the sky during a gentle shower. No whirlwinds were reported which could have swept the fish up from the nearest stretch of water, the Gulf of Mexico, over 80 miles away. Another fish storm took place at ABERDARE, MID-GLAMORGAN, on 9 February 1859, bringing minnow and smooth-tailed stickleback to earth.

2. Following several weeks of drought, a fierce storm broke one afternoon in August 1814 over FREMONTIERS, near Amiens in France. In the rain which accompanied the storm were dozens of tiny frogs which proceeded to hop around on the ground. Live frogs also fell on LEICESTER, MASSACHUSETTS, on 7 September 1953, landing in gutters and on roofs — proof that they hadn't merely escaped from an overflowing pond.

3. On 11 May 1894, at the height of a hailstorm, a gopher turtle encased in ice fell on BOVINA, eight miles east of Vicksburg, Mississippi. During the same storm, a small block of alabaster, also encased in ice, landed on Vicksburg itself.

4. A deluge of dead birds tumbled from a clear sky on to the streets of BATON ROUGE, LOUISIANA, in November 1896. The only plausible explanation was that the birds, which included wild ducks, catbirds and woodpeckers, had been driven inland by a storm on the Florida coast and had been killed by a sudden temperature change over Baton Rouge.

5. Lumps of meat fell from a cloudless sky over a 100- by 50-yard area of BATH COUNTY, KENTUCKY, on 3 March 1876. When examined, the meat proved to be lung and muscle tissue, either from a child or a horse. It was thought that the meat may have been disgorged by buzzards but none had been seen in the area, and anyway it would have needed a vast number of birds to produce such a quantity of meat.

6. A 2ft-long alligator fell from the sky at EVANSVILLE, INDIANA, on 21 May 1911, landing on the front doorstep of the home of Mrs. Hiram Winchell. When

the creature tried to crawl indoors, it was clubbed to death by Mrs. Winchell and neighbours armed with bed slats.

7.   On 26 October 1956, the dead body of a small monkey was found in the back garden of a house in BROADMOOR, CALIFORNIA, by Mrs. Faye Swanson. The post holding her clothes-line had been damaged, presumably by the falling monkey. The only possible explanation for the incident was that the monkey had fallen from an aircraft, yet the local airport insisted that no planes had been carrying such a cargo that night.

8.   A rainfall of thousands of living snakes up to 18in long reportedly fell over the southern half of MEMPHIS, TENNESSEE, in 1877.

9.   A crop of peaches — hard, green and the size of golfballs — dropped on a building-site at SHREVEPORT, LOUISIANA, on 12 July 1961. The workmen confirmed that the fruit was coming from the sky and not being thrown. Weathermen said that conditions that day were not conducive to the peaches having been lifted by strong winds.

10.   A fall of maggots accompanied a heavy storm at ACAPULCO, MEXICO, on 5 October 1968. Craft assembled for the Olympic yachting events were covered in one-inch long maggots.

10 TURN-ONS WHEN BUYING A HOUSE (based on a U.K. bank survey)

1. SEDUCTIVE SMELLS such as fresh coffee or newly-baked bread.

2. FRESH FLOWERS.

3. CLEAN CARPETS.

4. A NEAT LAWN.

5. WARMTH from central heating or an open fire.

6. MIRRORS make a room seem spacious.

7. TABLE LAMPS giving a warm, homely effect.

8. A SMART FRONT DOOR — first impressions are all-important.

9. A CLEAN KITCHEN with no washing or dirty dishes.

10. BEING OFFERED A GLASS OF WINE by the vendor.

10 TURN-OFFS WHEN BUYING A HOUSE.

1. THE STENCH OF OLD CURRY and other food smells.

2. HAIR-FILLED PLUGHOLES in the bathroom.

3. DIRTY TOILETS .

4. THE TOILET SEAT LEFT UP.

5. COBWEBS in cupboards.

6. DAMP.

7. POOR LIGHTING.

8. NOISY NEIGHBOURS.

9. NOISY TRAFFIC.

10. A DEATH IN THE HOUSE — a lot of people believe in ghosts.

10 TERMS OF ENDEARMENT IN BRITISH LOCAL DIALECTS

1. MY LOVER (North Devon).

2. ME DUCK (Nottingham).

3. CHUCK (Manchester).

4. PET (North-east).

5. KIDDER (Lancashire).

6. FLOWER (Yorkshire).

7. HEN (Scotland).

8. SQUIRE (London).

9. 'BOR (Norfolk).

10. ME HANDSOME (Somerset).

10 CHRISTIAN NAMES AND THEIR MEANINGS

1. AMANDA — fit to be loved.

2. BARRY — javelin.

3. BENJAMIN — son of my right hand.

4. EDWARD — property guardian.

5. EMMA — all-embracing.

6. HAYLEY — hay-meadow.

7. KELLY — warlike one.

8. LINDA — serpent.

9. PHILIP — fond of horses.

10. WAYNE — wagon-maker.

THE 20 MOST POPULAR MALE NAMES IN THE U.K.

(based on a 1998 government survey)

1. JOHN.

2. DAVID.

3. MICHAEL.

4. JAMES.

5. ROBERT.

6. PAUL.

7. PETER.

8. WILLIAM.

9. ANDREW.

10. CHRISTOPHER.

11. THOMAS.

12. STEPHEN.

13. RICHARD.

14. MARK.

15. ANTHONY.

16. GEORGE.

17. ALAN.

18. DANIEL.

19. IAN.

20. BRIAN.

THE 20 MOST POPULAR FEMALE NAMES IN THE U.K.

(based on a 1998 government survey)

1. MARGARET.

2. MARY.

3. SUSAN.

4. ELIZABETH.

5. SARAH.

6. PATRICIA.

7. JOAN.

8. JEAN.

9. CHRISTINE.

10. KATHLEEN.

11. DOROTHY.

12. HELEN.

13. BARBARA.

14. EMMA.

15. JULIE.

16. LINDA.

17. JANET.

18. KAREN.

19. ANN.

20. JENNIFER.

A total of 823,652 forenames are currently in use in Britain, 562,030 of which are unique to one person. Examples of these one-offs include Attila, Begonia, Dimple, Firestar, Cadillac, Porsche, Cortina and Zebedee..

10 REPORTED MONSTERS

1. THE BEAST OF LE GEVAUDAN. Between 1764 and 1767, the village of Saint Etienne de Lugdares in the mountainous region of France known as Le Gevaudan was terrorised by a ferocious creature which went around killing and mutilating local children. A witness described it as walking on two legs like a man, but having short red hair and a pig-like snout. It was about the size of a donkey. Even the arrival of royal troops failed to quell the beast's appetite until a local nobleman shot it dead with a gun loaded with silver bullets. Some said it was a very large wolf; others insisted that it was a werewolf.

2. THE BEAST OF TRURO. A distant relative of our own Surrey Puma and Beast of Bodmin, the Beast of Truro lurked around the Cape Cod area of Massachusetts in the early 1980s. As pet cats were found slaughtered, speculation grew as to whether the beast was a mountain lion even though none exist in the region. Its identity remains a mystery.

3. CHINESE WILDMAN. Over the years there have been frequent reports of a hairy ape-like creature from Hubei Province in central China. The most convincing sighting was reported in 1940 by Wang Zelin. Travelling along a road in the Shennongija region he heard gunshots in the distance and found a crowd surrounding the corpse of a wild woman. He described the body as being covered in a coat of thick grey/red hair. The face had deep-set eyes and protruding lips.

4. THE FLATHEAD LAKE MONSTER. Visitors to Flathead Lake, Montana, have sometimes spotted something 'huge and black' in the water. A major sighting was in 1963 by Ronald Nixon who calculated the creature to be around 25ft long. Divers scoured the lake in vain and a reward offered for the first good photograph of the monster went unclaimed.

5. GOATMAN. Described as having the upper body of a human, the legs of a goat and cloven hooves, Goatman has been known to leap out on unsuspecting courting couples parked in lovers' lanes in Prince George's County, Virginia. One theory is that the creature was a scientist experimenting on goats at a nearby research station when things went wrong.

6. THE JERSEY DEVIL. The story goes that somewhere in the wooded Pine Barrens area of New Jersey lurks a monster with a large horse-like head, wings and a long serpent's body. In January 1909, thousands of people claimed to see the

Devil or its footprints. Then in 1951 strange screams were apparently heard coming from the woods — the cry of the Jersey Devil.

7.   THE LAKE WORTH MONSTER. The sighting in 1969 of a 7ft-tall biped covered in short white fur and with a white goat-like beard sparked a massive monster hunt around Lake Worth, near Fort Worth in Texas. The monster was never found but one tall teenager, wearing white overalls, was shot in the shoulder by an over-zealous hunter.

8.   MO-MO. In the summer of 1971 two girls had stopped for a picnic near the town of Louisiana, Missouri, when a half-ape, half-human emerged from some bushes and tried to break into their car. Monster hunts in the area failed to reveal the culprit.

9.   MOTHMAN. A weird figure with large wings folded against its back and luminous red eyes appeared to two young couples in 1966 at a roadside outside Point Pleasant, West Virginia. As they drove away in fear, it flew off after them. Other sightings were reported in the area, describing how the creature rose into the air 'like a helicopter'. One caller to the police department in nearby Clarkton insisted that Batman was standing on the roof of the house next door. The following year a bridge over the Ohio River collapsed killing nearly 50 people. The locals blamed Mothman, citing him as an omen of doom. Following the disaster, Mothman seemed to disappear as suddenly as he had arrived.

10. SPRING-HEELED JACK. In 1838, a seemingly respectable man walked into a London police station and recounted how his daughter had been savaged by a cloaked figure which had metallic claws and blue and white flames shooting from his mouth. Renowned for his ability to leap remarkable heights, often by way of escape, Spring-Heeled Jack continued to fascinate and terrify Victorian London. There was even a stage play in his honour in 1863. Who or what he was will almost certainly never be known.

10 EVERYDAY PHRASES AND THEIR ORIGINS

1. BACK TO THE DRAWING-BOARD. From a wartime cartoon by Peter Arno in the *New Yorker*. An official with a rolled-up engineering plan under his arm is seen walking away from a crashed plane and saying: 'Well, back to the old drawing-board.'

2. THE COLD SHOULDER. To deter an uninvited dinner guest from repeating the social gaffe, a hostess would serve up the remains of the last meal, such as cold shoulder of lamb. Alternatively, according to novelist Sir Walter Scott, she would turn her back on the interloper, exposing a bare shoulder and cold disdain.

3. THE FULL MONTY. This phrase has its roots in the north of England and is thought to be a reference to Field Marshal Montgomery wearing all his medals. Another theory is that it refers to the hire of a full set of formal clothes from the gents' outfitters which began life as Montague Burton's.

4. HAIR OF THE DOG. Taking 'a hair of the dog that bit you' stems from the old belief that if you were bitten by a mad dog you should take one of its hairs and lay it across the wound to heal it. Thus the best way to cure a hangover is said to be to have another drink.

5. LEFT IN THE LURCH. This stems from the French verb *lacher*, meaning to jilt a lover. A *lacheur/lacheuse* is still a person who lets you down in modern France.

6. LETTING THE CAT OUT OF THE BAG. In the 17th century a piglet would be sold at market in a poke (or bag). The wise buyer would insist on opening the bag first in case the crooked salesman had substituted a cat for the pig.

7. LIKE CHALK AND CHEESE. In the 14th century cheese was always soft and white — the colour of chalk — so the visible distinction was not obvious, although their qualities were totally different. In the same way, two relatives may look or sound the same but have wildly opposing tastes in just about everything.

8. LOSING YOUR MARBLES. According to the ancient Greeks, losing your mental faculties was like losing your furniture, which is how they described the

arrangement of the brain. The French for furniture is *meubles* and so the phrase is a corruption of that.

9.   SETTING YOUR CAP AT SOMEONE. The basic little mob caps which women used to wear in the privacy of their own homes were considered woefully inadequate to be seen by a prospective suitor. So whenever a lady ventured out of doors she would set a pretty bonnet over the offending cap in the hope of attracting the man of her dreams. Therefore she was said to be setting her cap at him.

10. A WHITE ELEPHANT. The discarded gifts which end up on a white elephant stall at the summer fête recall the ancient kings of Siam who wished to punish courtiers without actually appearing to do so. The means of punishment was for the king to give the offender a rare albino elephant, knowing that it was an offer which dare not be refused. The poor man was therefore left with something he didn't want and which he couldn't afford to keep.

10 DISTINCTIVE BRAS

1.   The Loving Cup bra of 1979 featured a tiny electronic circuit which signalled when it was safe for sex. Its lights flashed red or green indicating whether sex could result in pregnancy.

2.   During the 1970s, cherry-flavoured edible bras were introduced as a tasty tit-bit. Men could also get their teeth into a liquorice-flavoured bra.

3.   In 1992, a Somerset man invented a water-filled double-D cup bra. He said that the wearer should add wallpaper paste for an even firmer frontage.

4.   From Paris in the 1980s came the Joli'bust, a self-adhesive bra consisting of nothing more than two shaped pieces of sticky plastic fixed beneath the breasts to show off the curves.

5.   A new bra on the market is made of hologrammatic fibres, the surface of which creates a 3D impression to make the breasts appear a better shape.

6.   Designer André Van Pier created a bra adorned with 3,250 diamonds. It cost £641,000.

7.   Scented bras are on the way. The bra of the future will contain micro-pockets of fragrance which will be gradually released throughout the day.

8.   There are also plans to introduce a mirrored bra and one impregnated with insect repellent to keep mosquitoes at bay.

9.   Another bra of the future is the Smart Bra, featuring nickel-titanium alloys which, according to manufacturers, would 'remember the exact shape of the individual woman's breast'. The technique for using these 'shape-changing' alloys is so sensitive that it has only recently been declassified by the American military.

10. Madonna's famous 'Bullet Bra', worn during her Blonde Ambition tour of 1990, was based on an antique breastplate worn by Italian soldiers.

10 EXPLETIVES AND THEIR ORIGINS

1.   BOB'S YOUR UNCLE! This stems from Arthur Balfour's surprising appointment in 1886 as Chief Secretary for Ireland by his uncle, Robert Arthur Talbot Gascoyne-Cecil, Third Marquis of Salisbury, the Prime Minister.

2.   BY JINGO! From G.W. Hunt's anti-Russian song of 1877, 'We Don't Want to Fight (But By Jingo If We Do...)'.

3.   GERONIMO! This is said to have been used by the Apache Geronimo who, when pursued by soldiers, would leap on horseback over a steep cliff into the water below, shouting 'Geronimo' in mid-air. It was a cry of exultation because he knew that the troops didn't dare follow him.

4.   GORDON BENNETT! Derived from James Gordon Bennett III (1841-1918), the eccentric and wealthy editor-in-chief of the *New York Herald.*

5.   GREAT SCOTT! From the American General Winfield Scott, hero of the 1847 Mexican War.

6.   I'M ALL RIGHT, JACK! A naval term from the 19th century, 'Jack' being a traditional name for a sailor.

7.   NO PEACE FOR THE WICKED! This has Biblical origins, from Isaiah 48:22 'There is no peace, saith the Lord, unto the wicked.'

8.   SILLY BILLY! The nickname of William Frederick, Second Duke of Gloucester (1776-1834), the uncle of William IV.

9.   WAKE UP, ENGLAND! This was a Press summary of a speech made by the future King George V at London's Guildhall in 1901 when, on returning from a tour of the Colonies, he warned against taking the Empire for granted.

10. WHAT THE DICKENS! This has nothing to do with the novelist but is a substitute for 'What the devil'. Shakespeare used the phrase 'What the dickens' in *The Merry Wives of Windsor.*

20 NEWSPAPER MISPRINTS

1. 'In the handicrafts exhibition at Wordsley Community Centre, the contribution of the Misses Smith was "smocking and rugs" and not "smoking drugs" as stated in last week's report.' (*County Express*, Stourbridge).

2. 'Arthur Kitchener was seriously burned Saturday afternoon when he came in contact with a high voltage wife.' (Surrey paper).

3. 'A heavy pall of lust covered the upper two-thirds of Texas last night and was expected to drift south-east over the state by morning.' *(Yankton Press)*.

4. 'The goalkeeper was then troubled by a 20-yard shit from Macdonald.' *(Sunday Post)*.

5. 'For sale. Lovely rosewood piano. Owner going abroad with beautiful twisted legs.' *(North Wales Advertiser)*.

6. 'PARKYNS — to the memory of Mr. Parkyns, passed away September 10. Peace at last. From all the neighbours of Princes Avenue.' *(Leicester Mercury)*.

7. 'On 28th inst. To Mr and Mrs Arthur French, a bony daughter.' (South African paper).

8. 'The bride wore a gown of heavy Oldham Corporation Gasworks.' *(Manchester Evening News)*.

9. 'Fire broke out on the prairie near the C.P.R. viaduct on Monday evening but the blaze was extinguished before damage could be done by the local fire brigade.' (Canadian paper).

10. 'The local ladies, who were on duty in the church and elsewhere, were by no means ornamental additions to the gathering.' (Hertfordshire paper).

11. 'The Vicar, the Rev. C.O. Marston, reported an increased number of communicants during the year. He also stated that the death watch beetle had been confirmed in the church.' *(Banbury Guardian)*.

12. 'The constable now preferred a further charge against the two girls of stealing a carving knife, a fork and two ornamental judges which he found on top of a wardrobe in the hotel bedroom.' *(Dublin Evening Mail)*.

13. 'Miss Mary Salter rendered three vocal solos and a return to orchestral

music was greatly appreciated.' (Surrey paper).

14. '3.0. Greenwich Time Signal.

Conducted by.

Lt. Col. S. Rhodes M.B.E.

Edith Lewin (mezzo-soprano)'. *(Radio Times)*.

15. '1959 Austin A35, black, heater, new tyres, immaculate, elderly owner exchanged for bath chair.' *(Cambridge Daily News)*.

16. 'Belcoo police seized 20 cattle and 30 small pigs on suspicion of having been smuggled, assisted by Miss K. McDermott (violin) and Mrs. P. O'Rourke (percussion and effects).' *(Fermanagh Herald)*.

17. 'If the motion were passed, no strike action would be taken by NALGO without a ballet of all its members.' *(Bristol Evening Post)*.

18. 'Complete home for sale; two double, one single bed, dining-room threepiece suite, wireless, television, carpets, lion, etc.' *(Portsmouth News)*.

19. 'Wrap poison bottles in sandpaper and fasten with scotch tape or a rubber band. If there are children in the house, lock them in a small metal box.' *(Philadelphia Record)*.

20. 'At the fair they will be exhibiting a full range of shoes for girls with low-cut fancy uppers.' *(Leicester Mercury)*.

10 NEWSPAPER HEADLINES

1. STRIP CLUBS SHOCK — Magistrates May Act On Indecent Shows *(Daily Mirror)*.

2. AUDIENCE TRIED TO SPOIL PLAY — But St. Chad's Players Succeeded *(Sunderland Echo)*.

3. A FARMER'S WIFE IS BEST SHOT *(Glasgow Evening Citizen)*.

4. NUDIST NABBED — Unclothed Man Who Admits Brandishing Pistol Is Charged With Carrying Concealed Weapon *(Providence Journal)*.

5. MAGNATE USED TO REMOVE NAIL IN STOMACH *(Los Angeles Times)*.

6. PUBLIC HEALTH PROBLEM — Special Committee To Sit On Bed Bug *(Liverpool Echo)*.

7. PIPELINE RAPTURED *(Ghanaian Times)*.

8. UNDERTAKER'S FAILURE — Let Down By Customers (Yorkshire paper).

9. CHANNEL SWIM ATTEMPT — Boston Girl's Arrival in Liverpool *(Liverpool Echo)*.

10. POLICE FOUND SAFE UNDER BLANKET *(Gloucestershire Echo)*.

CHAPTER

SPORT

SPORT

10 DISCONTINUED OLYMPIC SPORTS

1. CRICKET (1900).

2. CROQUET (1900).

3. GOLF (1900, 1904).

4. JEU DE PAUME (1908).

5. LACROSSE (1904, 1908).

6. MOTORBOATING (1908).

7. POLO (1900, 1908, 1920, 1924, 1936).

8. RACKETS (1908).

9. ROQUE (1904).

10. RUGBY UNION (1900, 1908, 1920, 1924).

These sports were usually included because they were of interest to the host country. So croquet made its solitary appearance in the 1900 Games in Paris. All of the competitors were French, thus giving the host nation a fighting chance of winning gold. Similarly when roque, a form of croquet which was popular in the United States, featured in the 1904 Olympics at St. Louis, all of the players were American. The other obscure sport, *jeu de paume,* is a French variation of tennis, invariably played with the hand. For the one and only Olympic cricket contest, Britain was represented by Devon Wanderers CC who beat a French team composed principally of expatriate Britons in a five-a-side match. And how many people realise that the United States are the reigning Olympic rugby union champions after beating France in 1924...?

10 OLYMPIC DEMONSTRATION SPORTS

1. BICYCLE POLO (1908).

2. KORFBALL (1920).

3. AMERICAN FOOTBALL (1932).

4. DOG SLED RACING (1932).

5. GLIDING (1936).

6. BANDY (1952).

7. AUSTRALIAN RULES FOOTBALL (1956).

8. BUDO (1964).

9. WATER SKIING (1972).

10. ROLLER HOCKEY (1992).

As the name implies, demonstration sports were Olympic exhibition events for which no medals were awarded. The 1952 Helsinki Olympics featured a demonstration of bandy, which is like field hockey but played on an ice-covered soccer pitch. A popular sport in neighbouring Sweden, it came as little surprise when the Swedes triumphed. A demonstration of Australian Rules Football at Melbourne in 1956 produced an entertaining 250-135 result while Émile St. Goddard of Canada emerged victorious in the 1932 dog sled racing. But the most bizarre Olympic demonstration sport was surely bicycle polo, back in 1908, even though the Irish won't hear a word against it — for they defeated the might of Germany 3-1.

20 SPORTING FAILURES

1. WALLACE WILLIAMS (Virgin Islands) ran in the 1979 Pan-American Games marathon, but was so slow that by the time he reached the stadium it was locked and everyone had gone home.

2. Boxer RALPH WALTON of the United States was still adjusting his gumshield when he was knocked out by Al Couture just half a second into their 1946 bout at Lewiston, Maine.

3. ROBERTO ALVAREZ (Mexico) finished so far behind in the 50-kilometre cross-country skiing at the 1988 Winter Olympics that worried officials sent out a search party to look for him.

4. Playing the 130-yard 16th hole at the 1912 Shawnee Invitational for Ladies, American golfer MAUD MCINNES saw her drive land in the Binniekill River and float downstream. Undeterred, she clambered into a boat and, with her husband at the oars, set off in pursuit of her ball. After a number of unsuccessful attempts, she managed to hit the ball on to dry land. Two hours after her tee shot, she holed out for a 166 — 163 over par for the hole.

5. Film star TREVOR HOWARD was an ardent cricketer. One day in 1960 he got up at 5am to drive 180 miles to Buxton, Derbyshire, for a match only to be out first ball.

6. To combat the heat in the 1950 Tour de France, ABD-EL KADER ZAAG drank a bottle of wine and promptly fell off his bike. After sleeping it off by the roadside, he climbed back in the saddle and sped off...in the wrong direction.

7. ANTONIN MILORDIS (Greece) fell 18 times during his slalom ski run at the 1952 Winter Olympics. His time for one run was longer than the winner's two-run total.

8. In May 1986, 52-year-old PEDRO GATICA cycled from his home in Agentina to Mexico for the soccer World Cup, only to find on arrival that he couldn't afford to get in. While he haggled for a ticket, thieves stole his bike.

9. Cuban postman FELIZ CARVAJAL was denied a medal in the 1904 Olympic marathon when he stopped en route to talk to spectators and eat unripe fruit. The resulting indigestion relegated him to fourth place.

10. Russian athlete IVANON VYACHESLAV was so thrilled to win a medal at the 1956 Melbourne Olympics that he hurled the medal high into the air in

jubilation. Unfortunately it came down in Lake Wendouree where, despite a frantic search by Vyacheslav and his team-mates, it remains to this day.

11. Goalkeeper ISADORE IRANDIR of Brazilian team Rio Preto was on his knees in the goalmouth saying his traditional pre-match prayers as opponents Corinthians kicked off. Three seconds later, he was just concluding his beseechments to the Almighty when a 60-yard shot from Roberto Rivelino flew past his ear into the net.

12. Batting at Kalgoorlie, Australia, in the 1970s cricketer STAN DAWSON was hit by a delivery which ignited a box of matches in his pocket. As he tried to beat down the flames, he was run out.

13. Waving to the crowds after finishing fourth in the 500cc US Motor Cycle Grand Prix at Laguna Seca, California, in 1989, Australia's KEVIN MAGEE fell off his machine on his lap of honour and broke a leg.

14. Driving off at the 17th tee at Lyme Regis, Dorset, 69-year-old DEREK GATLEY was half-way through his backswing when the steel shaft snapped and the club struck him on the back of the head, knocking him out. When he came to, a rueful Mr. Gatley admitted: 'It was the first thing I'd hit all day!'.

15. At the 1929 American Football Rosebowl, California centre ROY RIEGELS ran nearly half the length of the field with the ball — but in the wrong direction, towards his own goal. 'Wrong-Way Riegels' became an overnight celebrity, receiving an offer of marriage in which he and his bride would walk up the aisle instead of down!.

16. Preparing for a bout at the 1992 New York Golden Gloves Championships, boxer DANIEL CARUSO psyched himself up by pounding his gloves into his face. In doing so, he broke his nose and was declared unfit to box.

17. After travelling all the way from New York to Sandwich, Kent, for the 1937 Amateur Golf Championship, BRIGADIER-GENERAL CRITCHLEY arrived six minutes late and was disqualified.

18. Reigning Tour de France champion PEDRO DELGADO of Spain only finished third in 1989 after losing three minutes at the start signing autographs.

19. Referee HENNING ERIKSTRUP was about to blow the final whistle at a 1960 Danish League match between Norager and Ebeltoft when his dentures fell out. As he scrambled around on the pitch trying to recover them, Ebeltoft equalised. However Mr. Erikstrup disallowed the goal, replaced his teeth and blew for full-time.

20. After beating 1,000 rivals in a 500-mile race, PERCY the racing pigeon flopped down exhausted in his Sheffield loft and was promptly eaten by a cat.

10 BIZARRE SPORTING EVENTS

I.   An ingenious alternative to England's famous Henley-on-Thames Regatta is
staged each October at Alice Springs in Australia's Northern Territory. It is the
HENLEY-ON-TODD REGATTA, the difference between the Thames and the
Todd being that the Todd River is invariably dry. The competing canoes are
bottomless, the crews' legs protruding through the holes so that the teams run
along the river bed.

2.   Back in the 19th century, Yorkshire folk bound for Blackpool would stop off
at the Corner Pin public house at ramsbottom near Manchester. One day they
started throwing stones at the Yorkshire puddings which had been left to cool
down on the ledges of the pub roof prior to lunch. Seeing this, the landlord
decided to instigate a War of the Roses with Lancashire black puddings replacing
stones. Thus since 1837, competitors have hurled black puddings on to the roof
of the Corner Pin in a bid to dislodge the Yorkshire puddings nestling there. The
contests has acquired the title of the WORLD BLACK PUDDING
KNOCKING CHAMPIONSHIPS and attracts entrants from as far afield as the
United States, Australia, Canada and Germany. Each competitor is permitted
three lobs, a ladder being used to replace the fallen Yorkshire puddings. The first
prize is the winner's height in beer.

3.   Tobacco-spitting is the name of the game at the annual CALICO
TOBACCO CHEWING AND SPITTING CHAMPIONSHIPS near Barstow,
California. Wads have been known to be ejected distances of over 47 feet.

4.   The sport of brick-throwing is recognised by an international contest held
each July at STROUD, NEW SOUTH WALES, between teams representing the
Australian, English, American and Canadian towns named Stroud. So that the
ladies don't feel left out, there is also a rolling-pin-throwing contest.

5.   The WORLD FLOUNDER-TRAMPING CHAMPIONSHIPS were first
staged in 1976 to settle a wager as to who could catch the biggest flounder in
Scotland's Urr estuary. The flounder, a flat-fish, lies on the bottom of the shallow
estuary and buries itself in the mud when the tide goes out. Some 200
competitors wade chest-high into the water with bare feet, searching for the tell-
tale wriggle of the flounder beneath their toes. The fish can then be captured
either with a three-pronged spear called a leister or by manual dexterity. The

flounder must be alive at the weigh-in.

6.   The BEER CAN REGATTA is raced each June off Mindil Beach at Darwin in Australia's Northern Territory. All of the craft are assembled from beer and soft drinks cans, the result being anything from a simple raft to an intricate galleon.

7.   Bed-pushers from all over Britain converge on North Yorkshire each year for the KNARESBOROUGH BED RACE. The main obstacle on the gruelling two-mile course is the River Nidd.

8.   The inaugural WORLD WORM-CHARMING CHAMPIONSHIPS took place at Willaston, Cheshire, in 1980. The winner charmed 511 worms out of his three-metre-square plot in the allotted half-hour. The worms are coaxed to the surface by vibrating garden forks and other implements in the soil. Water may also be employed but competitors must drink a sample before use. This rule follows a spate of unsavoury incidents where the water was laced with washing-up liquid, a banned stimulant which irritates the worm's skin and drives it illegally to the surface.

9.   The highlight of the VANCOUVER SEA FESTIVAL each July is the Nanaimo to Vancouver bathtub race across the choppy waters of the Strait of Georgia.

10. Llanwrtyd Wells in Powys, Wales, is the venue for the annual WORLD BOG-SNORKELLING CHAMPIONSHIPS. Entrants must swim 60 yards with their snorkels through a murky, weed-infested peat bog in as fast a time as possible. There is rarely any great rush to hug the winner....

20 SPORTS STARS WHO HAVE APPEARED IN FILMS

1. MUHAMMAD ALI. The world heavyweight boxing champion played himself in *The Greatest* (1977) and *Body and Soul* (1981). He also appeared as a young fighter in *Requiem for a Heavyweight* (1962) and as Gideon Jackson, the first black U.S. Senator, in the 1979 TV movie *Freedom Road*.

2. VIJAY AMRITRAJ. The Indian tennis player appeared as himself in the 1983 James Bond movie *Octopussy*.

3. MARIO ANDRETTI. The American racing driver who became world champion in 1978 played himself in a film of that year, *Speed Fever*. Austrian ace NIKKI LAUDA appeared in the same picture.

4. DANNY BLANCHFLOWER. The former Tottenham and Northern Ireland soccer international portrayed himself in the 1983 movie *Those Glory Glory Days*.

5. BJORN BORG. The Swedish tennis champion appeared as himself in the 1979 production *Racquet*.

6. JACK BRABHAM. The Australian three-times world motor racing champion played himself in the 1961 production *The Green Helmet*.

7. HENRY COOPER. In 1975, the former British heavyweight boxing champion starred as prizefighter John Gully in *Royal Flash*.

8. BUSTER CRABBE. The 1932 Olympic 400-metre freestyle swimming champion made his film debut the following year as Karpa the Lion Man in *King of the Jungle*. He went on to appear in a further 52 movies, most notably as Flash Gordon and Buck Rogers.

9. STEVE DONAGHUE. The American jockey played Steve Baxter, hero of four 1926 films about horse-racing, *Riding for a King*, *Beating the Book*, *The Golden Spurs* and *The Stolen Favourite*.

10. BRUCE JENNER. The American decathlete who won gold at the 1976 Olympics played an uptight lawyer in the 1980 flop *Can't Stop the Music*.

11. JEAN-CLAUDE KILLY. The French skiing ace appeared as a devious ski instructor in the 1972 movie *Snow Job*.

12. JIM LAKER. The English off-spinner appeared with team-mates DENIS COMPTON, LEN HUTTON and ALEC BEDSER in the 1953 cricketing epic *The Final Test.* They all played themselves.

13. SUZANNE LENGLEN. The French tennis champion appeared as herself in the 1935 film *Things Are Looking Up.*

14. JOE LOUIS. The newly-crowned world heavyweight boxing champion played a hungry young fighter in the all-black *Spirit of Youth* in 1938. .

15. STIRLING MOSS. The charismatic British motor-racing driver appeared alongside DAVID NIVEN in the 1967 film *Casino Royale.*

16. ILIE NASTASE. The Romanian tennis champion appeared as himself in the 1979 movie *Players.*

17. PELÉ. The Brazilian soccer star played the footballing hero in *Hotshot* (1987).

18. DENNIS RODMAN. The colourful Chicago Bulls basketball star appeared in the 1997 film *Double Team.*

19. BARRY SHEENE. The world motorcycling champion played himself in the 1983 film *Space Riders.*

20. BOMBARDIER BILLY WELLS. The British heavyweight boxing champion starred as the pilot in the 1919 film *The Silver Lining* and played the hangman in the 1952 film *The Beggar's Opera* which starred Laurence Olivier.

10 SPORTS STARS WHO HAVE BEEN THE SUBJECT OF FILMS

1.   HAROLD ABRAHAMS. The 1924 Olympic 100 metres champion was played by Ben Cross in the 1981 hit *Chariots of Fire*.

2.   NADIA COMANECI. The tiny Romanian gymnast, star of the 1976 Montreal Olympics, was played by Leslie Weiner (as a youngster) and Johann Carlo (in adulthood) in the 1984 movie *Nadia*.

3.   DAWN FRASER. The Australian triple gold-medallist swimmer, later banned for stealing a flag at the Tokyo Olympics, was portrayed by Bronwyn Mackay-Payne in the 1979 movie *Dawn*.

4.   BEN HOGAN. Glenn Ford played the legendary U.S. golfer in the 1951 film *Follow the Sun*.

5.   ANNETTE KELLERMAN. Esther Williams starred as Australian swimmer Annette Kellerman in the 1952 movie *Million Dollar Mermaid*.

6.   BOB MATHIAS. The double Olympic decathlon-winner (1948 and 1952) played himself in the 1954 movie *The Bob Mathias Story*.

7.   KNUTE ROCKNE. The celebrated American Football coach was played by Pat O'Brien in the 1940 biopic *Knute Rockne, All American*. Ronald Reagan co-starred. .

8.   WILMA RUDOLPH. Shirley Jo Finney played the brilliant American Olympic sprinter in the 1977 TV movie *Wilma*.

9.   JOHN L. SULLIVAN. The 'Boston Strong Boy', world heavyweight boxing champion from 1882 to 1892, was played by Greg McClure in the 1945 film *The Great John L*.

10. JIM THORPE. The man who completed the decathlon/pentathlon double at the 1912 Olympics but was later forced to return his medals over claims of professionalism, was played by Burt Lancaster in the 1951 film *All-American*.

10 SURPRISING SPORTSMEN

1.   MATTHEW ARNOLD. The poet was an accomplished high-jumper and once vaulted a set of 5ft 3in high spiked railings at Oxford for a bet.

2.   ARNOLD BENNETT. The author was no mean footballer and played for his school's First Eleven.

3.   SIR ARTHUR CONAN DOYLE. The creator of Sherlock Holmes played soccer for Portsmouth and cricket for the M.C.C. He hit a century on his debut, had bowling figures of 7-51 against Cambridgeshire and once bowled out the great W.G. Grace.

4.   BILLY JOEL. The American singer was a welterweight boxing champion in his youth.

5.   HUGH LAURIE. The comedian rowed for the defeated Cambridge crew in the 1980 University Boat Race.

6.   JOHNNY MATHIS. In 1955, the singer was ranked joint 85th in the world for the high jump.

7.   LIAM NEESON. The Irish actor was a keen boxer in his younger days.

8.   RYAN O'NEAL. The Hollywood star boxed as a teenager in Golden Gloves contests.

9.   EDGAR ALLAN POE. The American author was an accomplished exponent of the long jump.

10. JAMES WHALE. Broadcaster Whale is a former Surrey Junior Archery Champion.

10 SUPERSTITIOUS SPORTSMEN

1.   JACK BERRY. The English racehorse trainer is never seen in public without his trademark red shirt. The superstition began in his early twenties when Berry was an aspiring jockey. He bought a red shirt prior to a meeting at Ayr and the next day he wore the shirt and rode a winner. After that, whenever he rode a fancied horse, he put on the red shirt to bring him luck. He now has a vast collection, sent to him by well-wishers and owners who would be most aggrieved if he was wearing anything but a red shirt on race day.

2.   BJORN BORG. The Swedish tennis maestro always stopped shaving four days before a major championship. Then before each match he would pack his bag so that all ten racquets were arranged in descending order of tension. The tension testing would take up to an hour. When travelling to Wimbledon, he was always driven over Hammersmith Bridge, never Putney Bridge — and the car had to possess a radio. His parents were equally superstitious. Every year, they alternated between watching their son at Wimbledon and at the French Open in Paris, convinced that to attend both championships in the same year would bring his run of success to an end. Borg's mother, Margarethe, always made a point of sucking a sweet during the final set. At Wimbledon in 1979, after Borg had reached three match points, opponent Roscoe Tanner rallied to deuce. Mrs. Borg decided to spit the sweet on the floor but quickly realised the folly of her actions, picked it up and slipped it back in her mouth. For mother and son there was soon the delicious taste of another victory.

3.   STEVE CLARIDGE. The much-travelled footballer has a curious pre-match ritual when the team stays in a hotel. He always has to have a room on his own and the first thing he does is to remove the hotel sheets from the bed and replace them with ones he has brought from home. His favourite pre-match meal is Rice Krispies and baked beans — sometimes together.

4.   PHIL GRIDELET. Footballer Phil Gridelet always insists on being the last player to come out onto the pitch at the start of each half. Usually this presents no problem but when his team, Southend United, met Ipswich in February 1997 his superstition was really put to the test — for team-mate Andy Rammell was having problems with his contact lenses at half-time and was late out for the second half. Instead of bolstering the numbers, Gridelet steadfastly stayed with him in the dressing-room, forcing Southend to kick off with just nine players.

Manager Ronnie Whelan labelled Gridelet's decision 'crazy'.

5. ALBERT KNIGHT. The Leicestershire cricketer who played for England in 1903 was a lay preacher and before each innings would go down on his knees at the crease to pray for help from above. Playing at Middlesex, his antics brought a new meaning to the Lord's Prayer.

6. JACK NICKLAUS. The great American golfer always carries three pennies in his pocket at tournaments and, when he marks the ball, always does it with the tails side up.

7. GARY PLAYER. When the little South African opens a brand-new box of golf balls, he immediately discards all the odd-numbered balls and plays only with the even-numbered ones.

8. GRAHAM THORNER. Former jump jockey Graham Thorner hated using anything new. He would always get someone else to break in a new saddle or a new pair of breeches for him, and rather than wear a new set of colours he would often jump up and down on them first, just to create that 'used' look. He also insisted on wearing the same lucky underpants and would never ride with a green saddle-pad until he rode a winner with one at Newton Abbot and thereafter demanded a green saddle-pad for every race.

9. JACK TINN. The diminutive Geordie who guided Portsmouth Football Club to three FA Cup finals attributed his success to his lucky spats. Throughout the 1939 Cup run, which ended in a 4-1 victory over Wolves at Wembley, Tinn wore the magical spats, which were religiously put on for him by the same player before every match.

10. LEV YASHIN. The former Russian international goalkeeper always took two caps to a match. He wore one and put the other behind him in the net for luck.

10 CELEBRITIES WHO HAD SOCCER TRIALS

1. STAN BOARDMAN (Liverpool, Tranmere Rovers).

2. ANGUS DEAYTON (Crystal Palace).

3. JULIO IGLESIAS (Real Madrid).

4. EDDIE LARGE (Manchester City).

5. GLEN MURPHY (Charlton Athletic).

6. DES O'CONNOR (Northampton Town).

7. BRIAN REGAN (Liverpool).

8. ROD STEWART (Brentford).

9. BRADLEY WALSH (Brentford).

10. CHARLIE WILLIAMS (Doncaster Rovers).

Former Brookside star Brian Regan was a promising young goalkeeper with Liverpool, while both singer Julio Iglesias and comedian Eddie Large saw their careers wrecked by injury. Iglesias was goalkeeper with Real Madrid's reserve team but a car crash ended his playing career, and Large was a midfield dynamo with his beloved Manchester City until, when he was 15, he fell off his bike and a bus ran over his ankles. Comedian Charlie Williams had a reputation as a bit of a hard man with Doncaster in the 1950s; crooner Des O'Coonor had a stint as a winger with Northampton and 16-year-old Rod Stewart was an apprentice with Brentford for three weeks. 'It was my dad's idea,' he recalled. 'I signed on as a professional and they paid me £8 for a seven-day week. I cleaned the first team's boots and cleaned out the lockers and that's about all. I gave it up after three weeks, never having kicked a ball.'

20 ROCK STARS' FAVOURITE SOCCER TEAMS

1. STUART ADAMSON, Big Country (Dunfermline Athletic).

2. JAMES DEAN BRADFIELD, the Manic Street Preachers (Nottingham Forest).

3. GEEZER BUTLER, Black Sabbath (Aston Villa).

4. DAVID BYRNE, Talking Heads (Dumbarton).

5. ROB CIEKA, the Boo Radleys (Crewe Alexandra).

6. ELVIS COSTELLO (Liverpool).

7. RAY DAVIES, The Kinks (Arsenal).

8. LIAM and NOEL GALLAGHER, Oasis (Manchester City).

9. FISH, Marillion (Hibernian).

10. PAUL HEATON, The Beautiful South (Sheffield United).

11. JIM KERR, Simple Minds (Celtic).

12. MEL B, The Spice Girls (Leeds United).

13. ALISON MOYET (Southend United).

14. CHRIS REA (Middlesbrough).

15. SHAKIN' STEVENS (Cardiff City).

16. DAVE STEWART, The Eurythmics (Sunderland).

17. STING (Newcastle United).

18. SUGGS (Chelsea).

19. LOUISE WENER, Sleeper (West Ham United).

20. ROBBIE WILLIAMS (Port Vale).

10 FAMOUS MANCHESTER UNITED FANS

1. MIKE ATHERTON.

2. ZOE BALL.

3. TERRY CHRISTIAN.

4. STEVE COOGAN.

5. ANGUS DEAYTON.

6. EAMONN HOLMES.

7. ULRIKA JONSSON.

8. MICK HUCKNALL.

9. MORRISSEY.

10. GARY RHODES.

10 POLITICIANS' FAVOURITE SOCCER TEAMS

1. JEFFREY ARCHER (Bristol Rovers).

2. GORDON BROWN (Raith Rovers).

3. KENNETH CLARKE (Nottingham Forest).

4. ROY HATTERSLEY (Sheffield Wednesday).

5. GLENDA JACKSON (Tranmere Rovers).

6. NEIL KINNOCK (Brentford).

7. NORMAN LAMONT (Grimsby Town).

8. JOHN MAJOR (Chelsea).

9. CECIL PARKINSON (Preston North End).

10. RICHARD RYDER (Ipswich Town).

10 GOALSCORING GOALKEEPERS

1. PAT JENNINGS (Tottenham Hotspur) v ALEX STEPNEY (Manchester Utd), 1967.

2. PETER SHILTON (Leicester City) v CAMPBELL FORSYTH (Southampton), 1967.

3. RAY CASHLEY (Bristol City) v JEFF WEALANDS (Hull City), 1973.

4. STEVE SHERWOOD (Watford) v RADDY AVRAMOVIC (Coventry City), 1984.

5. STEVE OGRIZOVIC (Coventry City) v MARTIN HODGE (Sheffield Wednesday), 1986.

6. ANDY GORAM (Hibernian) v DAVID WYLIE (Morton), 1988.

7. ANDY MCLEAN (Cliftonville) v GEORGE DUNLOP (Linfield), 1988.

8. ALAN PATERSON (Glentoran) v GEORGE DUNLOP (Linfield), 1989.

9. RAY CHARLES (East Fife) v BERNARD DUFFY (Stranraer), 1990.

10. CHRIS MACKENZIE (Hereford United) v MAIK TAYLOR (Barnet), 1995.

10 MAD GOALKEEPERS

1. JOHN BURRIDGE. Veteran English goalkeeper John Burridge used to live, eat and sleep football. He has been known to take a football to bed at night and to wake up in the middle of the night and conduct imaginary interviews. He also had a penchant for watching *Match of the Day* in his full goalkeeping kit, complete with jersey, gloves and boots.

2. JOSÉ JUIS CHILAVERT. The extrovert Paraguayan wears the image of a snarling bulldog emblazoned on his goalkeeper's jersey and loves to wander from his own area and score spectacular goals. In 1996 he scored eight for his club, Velez Sarsfield of Argentina, including a 60-yard free-kick against River Plate which caught the opposing keeper, German Burgos, off his line.

3. WILLIAM FOULKE. Known to all as 'Fatty' on account of the fact that he weighed 25 stone towards the end of his career, Foulke used his size to intimidate opposing forwards and referees alike. Playing for Sheffield United against Liverpool in the 1898-99 season, he picked up opposing centre-forward George Allan, turned him upside-down and stood him on his head in the penalty area mud. The resultant penalty cost United the game and Foulke apologised to his team-mates afterwards before adding mischievously: 'I made a right toffee-apple out of him, didn't I?' After United's 1902 FA Cup final defeat, Foulke was so aggrieved that, stark naked, he chased referee Tom Kirkham along the corridors at Crystal Palace, forcing the terrified official to lock his dressing-room door. Foulke used to say: 'I don't mind what they call me, as long as they don't call me late for lunch.' To prove his point, he once sat down at the table before his Chelsea team-mates had arrived and proceeded to eat the food intended for the whole team.

4. RENÉ HIGUITA. The Colombian stunned Wembley in September 1995 with his remarkable 'scorpion' save. To keep out a shot from England's Jamie Redknapp, Higuita did a handstand, arched his back and knocked the ball off the goal-line with the studs of his upturned boots.

5. ALBERT IREMONGER. The Notts County and England goalkeeper of the period either side of the First World War used to venture from his area to take throw-ins. His most dramatic expedition was to take a penalty against Blackburn. His shot thundered against the bar and rebounded towards the half-way line. Iremonger hared back towards his exposed goal in a desperate race with the Blackburn winger. With a late lunge, Iremonger got to the ball first but merely

succeeded in slicing it into his own net. .

6. DICK PYM. The Bolton and England keeper of the 1920s would refuse to travel if the numbers on his rail ticket added up to 13. He also used to carry a lump of coal in his pocket at all times, even during matches.

7. RAMON QUIROGA. Christened 'El Loco' by his Peruvian team-mates, Quiroga was another South American goalkeeper who was liable to be found tackling opponents on the half-way line. He liked to juggle the ball in dangerous situations and had a penalty-saving technique which involved standing nonchalantly with his hands on his hips.

8. DR. LEIGH RICHMOND ROOSE. The Welshman who won 24 caps for his country between 1900 and 1911 was a born practical joker. He turned up for a match against Ireland with one hand heavily bandaged and was hailed a hero for defying the pain barrier. Then just as the match was about to start, he whipped off the bandages to reveal a perfectly healthy set of fingers. On another occasion, Roose doubled as goalkeeper and full-back when the latter was injured. And throughout his career, he never had his undershirt washed, convinced that a trip to the laundry would bring him bad luck.

9. JIMMY TRAINOR. When Preston trounced Reading 18-0 in 1893-94 Trainor, their Welsh international keeper, was so under-employed that he wore a mackintosh in the second half to keep out the driving rain.

10. TIM WILLIAMSON. To make himself look more imposing to forwards Williamson, who won seven England caps between 1905 and 1913, used to wear several jerseys under the official one.

10 SOCCER PERSONALITIES WHO HAVE APPEARED IN TV ADVERTS

1. RON ATKINSON (Royal Insurance).

2. JOHN BARNES (Lucozade).

3. GEORGE BEST (Fore grooming aids for men).

4. PETER SCHMEICHEL (Danepak Bacon).

5. RYAN GIGGS (Quorn).

6. RUUD GULLIT (Pizza Hut).

7. GLENN HODDLE (Shredded Wheat).

8. KEVIN KEEGAN (Brut, Sugar Puffs).

9. GARY LINEKER (Walkers Crisps).

10. DAVID PLATT (McDonald's).

When Kevin Keegan was managing Newcastle United and promoting Sugar Puffs, fans of north-east rivals Sunderland abandoned the product in droves. Sainsbury's in Sunderland reported a 20 per cent drop in sales of Sugar Puffs.

20 FORMER SOCCER CLUB HOMES

1. ANFIELD (Everton).

2. THE ANTELOPE GROUND (Southampton).

3. BANK STREET (Manchester United).

4. BLINKBONNY (Falkirk).

5. BULL STOB CLOSE (Berwick Rangers).

6. THE CHANONRY (Aberdeen).

7. THE CHUCKERY (Walsall).

8. COCKLE'S FIELD (Bolton Wanderers).

9. THE COW PAT (Lincoln City).

10. THE INVICTA GROUND (Arsenal).

11. THE NEST (Norwich City).

12. THE OLD ARCHERY GROUND (Middlesbrough).

13. OLIVE GROVE (Sheffield Wednesday).

14. THE PRAIRIE (Mansfield Town).

15. RAIKES HALL GARDENS (Blackpool).

16. RANDYFORD PARK (East Stirlingshire).

17. SHORTROODS (St. Mirren) .

18. SIEMENS MEADOW (Charlton Athletic).

19. THE TROTTING TRACK (Stranraer).

20. WHITTLES WHIPPET GROUND (Leyton Orient).

Everton were the original tenants of Anfield from 1884 to 1892 until they fell out with their landlord, local MP John Houlding, over a rent increase. Houlding gave Everton notice to quit and, in their place, established his own club, Liverpool FC, at Anfield, where they remain to this day.

20 SOCCER CLUBS' FORMER NAMES

1. ARDWICK (Manchester City).

2. BAINSFORD BRITANNIA (East Stirlingshire).

3. BLACK ARABS (Bristol Rovers).

4. BRUMBY HALL (Scunthorpe United).

5. CHRIST CHURCH (Bolton Wanderers).

6. DIAL SQUARE FC (Arsenal).

7. DUNDEE HIBERNIAN (Dundee United).

8. EXCELSIOR FC (Airdrieonians).

9. FERRANTI THISTLE (Livingston).

10. HEATON NORRIS ROVERS (Stockport County).

11. L&Y RAILWAY FC (Manchester United).

12. NEW BROMPTON (Gillingham).

13. ST. DOMINGO'S FC (Everton).

14. ST. JUDE'S INSTITUTE (Queen's Park Rangers).

15. ST. MARY'S YMCA (Southampton).

16. SINGERS FC (Coventry City).

17. SMALL HEATH ALLIANCE (Birmingham City).

18. STANLEY (Newcastle United).

19. SUNDERLAND AND DISTRICT TEACHERS AFC (Sunderland).

20. THAMES IRONWORKS (West Ham United).

West Ham started out as a works team but at the turn of the century when they decided to pay their players they fell foul of the head of Thames Ironworks, who severed the football club from the firm. The footballers changed their name to West Ham and secured a potato-field as their new ground.

THE FIRST 10 ENGLISH AND SCOTTISH LEAGUE SOCCER CLUBS TO INSTALL FLOODLIGHTS

1. OXFORD UNITED (then known as Headington) December 1950.

2. SWINDON TOWN April 1951.

3. ARSENAL September 1951.

4. SOUTHAMPTON October 1951.

5. STENHOUSEMUIR November 1951.

6. CARLISLE UNITED February 1952.

7. SUNDERLAND December 1952.

8. BRISTOL CITY January 1953.

9. HULL CITY January 1953.

10. NEWCASTLE UNITED February 1953.

The very first floodlit match took place in October 1878 when two Sheffield representative teams met at Bramall Lane before a crowd of 20,000. The four lights were mounted on 30ft poles and produced power to the equivalent of 8,000 candles. The experiment was so successful that others followed suit. In Scotland, Third Lanark entertained Vale of Leven in a floodlit friendly where a single beam, mounted on a platform, was directed at the ball to spotlight the play. But at Chorley, Lancashire, a crowd of 8,000 went home disappointed after waiting two hours in torrential rain. The electrician couldn't switch on the lights! The Football Association banned the use of floodlights for competitive games until the end of 1950 but the first Cup tie under lights did not take place until 1955. In that same year, Scottish club Arbroath proudly switched on their lights against Dundee United, only for one of the precious lamps to be smashed by a mighty clearance from an Arbroath player.

10 INFAMOUS SOCCER SENDINGS-OFF

1. Former blacksmith FRANK BARSON was sent off at least a dozen times in his football career between the wars. While playing for Aston Villa, he is even reputed to have pulled a gun on the manager.

2. JOSÉ BATISTA of Uruguay was dismissed after only 55 seconds of the World Cup tie against Scotland in 1986.

3. AMBROSE BROWN of Wrexham was sent off 20 seconds after the start of the Third Division (North) match versus Hull City in 1936.

4. Charlton pair DEREK HALES and MIKE FLANAGAN were sent off for fighting each other during the FA Cup tie with Maidstone United in 1979.

5. Former Scottish winger WILLIE JOHNSTON holds the unenviable record of being sent off 21 times in his career.

6. Liverpool's KEVIN KEEGAN and Leeds United's BILLY BREMNER left the field in disgrace after being sent off for fighting in the 1974 Charity Shield at Wembley.

7. Owing to an injury crisis, 37-year-old DAVID LANE, chairman of Tring Town, was named as a substitute for their game against Berkhamsted Town in 1990-91. Called off the bench, he was sent off without kicking the ball.

8. Bologna's GIUSEPPE LORENZO set a new world record when he was sent off for striking an opponent after just ten seconds of an Italian League game against Parma in 1990.

9. Manchester United's KEVIN MORAN became the first player to be sent off in an FA Cup final when he received his marching orders against Everton in 1985.

10. ALAN MULLERY was the first player to be sent off for England when he was dismissed against Yugoslavia in a 1968 European Championship match in Florence.

10 FOOTBALLERS' NICKNAMES

1. THE BLACK PANTHER (Eusebio).

2. BUDGIE (Johnny Byrne).

3. THE CAT (Peter Bonetti).

4. CRAZY HORSE (Emlyn Hughes).

5. THE FLYING PIG (Tommy Lawrence).

6. THE GIRAFFE (Jack Charlton).

7. LITTLE BIRD (Garrincha).

8. SNIFFER (Allan Clarke).

9. SPARKY (Mark Hughes).

10. THE VULTURE (Emilio Butragueno).

10 BOXERS' NICKNAMES

1. THE AMBLING ALP (Primo Carnera).

2. THE BROCKTON BLOCKBUSTER (Rocky Marciano).

3. THE BROWN BOMBER (Joe Louis).

4. THE FIGHTING MARINE (Gene Tunney).

5. GENTLEMAN JIM (James J. Corbett).

6. THE LIVERMORE LARRUPER (Max Baer).

7. THE LOUISVILLE LIP (Muhammad Ali).

8. THE MANASSA MAULER (Jack Dempsey).

9. THE MICHIGAN ASSASSIN (Stanley Ketchel).

10. ORCHID MAN (Georges Carpentier).

10 FATHER AND SON GOLFERS

1. When BUDDY ALEXANDER won the 1986 U.S. Amateur Championship, he was not the first in the family to taste golfing success. His father SKIP won two PGA events back in 1948 and played for the United States Ryder Cup team in 1949 and 1951.

2. PERCY ALLISS and his son PETER both played for Britain in the Ryder Cup, the former three times and the latter eight.

3. The final of the 1952 Swiss Amateur Championship was contested by father and son ANTOINE and ANDRÉ BARRAS. The son won.

4. JOE CARR and his sons RODDY and JOHN have all represented Ireland at golf.

5. CLAYTON HEAFNER was a member of the American Ryder Cup teams of 1949 and 1951 and his son VANCE played for the 1977 American Walker Cup team.

6. American Ryder Cup player DAVIS LOVE III is, unsurprisingly, the son of DAVIS LOVE II who finished equal sixth in the 1969 British Open.

7. OLD TOM MORRIS (1861, 1862, 1864, 1867) and YOUNG TOM MORRIS (1868, 1869, 1870, 1872) both won the British Open. Young Tom's triumph in 1868 meant that he succeeded his father as champion, the only time this has ever happened in a major tournament.

8. WILLIE PARK SR. (1860, 1863, 1866, 1875) and WILLIE PARK JR. (1889) also both won the British Open.

9. GARY PLAYER's son WAYNE played for South Africa in the 1980 World Amateur Team Championship.

10. HARRY VARDON, six times winner of the British Open, had a younger brother TOM who finished runner-up to him in the 1903 championship at Prestwick.

10 BROTHERLY GOLFERS

1. When MIGUEL BALLESTEROS won the 1983 Timex Open in Biarritz, he was beginning to emerge from the shadows of illustrious brother SEVERIANO who had already won the U.S. Masters and British Open.

2. Brothers JAY and LIONEL HEBERT both played for the United States in the Ryder Cup — Lionel in 1957, Jay in 1959 and 1961. They have also both won the U.S. PGA Championship — Lionel in 1957 and Jay in 1960.

3. HAROLD and ALAN HENNING are both former winners of the South African Open.

4. In 1963, brothers BERNARD and GEOFFREY HUNT represented Great Britain and Ireland in the Ryder Cup in Atlanta.

5. ANGEL and SEBASTIAN MIGUEL both won the Spanish Open in the early 1960s.

6. In 1910, ALEX SMITH defeated his brother, MACDONALD, in a play-off for the U.S. Open. Another brother, WILLIE, had won the title in 1899. And in 1906, Alex had finished first with Willie as runner-up.

7. In 1954, PETER TOOGOOD won the Australian Amateur Championship just ahead of brother JOHN. Two years later, they finished first and third in the Tasmanian Open. Sandwiched between them in second place was their father ALFRED.

8. After JOE TURNESA had finished second in the U.S. PGA Championship of 1927, brother JIM went one better, winning the title in 1952. A third brother, WILLIE, twice won the U.S. Amateur Championship.

9. America's LANNY WADKINS was U.S. PGA champion in 1977 and the following year younger brother BOBBY won the inaugural European Open.

10. CHARLES, ERNEST and REG WHITCOMBE all played for Britain in the Ryder Cup, Charles and Ernest being paired together in the 1935 foursomes.

THE 10 HIGHEST POINTS SCORERS IN THE RYDER CUP

1.	NICK FALDO (GB and Europe, 1975-97)	25.
2.	BILLY CASPER (U.S., 1961-75)	23.
3.	ARNOLD PALMER (U.S., 1961-73)	23.
4.	SEVERIANO BALLESTEROS (GB and Europe, 1979-95)	22.
5.	LANNY WADKINS (U.S., 1977-93)	21.
6.	BERNHARD LANGER (GB and Europe, 1981-97)	20.
7.	LEE TREVINO (U.S., 1969-81)	20.
8.	JACK NICKLAUS (U.S., 1969-81)	18.
9.	GENE LITTLER (U.S., 1961-75)	18.
10.	TONY JACKLIN (GB and Europe, 1967-79)	17.

THE WORLD'S FIRST 10 GOLF CLUBS

1.	HONOURABLE COMPANY OF EDINBURGH GOLFERS	1744.
2.	GOLF CLUB OF ST. ANDREWS (later the Royal And Ancient)	1754.
3.	BRUNTSFIELD LINKS GOLFING SOCIETY	1761.
4.	ROYAL BLACKHEATH	1766.
5.	ROYAL MUSSELBURGH	1774.
6.	ROYAL ABERDEEN	1780.
7.	GLASGOW	1787.
8.	DUNBAR	1794.
9.	BURNTISLAND	1797.
10.	ROYAL ALBERT, MONTROSE	1810.

THE FIRST 20 COUNTRIES TO TAKE UP GOLF

(based on the date of the oldest club to have enjoyed continuous existence)

1. SCOTLAND (1744) — Honourable Company of Edinburgh Golfers.

2. ENGLAND (1766) — Royal Blackheath .

3. INDIA (1829) — Royal Calcutta .

4. FRANCE (1856) — Pau.

5. PAKISTAN (1857) — Lahore Gymkhana.

6. JAMAICA (1868) — Manchester.

7. INDONESIA (1872) — Jakarta.

8. CANADA (1873) — Royal Montreal.

9. SRI LANKA (1879) — Royal Colombo.

10. IRELAND (1881) — Royal Belfast.

11. ITALY (1885) — Roma.

    SOUTH AFRICA (1885) — Royal Cape.

13. WALES (1888) — Tenby.

    = BELGIUM (1888) — Royal Antwerp.

    = UNITED STATES (1888) — St. Andrews (Yonkers), New York.

    = MALAYSIA (1888) — Perak at Taipang.

17. HONG KONG (1889) — Royal Hong Kong .

    = ARGENTINA (1889) — Lomas, Buenos Aires.

19. PORTUGAL (1890) — Oporto.

    = THAILAND (1890) — Royal Bangkok.

10 NEAR-MISSES IN THE MAJORS

1. At the 1949 British Open at Sandwich, Irishman HARRY BRADSHAW saw his drive at the fifth hole in Round Two land in a broken bottle. Opting to play it as it lay, he ended up taking a double-bogey 6, as a result of which he could only tie for first place with Bobby Locke of South Africa. Locke then went on to win the play-off.

2. In the third round of the 1946 U.S. Open at Canterbury, Ohio, BYRON NELSON's caddie, Eddie Martin, accidentally kicked his player's ball while climbing beneath the spectator rope on the edge of the 15th fairway. It cost Nelson a one-stroke penalty and the championship — for he lost in the play-off to Lloyd Mangrum.

3. Needing to hole a three-foot putt to win the 1970 British Open at St. Andrews, America's DOUG SANDERS missed and went in to a play-off with Jack Nicklaus. The disappointment of the missed putt proved too much for Sanders and Nicklaus won the play-off.

4. On the same St. Andrews green in 1933 another American, LEO DIEGEL, had missed a putt of similar length which would have got him into a play-off for the British Open with fellow-countrymen Densmore Shute and Craig Wood.

5. Argentina's ROBERTO DE VICENZO left the final green at the 1968 U.S. Masters convinced that his last-round 65 had earned him a play-off against American Bob Goalby. But de Vicenzo had inadvertently signed for a card of 66 after playing partner Tommy Aaron had incorrectly written down a 4 when de Vicenzo took a birdie 3 on the 17th.

6. In the 1961 U.S. PGA Championship DON JANUARY was four ahead with three to play but 45-year-old Jerry Barber holed putts of 20, 40 and 60 feet to force a tie. Barber then won the play-off.

7. In the 1983 British Open at Royal Birkdale, American HALE IRWIN contrived to miss a one-inch putt at the 14th in Round Three. Irwin took his eye off the ball as he went to tap it in and missed the ball completely. Sportingly, he called a one-shot penalty on himself — and it was to prove a costly lapse, as he finished joint second, just one stroke behind the winner, Tom Watson.

8. In 1937 Densmore Shute retained his U.S. PGA title, largely as a result of the misfortune which befell HAROLD MCSPADEN. The latter had a four-foot putt for victory at the final hole but was interrupted by photographers, missed the putt and lost the first extra hole.

9. ED 'PORKY' OLIVER missed out on a play-off for the 1940 U.S. Open for teeing off too early. In a bid to counter a forecast of adverse weather he had started before his allotted time and, in doing so, became one of six players to be disqualified. He played on, however, and shot 72 for a total of 287, a score which would have tied for first place.

10. English golfer ROGER WETHERED was left to rue a careless moment in the 1921 British Open at St. Andrews — one which was to cost him the championship. Weighing up a shot to the 14th in the third round, Wethered was walking backwards when he accidentally trod on his ball, thus incurring a one-stroke penalty. How costly that shot was; for at the end of 72 holes he was left tied for first place with American 'Jock' Hutchison — and it was Hutchison who went on to win the play-off.

10 BAD-TEMPERED GOLFERS

1. Former British Ryder Cup player BRIAN BARNES 12-putted a hole in the 1968 French Open at St. Cloud after losing his temper. Playing the second round, he had taken three shots to the eighth and was left with a putt of less than a yard. But when he missed it, he began angrily stabbing at the ball while it was still moving, incurring a further penalty for standing astride the line of a putt. He ended up taking 15 before the ball finally dropped into the hole.

2. After his Florida University team had lost to Wake Forest University, young ANDY BEAN took out his frustration on a golf ball by trying to eat it. He sank his teeth into the cover of the ball, bit off a large chunk and handed it to a friend with the words: 'Here, take it. I've eaten my last golf ball. I'm going off the diet.'

3. TOMMY BOLT had a reputation for hurling his clubs around when things went wrong. Nicknamed 'Thunder-Bolt', he threw his driver into a lake at the 1960 U.S. Open at Cherry Hills, Colorado and another time had to pay a deep-sea diver $75 to retrieve the driver from the bottom of a canal. After one particularly volatile round, partner Jimmy Demaret remarked that Bolt's putter had spent 'more time in the air than Lindbergh.'

4. After missing two simple putts at Oakmont Country Club in 1919, American golfer CHICK EVANS was so angry with himself that he holed out with the handle of his umbrella.

5. Frustrated by the slow play of his partners at the 1968 Los Angeles Open, fiery American BOB GOALBY abandoned them half-way round and went off and finished alone. On another occasion he was so disgusted with one shot that he threw himself, fully-clothed, into a water hazard!.

6. According to Sam Snead, American CLAYTON HEAFNER was 'the most even-tempered golfer I ever saw. He was mad all the time.' Heafner once stormed off the first tee because the starter pronounced his name incorrectly, while another starter incurred his wrath by referring to a shot from a tree which Heafner had been forced to play in the corresponding event the previous year. To ensure there was no repetition Heafner marched off the tee, threw his clubs in the car and drove out of the event in a cloud of dust.

7. American golfer KY LAFFOON, who played in the 1935 Ryder Cup, had a love-hate relationship with his putter. After one missed putt he was seen trying

to strangle the club and, when that failed, he attempted to drown it — not by hurling it into a lake but by actually holding it down under water! Finally he decided to punish it by tying it with string to the bumper of his car and allowing it to bruise itself on the tarmac as he drove to the next tournament. On another occasion, he angrily broke his putter by smashing it against his foot. Unfortunately the impact also broke his toe.

8. NORMAN VON NIDA, an Australian post-war professional, exploded in a bunker during a tournament in England. Unable to extricate his ball, he vented his anger on the lump of turf which formed the insurmountable overhang. Hacking away at it with his clubs until he had completely destroyed it, he proceeded to hide the pieces in nearby bushes. When challenged about his behaviour, he insisted that he had been merely been 'tidying up'.

9. Texan golfer LEFTY STACKHOUSE punished himself after one poor shot by throwing himself into a thorn hedge. He was also seen to thrash an entire set of clubs into pieces against a tree stump.

10. Putting at Bethesda Congressional Country Club, Maryland, in 1979, 66-year-old physician Dr. SHERMAN A. THOMAS was so distracted by the honking of a nearby Canadian goose that he chased the bird and felled it with a blow to the head. Up before the local beak, he was fined $500 for killing a goose out of season.

10 ROYAL GOLFERS

Although the first golf clubs were not founded until the 18th century the game had been played long before that, especially by royalty.

1.   JAMES IV OF SCOTLAND was a keen golfer until he died at Flodden Field in 1513.

2.   MARY QUEEN OF SCOTS is believed to have played golf at St. Andrews in 1563 and, bringing a new meaning to the term 'golf widow', was criticised for playing only a day or so after her husband Darnley was murdered in 1567.

3.   CHARLES I was playing golf at Leith in 1642 when news of the Irish Rebellion was brought to him. The story goes that he insisted on finishing the game before returning to matters of state.

4.   CHARLES II played a little golf in Scotland.

5.   JAMES II played frequently at Leith while living in Edinburgh as Duke of York.

6.   EDWARD VII was introduced to golf at Musselburgh when he was at Edinburgh University as Prince of Wales. Putting was said to be his strength. He was also patron of several clubs.

7.   THE DUKE OF CONNAUGHT, Edward VII's younger brother, was a modest golfer who always counted two on greens to avoid putting!

8.   GEORGE V, when still the Duke of York, played at Windsor with Ben Sayers, the North Berwick professional. Sayers' brother, George, gave lessons to the Duke's wife, later Queen Mary.

9.   EDWARD VIII, when Prince of Wales, reached the final of the Parliamentary Handicap in 1933.

10. GEORGE VI was Captain of the Royal and Ancient and an enthusiastic player and spectator, attending the 1948 British Open at Muirfield.

THE 10 LONGEST WINNING SEQUENCES BY A RACEHORSE

1. CAMARERO (56). From April 1953 to August 1955, won his first 56 races in Puerto Rico. He eventually finished with a career record of 73 wins from 77 races over distances from five to nine furlongs.

2. KINCSEM (54). The Hungarian-bred mare was never beaten, winning ten races as a two-year-old in 1876, 17 at three years, 15 at four years and 12 at five. She raced all over the world at distances of anything from five furlongs to two and a half miles.

3. GALGO JR. (39). Between 1930 and 1931, Galgo Jr. won 39 successive races in Puerto Rico.

4. LEVIATHAN (23). Racing almost exclusively in Virginia, Leviathan chalked up an impressive sequence in long-distance events between 1797 and 1801. He retired with 24 wins from 30 starts.

5. MISS PETTY (22). A sharp sprinter, Miss Petty remained unbeaten in minor Queensland events between 1985 and 1989.

6. POOKER T (22). Competing in modest claiming races in Puerto Rico in 1962, Pooker T notched up 24 wins, 22 of them in succession.

7. BOND'S FIRST CONSUL (21). The champion of the northern states of America, Joshua Bond's horse won the first 21 races of his career from 1801 to 1806.

8. LOTTERY (21). An outstanding American mare, Lottery lost only the first of her 22 races, winning major Jockey Club races at South Carolina in 1808 and 1810.

9. METEOR (21). Although small in stature, British-trained Meteor won 30 of his 33 starts from 1786, mostly at Newmarket.

10. PICNIC IN THE PARK (21). This horse broke the Australasian record of 19 consecutive wins which had stood for over 60 years when trotting up in 21 successive sprint races at lowly Queensland 'bush' tracks between 1984 and 1985.

10 OUTSIDERS WHICH HAVE WON THE DERBY

1. JEDDAH (1898, 100-1).

2. SIGNORINETTA (1908, 100-1).

3. ABOYEUR (1913, 100-1).

4. HERMIT (1867, 1,000-15).

5. PSIDIUM (1961, 66-1).

6. AZOR (1815, 50-1).

7. SPANIEL (1831, 50-1).

8. LITTLE WONDER (1840, 50-1).

9. AIRBORNE (1946, 50-1).

10. SNOW KNIGHT (1974, 50-1).

The victory of Signorinetta was the result of a true equine love story. The horse was trained by the extrovert Italian, Odorado Ginistrelli, who came to Newmarket from his homeland in the 1880s. His unorthodox methods meant that he was not taken seriously by the racing fraternity, even after Signorina had won the 1889 Middle Park Stakes. She was retired to stud but remained barren for ten years until producing the Derby third Signorino. In 1904 she was due to be covered by a fine stallion called Cyllene but, on a whim, Ginistrelli sent her instead to the vastly inferior Chaleureux. His reasoning was that he was convinced the two horses were in love! Ginistrelli maintained that whenever Chaleureux was led past Signorina's paddock he whinnied and she answered. The union produced a foal, Signorinetta, who, despite showing little form as a two-year-old, persuaded the trainer that she was good enough to win the Derby. And sure enough, unfancied by all but Ginistrelli, she won the 1908 Derby and two days later completed a remarkable double by winning the Oaks too.

20 RACEHORSES WITH BRITISH PUBS NAMED AFTER THEM

1. ALTISIDORA (won the St. Leger, 1813). Bishop Burton, Humberside.

2. AMATO (won the Derby, 1838). Epsom.

3. ARKLE (won the Cheltenham Gold Cup, 1964, 1965, 1966). Ashleworth, Gloucestershire.

4. BLENHEIM (won the Derby, 1930). Epsom.

5. BLINK BONNY (won the Derby, 1857). Christon Bank, Northumberland.

6. BRIGADIER GERARD (won the 2,000 Guineas, 1971). Horton Heath, Southampton.

7. CADLAND (won the 2,000 Guineas and the Derby, 1828). Chilwell, Nottingham.

8. COSSACK (won the Derby, 1847). Langstock, Hampshire.

9. CREMORNE (won the Derby, 1872). Sheffield.

10. ECLIPSE (unbeaten in 18 races, 18th century). Mansfield.

11. FLYING CHILDERS (unbeaten in two matches, 1715). Stanton-in-Peak, Derbyshire.

12. THE FLYING DUTCHMAN (won the Derby and the St. Leger, 1849). Summerbridge, near Harrogate.

13. GIMCRACK (18th-century racehorse). York.

14. HIGHFLYER (unbeaten in 12 races,18th century). Ely, Cambridgeshire.

15. LADAS (won the 2,000 Guineas and the Derby, 1894). Epsom.

16. LITTLE OWL (won the Cheltenham Gold Cup, 1981). Charlton Kings, near Cheltenham.

17. LITTLE WONDER (won the Derby, 1840). Harrogate.

18. SALAMANDER (won the Grand National, 1866). Dudley.

19. SMOKER (owned by the Prince Regent, 1790-93). Plumley, Cheshire.

20. VOLTIGEUR (won the Derby, 1850). Spennymoor, Durham.

THE FIRST 10 U.S. TRIPLE CROWN WINNERS

(the Triple Crown comprises the Kentucky Derby, the Preakness Stakes and the Belmont Stakes).

1. SIR BARTON (1919) arrived at the Kentucky Derby as a maiden after six starts and with the job of pacemaker for Billy Kelly. Instead Sir Barton won by five lengths, took the Preakness four days later by four lengths and within a month had romped home in the Belmont.

2. GALLANT FOX (1930) was a disappointment as a two-year-old but blossomed the following year. Retired after winning 11 of his 17 races.

3. OMAHA (1935). A Gallant Fox foal, Omaha completed the treble despite being beaten in the Withers Stakes in the short period between the Preakness and the Belmont.

4. WAR ADMIRAL (1937) remained unbeaten as a three-year-old, running up eight victories. Finished with a career record of 21 wins from 26 starts.

5. WHIRLAWAY (1941) was named U.S. Horse of the Year at both three and four. Despite a tendency to veer right under pressure, he retired with earnings of $561,161 but proved a flop as a sire.

6. COUNT FLEET (1943) was invincible as a three-year-old, culminating in a Belmont victory by 25 lengths. Unfortunately he suffered an injury in that race which forced his retirement.

7. ASSAULT (1946) won at 71-1 as a two-year-old but raced at much shorter prices as a successful three-year-old. He was still winning at six and retired the following year with 18 wins from 42 starts.

8. CITATION (1948) won nine out of ten as a juvenile and 19 out of 20 at three. Injury curtailed his subsequent appearances but he still won over $1 million.

9. SECRETARIAT (1973) set track records for both the Kentucky Derby and the Belmont, a race he won by a record 31 lengths.

10. SEATTLE SLEW (1977) fetched only $17,500 as a yearling but retired with 14 wins from 17 starts. He became America's champion sire in 1984.

MICHAEL SCHUMACHER'S 10 BEST CRASH EXCUSES

1. 1991 Australian GP with Jean Alesi: 'I got wheel spin over a puddle and went sideways. It didn't seem like a problem, but Alesi tried to pass me and hit my right front wheel.'

2. 1992 French GP with Ayrton Senna: 'I tried to pass, he came in and I just couldn't stop.'

3. 1993 Japanese GP with Damon Hill: 'I was trying to stay close to Gerhard Berger to stop Hill from moving inside, but he did and I hit his wheel.'

4. 1994 Australian GP with Damon Hill: 'I went over grass and hit a wall, then I just wanted to run into the next corner and suddenly saw Damon next to me. We just hit each other.'

5. 1995 British GP with Damon Hill: 'I think what Damon did was totally unnecessary. In fact it was really stupid. There was no room for two cars.'

6. 1995 Italian GP with Damon Hill: 'I felt a big bang and Damon crashed into me. It was not a slight touch — he really crashed into me.'

7. 1995 Australian GP with Jean Alesi: 'I don't understand what was going on in his brain. Was it switched off?'

8. 1997 Luxembourg GP with Ralf Schumacher: 'It's a shame that the incident happened with my brother but I don't think anyone is to blame.'

9. 1997 European GP with Jacques Villeneuve: 'He tried a rather optimistic attack. It worked for him but not for me.'

10. 1998 Argentinian GP with David Coulthard: 'I went for the gap but he seemed to close the door. I did not want to lift off because I felt I had the momentum to get through.'

10 DRIVERS WHO NEVER QUALIFIED FOR A FORMULA ONE GRAND PRIX

1.   GIOVANNA AMATA. Italian woman driver who launched unsuccessful bids to qualify in a Brabham for the 1992 Grands Prix of South Africa, Mexico and Brazil.

2.   GARY BRABHAM. Son of Sir Jack failed to qualify in 1990.

3.   COLIN CHAPMAN. The future Lotus supremo failed in his bid to qualify for the 1956 French Grand Prix at Reims driving a Vanwall.

4.   KEVIN COGAN. The U.S. Indy Car winner made futile attempts at the Grand Prix circuit in 1980 and 1981.

5.   BERNIE ECCLESTONE. The man who is now the driving force behind Formula One failed to qualify in a Connaught in 1958 at both Monaco and Silverstone.

6.   DIVINA GALICA. British lady skier who unsuccessfully tried her hand at Formula One in 1976 and 1978.

7.   NAOKI HATTORI. The Japanese motor sport journalist failed to make the starting grid in 1991.

8.   PERRY MCCARTHY. British enthusiast who, driving a Moda in 1992, entered eight Grands Prix. He didn't qualify in seven and missed the car weight check at the German GP, resulting in his exclusion.

9.   OTTO STUPPACHER. The Austrian missed his big chance at Monza in 1976 when, having apparently failed to qualify in his Tyrrell, he left the circuit. However James Hunt, Jochen Mass and John Watson had their times disallowed due to fuel irregularities, which would have allowed Stuppacher in the race. But by that time he was back in Vienna!

10. JACQUES VILLENEUVE. Younger brother of Gilles and uncle of World Champion Jacques, he tried in vain at Montreal and Las Vegas in 1981 and again at Montreal in 1983.

10 GRAND PRIX DRIVERS WHO DIED IN NON-RACING ACCIDENTS

1. GEORGES BOILLOT (1916): shot down in a plane by Germans.

2. ANDRÉ BOILLOT (1932): killed in a road crash.

3. WILBUR SHAW (1954): died in a plane crash.

4. MIKE HAWTHORN (1959): died in a car crash on the Guildford by-pass.

5. GUISEPPE FARINA (1966): killed in a road accident on his way to the French GP.

6. GRAHAM HILL (1975): killed in a plane crash on a golf course near Barnet, Hertfordshire.

7. CARLOS PACE (1977): died in a plane crash.

8. MIKE HAILWOOD (1981): died in a road crash near Tanworth-in-Arden, Warwickshire.

9. ELIO DE ANGELIS (1986): killed while testing at Paul Ricard, Provence.

10. DIDIER PIRONI (1987): died in a power-boat accident off the Isle of Wight.

10 GRAND PRIX DRIVERS KILLED IN PRACTICE SESSIONS

1. DAVID BRUCE-BROWN (1912): United States GP at Milwaukee.

2. ACHILLE VARZI (1948): Swiss GP at Berne.

3. HARRY SCHELL (1960): killed at Silverstone on Friday 13 May.

4. RICARDO RODRIGUEZ (1962): Mexican GP.

5. MIKE SPENCE (1968): Indianapolis 500.

6. JOCHEN RINDT (1970): Italian GP at Monza.

7. FRANÇOIS CEVERT (1974): United States GP, Watkins Glen.

8. PETER REVSON (1974): Kyalami, South Africa.

9. PATRICK DEPAILLER (1980): German GP at Hockenheim.

10. GILLES VILLENEUVE (1982): Zolder, Belgium.

10 SPORTSMEN WHO PLAYED CRICKET AND SOCCER FOR ENGLAND

1. JOHN ARNOLD (cricket 1931; soccer 1933).

2. ANDY DUCAT (cricket 1921; soccer 1910-21).

3. CHARLES (C.B.) FRY (cricket 1895-1912; soccer 1901).

4. LESLIE GAY (cricket 1894-95; soccer 1893-94).

5. BILLY GUNN (cricket 1886-99; soccer 1884).

6. WALLY HARDINGE (cricket 1921; soccer 1910).

7. RT. HON. ALFRED LYTTELTON (cricket 1880-84; soccer 1877).

8. ARTHUR MILTON (cricket 1958-59; soccer 1952).

9. JOHN SHARP (cricket 1909; soccer 1903-05).

10. WILLIE WATSON (cricket 1951-59; soccer 1950-51).

In addition to the above, a number of England Test cricketers represented their country at soccer as amateurs, including Laurie Fishlock, Dick Young, Reginald Foster (the only man to captain England at both sports) and Johnny Douglas, while Arsenal's Denis Compton appeared for England as a wartime soccer international. The pressures of the games mean that the days of cricketer/footballers have all but vanished. The last notable dual participant was Chris Balderstone who played cricket for Leicestershire and England and soccer for Huddersfield Town, Carlisle United, Doncaster Rovers and Queen of the South. On 15 September 1975 he turned out for Leicestershire against Derbyshire at Chesterfield and, at close of play at 6.30pm, dashed to Doncaster in time for a 7.30 kick-off against Brentford.

10 CRAZY CRICKETERS

1. In accordance with his wishes, Derbyshire batsman HARRY BAGSHAW was buried in 1927 dressed in his umpire's coat and clutching a cricket ball.

2. A heavy drinker, Derbyshire fast bowler BILL BESTWICK was given a team minder to monitor his behaviour. But Bestwick became an expert at giving him the slip and went absent during the 1922 fixture at Worcester. He later appeared, very drunk, and proceeded to barrack his own team from the stand.

3. Legendary umpire DICKIE BIRD constantly worried about being late. For his first county match — Surrey versus Yorkshire at The Oval in 1970 — he arrived at the ground at 5.30 am, nearly six hours before play was due to begin. Finding the gates locked he scaled them, only to be accosted by a passing policeman. Invited by the Queen for lunch at Buckingham Palace, Bird turned up at breakfast-time and whiled away the intervening five hours in a nearby café. As a young batsman, he was so nervous that he once inadvertently buckled his pads to each other and fell flat on his face as he went out to bat.

4. Left-arm bowler RAY EAST, who played for Essex from 1965 to 1984, was a born clown. One afternoon at the Scarborough Festival, the sound of cannon-fire from a nearby mock battle reverberated across the ground just as East was running in to bowl. He immediately collapsed at the umpire's feet, as if mortally wounded. On another occasion, batting against Lancashire on a hostile wicket, he anticipated a bouncer by diving to the ground and lying flat on his stomach with his hands on his head.

5. Australian left-arm spinner LESLIE O'BRIEN FLEETWOOD-SMITH would liven up a dull game by doing bird impersonations, often as he came in to bowl. His specialities were the screech of the magpie and the whoop of the whipbird. On Australia's 1938 tour of England, he eased the tension at a county game at Northampton by lapsing into an impression of a kookaburra on heat, complete with flapping wings and frenzied hops. When patrolling the boundary, he would often start singing 'I'm In the Mood for Love' to nobody in particular, or practise his golf swing. He was equally unpredictable on the golf course, preferring to tee the ball up, step back a few paces, trot in and hit the ball on the run.

6. The amazing W.G. GRACE once stunned his team-mates by suddenly declaring the innings closed with his own score on 93. He later explained that 93 was the only score he hadn't yet made between 0 and 100. He was a law unto

himself and, given out by one umpire, calmly replaced the bails and said: 'They've come to see me bat, not you umpiring.' With that, he continued with his innings. On another occasion, he lofted the ball towards the boundary where a fielder was waiting to take the catch. Before he could so, Grace declared the innings closed and forced the umpire to give him not out on the grounds that the ball had been caught after the declaration.

7.   Nottinghamshire batsman GEORGE GUNN was a clock-watcher. Playing at Southampton, Gunn was at the non-striker's end when the clock reached 1.30pm. Assuming it was lunch he headed off to the pavilion, only to be recalled by the umpire who informed him that lunch was at 2pm. Silently Gunn took guard, but as the first ball of the next over approached, he stepped aside, allowing it to hit his wicket. As he walked off, he announced: 'I take my lunch at 1.30.'

8.   Lancashire slow bowler CEC PARKIN used to delight in substituting an orange for the ball and sending it splattering into the wicket-keeper's gloves.

9.   Yorkshire's BOBBY PEEL was a slave to the bottle and was sacked by county captain Lord Hawke following an unfortunate incident at Sheffield in 1897. First he tried to bowl at the sightscreen, in the mistaken belief that it was a Middlesex batsman, and then he proceeded to urinate on the wicket. Fittingly, he became a pub landlord.

10. LIONEL, LORD TENNYSON, grandson of the poet, was the only county captain who employed his wicket-keeper as his butler. He liked to send messages from the pavilion to his Hampshire batsmen in the middle and, when the umpires objected, he arranged for an official telegram to be delivered by a boy in uniform. The telegram contained a terse inquiry as to what the recipient thought his bat was for.

10 CRICKETING POLITICIANS AND STATESMEN

1.   FRANCIS H.D. BELL, who played for Wellington 1873-77, became New Zealand Prime Minister for two weeks in 1925.

2.   SIR ALEC DOUGLAS-HOME. As Lord Dunglass, the former British Prime Minister played first-class cricket for Middlesex (1924-25) and went on the MCC tour to South America of 1926-27.

3.   LORD FOSTER OF LEPE played for Oxford University and Hampshire (1885-95) before becoming MP for Sevenoaks and Governor-General of Australia (1920-25).

4.   THOMAS FREEMAN of Cambridge University and Sussex (1886-90) went on to become Lord Willingdon, Governor-General of Canada from 1926-31.

5.   HON. SIR FRANCIS STANLEY JACKSON was a stylish middle-order batsman for Yorkshire and England (1893-1905) and was later appointed Governor of Bengal where he narrowly escaped assassination.

6.   HON. ALFRED LYTTELTON played for Middlesex and in four Tests for England, 1880-84. He was then made Britain's Colonial Secretary from 1903 to 1905.

7.   HON. CHARLES LYTTELTON captained Worcestershire from 1936 to 1939. Later, as Viscount Cobham, he served as Governor-General of New Zealand, 1957-62.

8.   SIR KYNASTON STUDD, a former Middlesex cricketer, was named Lord Mayor of London in 1928.

9.   HON. FREDERIC THESIGER played for Oxford University and Middlesex before, as Viscount Chelmsford, becoming Viceroy of India from 1916 to 1921.

10. THE DUKE OF WELLINGTON played for All Ireland against The Garrison in 1792, scoring just 5 and 1. He later became British Prime Minister.

10 RECOGNISED ENGLAND BATSMEN WITH A TEST AVERAGE OF FIVE OR UNDER

1. FRED GRACE (1880)   0.00.

2. GEORGE HEARNE (1891-92)   0.00.

3. JOSEPH MCMASTER (188-89)   0.00.

4. ARTHUR DOLPHIN (1920-21)   0.50.

5. ALEXANDER WEBBE (1878-89)   2.00.

6. ANDY DUCAT (1921)   2.50.

7. FRANCIS MACKINNON (1878-89)   2.50.

8. FRED PRICE (1938)   3.00.

9. GRAHAM BARLOW (1976-77)   4.25.

10. GEORGE EMMETT (1948)   5.00.

The youngest of the Grace brothers, Fred had an undistinguished England career. In his only Test, against Australia at the Oval, he made a 'pair' with the bat and didn't bowl. Sadly, two weeks later on his way to a match at Winchester, he died of lung congestion following a heavy cold. George Hearne also played in just one Test, as did younger brother Alec who finished up with the marginally better batting average of 9.00. Joseph McMaster's entire first-class career lasted a mere two days. Although he had a reputation as a sound batsman, the 29-year-old Irishman had no senior experience when he was picked to appear against South Africa at Cape Town. Going in at number nine, he was caught without scoring. His services were not required in the second innings (England cruising to victory) and he returned to obscurity. In addition to the above, a few England bowlers ended up with a batting average of zero, including Edwin Tyler (1895-96), Douglas Carr (1909) and Charles Marriott (1933).

SPORT

10 ENGLAND TEST CRICKETERS WHO MET UNTIMELY DEATHS

1.   CHARLES ABSOLOM. In 1889, ten years after his solitary Test appearance, Absolom was working as a purser on board the *SS Muriel* in Port-of-Spain when he was crushed by a crane loading sugar.

2.   After suffering a series of violent epileptic fits, JOHNNY 'BOY' BRIGGS was admitted to Cheadle Asylum where he is said to have indulged in imaginary bowling sessions up and down the ward, proudly announcing his full analysis at the end of the day. He died there in 1902, aged 39.

3.   HAROLD GIMBLETT. The former Somerset and England opening batsman committed suicide in 1978.

4.   REV. EDGAR THOMAS KILLICK died in 1953 at Northampton shortly after his 46th birthday while batting for St. Albans against Coventry in a diocesan clergy match.

5.   ALBERT RELF shot himself in 1937, depressed over his wife's ill-health. Ironically, she recovered.

6.   WILLIAM SCOTTON killed himself in 1893, depressed about losing his place in the Nottinghamshire team.

7.   ARTHUR SHREWSBURY was a hypochondriac who shot himself in 1903 because he was convinced that he was suffering from an incurable illness. In truth, he was completely healthy.

8.   ANDREW STODDART, who captained England at cricket and rugby, took his own life in 1915 in despair at his declining health and finances.

9.   ALBERT TROTT played for both his native Australia and England. In dire straits financially, he looked forward to his benefit match in 1907 but contrived to take four wickets in five balls so that the match finished a day early! Having shot himself in the foot metaphorically, in 1914 he shot himself in the head physically.

10. JOHNNY TYLDESLEY had just turned 57 when, in 1930, he collapsed and died as he was putting on his boots to go to work

10 CRICKETING INCOMPETENTS

1. Fielding against Lancashire in 1993, Leicestershire skipper NIGEL BRIERS sprained his thumb when he caught it in his trouser pocket.

2. Young Surrey batsman FREDERICK BUCKLE failed to distinguish himself against Middlesex in 1869. In the first innings he was recorded as 'Absent, not sent for in time — 0' and in the second as 'Absent unwell — 0'.

3. Bowled out for 0 in their 1952 fixture with Surrey villagers Bookham, the ELECTRICAL TRADES COMMERCIAL TRAVELLERS' ASSOCIATION CC lost the match when the first delivery of the Bookham innings flew past the wicket-keeper for four byes.

4. When Walsden entertained Rochdale in a Central Lancashire League match, Walsden bowler PETER GREEN was hit for a mighty six by Rochdale's Wilson Hartley. The ball smashed through the window of a nearby house — Peter Green's.

5. Bowling in a Queensland country match during the1968-69 season, R. GRUBB conceded 62 runs off one eight-ball over. The batsman hit nine sixes and two fours off the over which included four no-balls.

6. Last man in for Glamorgan against the Indian tourists, PETER JUDGE was bowled first ball by Sarwate. To save time when Glamorgan followed on, Judge kept his pads on and opened the batting. Once again, he was clean-bowled by Sarwate first ball for the quickest 'pair' in history.

7. Luncarty's JIM MCNICHOL enlivened a Haig National Village tie with fellow-Scots Manderston by running out three of his partners, including his captain, without facing a ball!

8. DR. R.L. PARK made a solitary Test appearance for Australia against England at Melbourne in 1920. He was out first ball in his only innings and bowled just one over which yielded an expensive nine runs.

9. In 1990, Northamptonshire tail-ender MARK ROBINSON went 12 first-class innings from 4 May until 15 September without scoring a run.

10. Gloucestershire batsman SIDNEY WELLS was selected for just one first-class game — against Kent at Bristol in 1927. It was abandoned without a ball being bowled.

CHAPTER

THE 20TH CENTURY

10 THINGS WHICH HAPPENED ON 1 JANUARY 1900

1. While the siege of Mafeking continued in the Boer War, the annual conference of the Incorporated Society of Musicians opened in Scarborough.

2. The Michigan-Mississippi canal was opened.

3. A verdict of accidental death was returned on the victims of the Brighton railway collision.

4. Nigeria became a British protectorate.

5. The South Goodwin Lightship was returned to its moorings after drifting in high winds.

6. Arthur Quiller-Couch's latest novel *The Ship of Stars* was published.

7. In honour of the famous explorer, the Livingstone Exhibition was opened at St. Martin's Town Hall, London.

8. Police investigated the death of 75-year-old Nicholas Theodore de Fischer who died after being mugged in Kensington.

9. In the First Division of the Football League, lowly Glossop surprised Newcastle United 3-2. Nevertheless Glossop went on to finish bottom of the table.

10. In Berlin the German emperor delivered a rousing speech to the German army extolling the strength of the German empire.

10 REASONS FOR NOT WEARING A MOUSTACHE

(as given to *The Hairdresser and Toilet Requisites Gazette* in 1909)

Women say:

1. 'I have a natural repulsion to seeing hair on a man's face.'

2. 'All nice men, actors, clergymen and other professional men are clean-shaven. Men without a moustache look more intelligent.'

3. 'A bad-tempered, cynical or criminal mouth may be hidden by a moustache.'

4. 'I much prefer a clean-shaven man. I do not consider a moustache hygienic.'

5. 'Decidedly give me a clean-shaven man if he has a good mouth and chin. Men with weak chins should be made to wear beards.'

Men say:

6. 'A moustache is a hive of bacilli.'

7. 'I have no courage to go through that awful stage when a moustache is merely bristles.'

8. 'I wear no moustache because I have a mouth I do not wish to hide. Only men of bad character need wear moustaches.'

9. 'I do not wear a moustache because I do not wish to appear a coward. The mouth is a truer index to character than the eyes, and men can hide emotion behind a moustache. I prefer to be able to control my lips and expression.'

10. 'I do not wear a moustache because my moustache would, when grown, have a green tomato shade. Also, I do not want to look old.'

20 DEFUNCT BRITISH RACECOURSES FROM THE 20TH CENTURY

1. NORTHAMPTON (1904).

2. PAISLEY (1907).

3. HULL (1909).

4. BOURNEMOUTH (1928).

5. BANBURY (1929).

6. PLYMOUTH (1930).

7. CHELMSFORD (1935).

8. TENBY (1936).

9. DERBY (1939).

10. TORQUAY (1940).

11. GATWICK (1940).

12. BUCKFASTLEIGH (1960).

13. HURST PARK (1962).

14. LEWES (1964).

15. LINCOLN (1964).

16. MANCHESTER (1964).

17. BIRMINGHAM (1965).

18. ALEXANDRA PARK (1979).

19. LANARK (1977).

20. STOCKTON (1981).

Manchester racecourse actually staged England's first evening meeting — on 13 July 1951.

10 MAMMALS WHICH BECAME EXTINCT IN THE 20TH CENTURY

1. GILBERT'S POTOROO (Western Australia, 1900).

2. PIG-FOOTED BANDICOOT (South Australia, 1907).

3. BURCHELL'S ZEBRA (South Africa, 1910).

4. NEWFOUNDLAND WHITE WOLF (Newfoundland, c. 1911).

5. BARBARY LION (North Africa, c. 1922).

6. BUBAL HARTEBEEST (Algeria, 1923).

7. SYRIAN ONAGER (Middle East, 1930).

8. SCHOMBURGK'S DEER (Thailand, 1932).

9. BALI TIGER (Bali, 1937).

10. CARIBBEAN MONK SEAL (Caribbean, 1952).

When martyrs were thrown to the lions in Roman times, it was to a huge Barbary lion, a creature whose mane covered almost half of its body. But then the Arabs hunted them, encouraged by governments which allowed any tribes that killed the lions to be exempt from taxation. The creature's last stronghold was in the Great Atlas Mountains and it was there that the last true Barbary lion was killed in 1922, although attempts have subsequently been made to reconstruct the species in zoos. Other creatures hunted to extinction include the Newfoundland white wolf, whose demise was the direct result of the Newfoundland government having set a bounty on wolves back in 1842, and Schomburgk's deer, a mysterious creature never seen in the wild by a European. It was hunted for its antlers which were said to contain magical and medicinal properties and were used in the lucrative Chinese pharmaceutical trade.

10 BIRDS WHICH BECAME EXTINCT IN THE 20TH CENTURY

1. BLACK MAMO (Hawaii, 1907).

2. HUIA (New Zealand, 1907).

3. SLENDER-BILLED GRACKLE (Mexico, 1910).

4. GUADELOUPE STORM-PETREL (West Indies, 1912).

5. CAROLINA PARAKEET (U.S.A., 1914).

6. PASSENGER PIGEON (U.S.A., 1914).

7. NORFOLK ISLAND STARLING (Australia, 1925).

8. GRAND CAYMAN THRUSH (West Indies, 1938).

9. NEW ZEALAND BUSH WREN (New Zealand, 1972).

10. COLOMBIAN GREBE (South America, 1977).

The Guadeloupe storm-petrel was wiped out by partly by imported domestic cats, while the loss of the huia was a particular blow since it was the only species in which the male and female had radically different-shaped beaks. But the most startling decline was undoubtedly that of the passenger pigeon. In 1810, it was just about the commonest bird in the world. A total of 2,230,272,000 passenger pigeons were estimated in a single flock and these huge gatherings used to darken the skies and break off hefty branches from trees, so great were their numbers. Yet a century later, the bird was extinct, its downfall hastened by American Indians who lit fires in the bird's breeding areas. In 1909, a reward of $1500 was offered for information on a nesting pair but all claims proved to be false, the majority turning out to be mourning doves. Five years later, the last passenger pigeon died in captivity in the Cincinnati Zoological Gardens.

20 NEW MAMMALS DISCOVERED IN THE 20TH CENTURY

1. OKAPI (Zaire, 1901).

2. ROTHSCHILD'S GIRAFFE (Uganda, 1901).

3. MOUNTAIN GORILLA (Zaire, 1902).

4. SEA MINK (U.S.A., 1903).

5. PACARANA (Ethiopia, 1904) — also known as 'the terrible mouse'.

6. MOUNTAIN NYALA (Ethiopia, 1910) — an antelope.

7. HERO SHREW (Uganda, 1910).

8. PYGMY HIPPOPOTAMUS (Liberia, 1913).

9. SCALY-TAILED POSSUM (Australia, 1917).

10. LONGMAN'S BEAKED WHALE (Australia, 1926).

11. PYGMY CHIMPANZEE (Zaire, 1928).

12. KOUPREY (Cambodia, 1937) — an ox-like creature.

13. SELEVIN'S DORMOUSE (Kazakhstan, 1938).

14. BLACK-SHOULDERED OPOSSUM (South America, 1950).

15. GOLDEN LANGUR (India, 1955) — a species of monkey.

16. COCHITO (Gulf of California, 1958) — a small porpoise.

17. RED GORAL (Southern Asia, 1964) — a goat-like relative of the antelope family.

18. CHACOAN PECCARY (South America, 1974) — a pig-like animal.

19. GOLDEN-CROWNED SIFAKA (Magagascar, 1989) — a species of lemur.

20. BLACK-FACED LION TAMARIN (Brazil, 1992) — a small monkey.

With its spine of bony knobs to prevent it from being crushed by rocks when burrowing, the little hero shrew can withstand tremendous weights. It is said that its backbone can bear the weight of a 12-stone human.

20 NEW BIRDS DISCOVERED IN THE 20TH CENTURY

1. FEARFUL OWL (Solomon Islands, 1901).

2. ROTHSCHILD'S PEACOCK PHEASANT (Borneo, 1902).

3. WAKE ISLAND RAIL (Wake Island, Pacific, 1903).

4. RUFOUS-HEADED ROBIN (China, 1905).

5. MIKADO PHEASANT (Taiwan, 1906).

6. NDUK EAGLE OWL (Tanzania, 1906).

7. AFRICAN BROADBILL (Zaire, 1908).

8. ROTHSCHILD'S MYNAH (Bali, 1911).

9. CRESTED SHELDUCK (Korea, 1913).

10. IMPERIAL PHEASANT (Vietnam, 1924).

11. BAKER'S REGENT BOWERBIRD (New Guinea, 1928).

12. RIBBON-TAILED BIRD OF PARADISE (New Guinea, 1938).

13. ARCHBOLD'S BOWERBIRD (New Guinea, 1939).

14. AFRICAN BAY OWL (Zaire, 1951).

15. SOKOKE SCOPS OWL (Kenya, 1965).

16. ALDABRAN WARBLER (Seychelles, 1968).

17. LONG-WHISKERED OWLET (Peru, 1976).

18. AMSTERDAM ALBATROSS (Amsterdam Island, Indian Ocean, 1978).

19. AMAZONIAN PARROTLET (Peru, 1985).

20. EL ORO PARAKEET (Ecuador, 1985).

Discovered in 1903, the Wake Island rail was extinct by 1946. It was wiped out when the island was occupied by Japanese soldiers during World War Two. With food supplies scarce, they found a tasty local delicacy in the rail and proceeded to eat every last bird.

10 BBC TELEVISION PROGRAMMES WHICH VIEWERS MISSED IN THE FIRST WEEK OF THE SECOND WORLD WAR

1. Beatrice Lillie at the piano (Monday 4 September, 1939).

2. 'A Cup of Happiness', a comedy play set on a farm, starring Leon M. Lion (Monday 4 September).

3. 'The Pelican', a drama starring Eric Portman (Tuesday 5 September).

4. Down on the Farm (Wednesday 6 September).

5. Style at Home — 'Bettie Cameron Smail will explain and illustrate how to achieve the professional touch in home dressmaking' (Wednesday 6 September).

6. Picture Page — the 263rd edition of the popular magazine show (Thursday 7 September).

7. Ken Johnson and his West Indian Dance Orchestra (Thursday 7 September).

8. 'Swans' — a ballet with Anton Dolin, music by Sibelius (Friday 8 September).

9. Bebe Daniels and Ben Lyon — comedy duo (Friday 8 September).

10. Blood Donors — a 20-minute film about giving blood (Friday 8 September).

Two days before war was officially declared, the BBC screens went blank without an announcement at midday on Friday 1 September, 1939 during a Mickey Mouse cartoon. A drama production of W. Somerset Maugham's 'The Circle', featuring a young James Mason and scheduled for Sunday 3 September, was halted mid-rehearsal. Like all other BBC programmes, it fell victim to the belief that signals from the mast at Alexandra Palace would attract enemy aircraft. The screens remained blank for seven years, service finally being resumed on 7 June 1946 with the same Mickey Mouse cartoon which had been interrupted.

10 SECOND WORLD WAR ADVERTISING AND PROPAGANDA SLOGANS

1. HITLER WILL SEND NO WARNING — SO ALWAYS CARRY YOUR GAS MASK.

2. DIG FOR VICTORY.

3. FOR A HEALTHY, HAPPY JOB, JOIN THE WOMEN'S LAND ARMY.

4. MOTHERS — SEND THEM OUT OF LONDON: GIVE THEM A CHANCE OF GREATER SAFETY AND HEALTH. (Government encouragement for parents to have their children evacuated).

5. MAKE DO AND MEND. (Handy hints from the Board of Trade to help women extend the life of clothes by renovating old items).

6. IS YOUR JOURNEY REALLY NECESSARY? (Railway posters urging passengers to think twice before travelling on busy lines).

7. KEEP A PIG. (Part of the push for self-sufficiency, pigs providing food).

8. CARELESS TALK COSTS LIVES.

9. PLOUGH NOW! BY DAY AND NIGHT. (Ministry of Agriculture advice to maintain food supplies).

10. UP HOUSEWIVES AND AT 'EM! (The Ministry of Supply urging women to put paper, metal and even bones out by their dustbin for collection as part of the war effort).

Another treasured wartime slogan was: 'Carrots Keep You Healthy and Help You To See in the Blackout.' As part of its nutrition campaign, the Ministry of Food created two cartoon characters, Dr. Carrot and Potato Pete, who helped promote the benefits of vegetables, especially the theory that carrots helped you see in the dark. The Ministry even insisted that top RAF night-fighter pilots lived on a diet of carrots, and it was not until the end of the war that it emerged that what really helped them shoot down enemy planes was not carrots but the secret new device — radar.

20 CODENAMES FROM WORLD WAR TWO

1. ATTILA. The German plan for occupying Vichy France following increasing French support for the Allies. The mission was undertaken in November 1942 and resulted in the scuttling of French warships at Toulon.

2. BINGO. A series of U.S. bomber attacks launched in November 1944 on electricity-producing plants supplying the railway system over the Brenner Pass. The aim was to block the main reinforcement route for German forces in Italy.

3. BRISK. The British plan to take the Azores (1940-41) in order to establish air and naval bases there and thus close the 'Atlantic gap' where German U-boats had been able to operate without fear of attack.

4. BUCCANEER. The British scheme to recapture the Andaman Islands in the Bay of Bengal during the spring of 1944. However, a lack of landing craft prevented it from being implemented.

5. BULLDOZER. The aborted British amphibious assault on Akyab, Burma, in the spring of 1944.

6. CROMWELL. The British codeword to be used to be signal any German invasion of Britain.

7. CROSSBOW. The 1943-44 British intelligence and photo-reconnaissance campaign to learn about the development, and halt production, of German secret weapons at Peenemünde.

8. FLOWER. A British low-level night intruder mission by de Havilland Mosquito aircraft over German airfields (1944-45).

9. HELLHOUND. The Allied plan for the bombing of Hitler's retreat at Berchtesgaden in the Alps in spring 1945.

10. HORLICKS. The American capture of Biak Island off the North-West coast of New Guinea in the summer of 1944. The exercise saw 5,093 Japanese and 524 Americans killed.

11. HURRICANE I. The Allied plan for a bombing offensive against targets in Germany's industrial Ruhr, 1944-45.

12. IMPERATOR. The British scheme to seize Boulogne (or a similar French coastal town) via an amphibious assault in the summer of 1942, the aim being to draw German troops from the Eastern front.

13. KREUZOTTER (viper). A German operation against Greek resistance forces.

14. MAGNET. The Allied exercise of 1942 to move U.S. ground forces into Northern Ireland in readiness for active service in Europe.

15. MUSTANG. The Allied contingency plan for a swift overland advance to Naples in the summer of 1943 in case of an Italian collapse after the Sicilian campaign.

16. PUMPKIN. The unsuccessful mission by the 17th Indian Light Division in central Burma in December 1943 to wreck the anticipated Japanese offensive.

17. SHRAPNEL. The British plan for the seizure of the Cape Verde Islands in spring 1941.

18. STRANGLE. An Allied air offensive in spring 1944, the aim of which was to cut all sea, rail and road communication to German troops south of Rome. Although some 20,000 tons of bombs were dropped on railway yards, bridges and tunnels, the operation was only a limited success.

19. TRUNCHEON. The 1941 British plan for a landing at Livorno in north-west Italy.

20. WINDOW. The release of tin foil strips by British bombers from August 1943. Dropped in bundles, the strips dispersed in mid-air to produce millions of echoes on German radar screens. Since these swamped the echoes produced by the bombers themselves, they served to protect the Allied aircraft.

10 BRITISH NEW TOWNS OF THE 1960S

1. SKELMERSDALE (1962).

2. LIVINGSTON (1962).

3. TELFORD (1963).

4. RUNCORN (1964).

5. WASHINGTON, Tyne & Wear (1964).

6. REDDITCH (1964).

7. IRVINE (1966).

8. MILTON KEYNES (1967).

9. NEWTOWN, Powys (1967).

10. PETERBOROUGH (1968).

10 MISS WORLD WINNERS OF THE 1960S

1. NORMA CAPPEGLI (Argentina, 1960).

2. ROSEMARIE FRANKLAND (U.K., 1961).

3. RINA LODDERS (Holland, 1962).

4. CAROLE CRAWFORD (Jamaica, 1963).

5. ANN SIDNEY (U.K., 1964).

6. LESLEY LANGLEY (U.K., 1965).

7. REITA FARIA (India, 1966).

8. MADELEINE HARTOG-BEL (Peru, 1967).

9. PENNY PLUMMER (Australia, 1968).

10. EVA RUEBER-STAIER (Austria, 1969).

20 WORDS INTRODUCED INTO THE ENGLISH LANGUAGE SINCE 1980

1. BOG-STANDARD (adj., 1980s).

2. CYBERSPACE (n., 1982).

3. DOWNLOAD (v., 1980).

4. DOWNSIZE (v., 1980s).

5. DROP-DEAD (adj., 1990).

6. FEEL-GOOD (adj., 1993).

7. FOODIE (n., 1992).

8. LUVVY (n., 1992).

9. ROLLOVER (n., 1994).

10. SADDO (n., 1992).

11. SCRATCH CARD (n., 1980s).

12. SEMI-SKIMMED (adj., 1980s).

13. SLAPHEAD (n., 1991).

14. SUSSED (v., pp., 1980s).

15. TOYBOY (n., 1980s).

16. TRAINSPOTTER (n., 1980s).

17. TOUCHY-FEELY (adj., 1992).

18. WANNABE (n., 1980s).

19. WAZZOCK (n., 1980s).

20. YOOF (adj., n., 1980s).

Some modern words date back further than you think. 'Babe' was in use as long ago as 1915 while 'bimbo' was slang for a prostitute in the late 1920s.

10 CURE-ALLS OF THE 20TH CENTURY

1. BILE BEANS — 'conquers disorders of the liver, stomach and bowels: a wonderful medicine that copies nature.'

2. BLAIR'S GOUT AND RHEUMATIC PILLS — 'the Great British Remedy'.

3. BUNTER'S NERVINE — 'the best remedy for toothache'.

4. CONGREVE'S ELIXIR — 'cures consumption, asthma, bronchitis, coughs'.

5. 'Fat folk should take FELL'S REDUCING TABLETS — guaranteed to reduce weight a pound a day'.

6. LLEWELLYN'S CUTICLE FLUID.

7. LOCKYER'S HAIR RESTORER.

8. DR. MACKENZIE'S SMELLING BOTTLE — 'for colds, influenza, catarrh, headaches etc'.

9. PHOSFERINE — 'the Remedy of Kings: supplied by Royal Command to the King of Greece, the Queen of Romania and the Empress of Russia.'

10. RANKIN'S HEAD OINTMENT — 'kills all nits and vermin'.

Even Marmite was once viewed as having remedial powers for a wide range of diseases. In the early 1950s, a special booklet was produced by the medical profession extolling the virtues of Marmite. Its high Vitamin B content meant that it was considered efficacious for those with diabetes, gastric ulcers and rheumatism as well as nervous and mental complaints. It was prescribed in the Eastern tropics where burning feet and beriberi were prevalent while the Medical Research Council's 1951 report on Deficiency Diseases in Japanese Prison Camps stated that Marmite yeast extract had proved effective in the treatment of scrotal dermatitis. The patients were presumably the original 'Marmite soldiers'...

10 PRODUCTS OF THE 20TH CENTURY NAMED AFTER THEIR INVENTOR

1. ADIDAS SHOES (German shoemaker Adolf 'Adi' Dassler).

2. ALMAY (American chemist and his wife, Al and May Schieffelin).

3. BERLEI (Australian businessman Fred Burley).

4. BIC (French inventor Marcel Bich).

5. BIRDS EYE (American businessman Clarence Birdseye).

6. COTY (Corsican-born industrialist Francois Coty).

7. HARPIC (London sanitary engineer Harry Pickup).

8. KENWOOD CHEF (British entrepreneur Ken Wood).

9. MARS BAR (American sweet manufacturer Forrest E. Mars).

10. RAWLPLUG (London building contractor John J. Rawlings).

A minor maintenance problem at the British Museum led to the invention of the humble Rawlplug in 1919. The museum needed electrical fittings to be fixed to the walls unobtrusively and without damaging the masonry but this was not easy using the traditional method of chiselling a hole, plugging it with wood and then screwing the fitting into the wood. Fortunately, Kensington builder John J. Rawlings solved the problem by inventing a fibre plug, made of jute bonded with animal blood. He called it the Rawlplug. Perrier Water was named after the inventor's doctor. Recuperating after a serious motor accident, Englishman St. John Harmsworth, brother of newspaper magnates Lord Northcliffe and Lord Rothermere, visited the French spa town of Vergeze in 1903. There he was introduced by his doctor, Louis Perrier, to the local spring, Les Bouillons. Harmsworth decided to market the bubbling water and named it after Dr. Perrier, moulding the famous green bottles on the Indian clubs he had been using to strengthen his arms and back following the car accident.

10 INNOVATIONS OF THE 20TH CENTURY WHICH WERE INITIALLY REJECTED.

1. BARBIE DOLL. A number of toy buyers wouldn't touch Barbie when she made her debut in 1959, considering her to be too adult. Barbie's creator, Ruth Handler, later admitted: 'The toy buyers didn't care for Barbie at first. And many of them did not order the doll. They did not think mothers would buy a doll with breasts.'

2. CORRECTION FLUID. The brainchild of Bette Nesmith Graham, mother of former Monkee Michael Nesmith, correction fluid was offered to IBM in 1956 under the brand name 'Mistake Out'. When they rejected it, Bette changed the name to 'Liquid Paper' and set up her own cottage industry, using the family kitchen as a laboratory and the garage as a bottling plant. By the end of 1957, she was settling 100 bottles of liquid paper a month.

3. FOLD-UP BICYCLE. Alex Moulton of Bradford-on-Avon, Wiltshire, designed the revolutionary folding bicycle in 1958 and offered it to Raleigh the following year. They promptly rejected it, maintaining that the public would never take to such an unusual machine. Moulton pressed on alone and by 1965, sales had reached 70,000. In 1967, Raleigh admitted their mistake and bought Moulton out.

4. HOVERCRAFT. By the late 1950s Christopher Cockerell had perfected the idea of the hovercraft and tried to sell his idea to industry. But aircraft companies showed little interest because it wasn't an aircraft and shipping firms rejected it because it wasn't a boat. The concept went nowhere for a year until, in 1958, Cockerell finally received the backing and financial support of the National Research Development Corporation.

5. MONOPOLY. Conceived by unemployed Philadelphia heating engineer Clarence B. Darrow, Monopoly was turned down flat by games manufacturers Parker Bros. as having '52 fundamental playing errors'. Convinced they were wrong, Darrow had 5,000 copies made up by a local box manufacturer and met with such success that in 1935 Parker Bros. reviewed their position and decided to take over production after all.

6. PHOTOCOPIER. Oklahoma office worker George C. Beidler thought up

the world's first photocopier back in 1903 but, because it was painfully slow, it attracted minimal attention. Then in 1938, American patent lawyer Chester Carlson improved upon the invention but he too struggled to find a research institute interested in developing his idea. It was not until 1959, 57 years after Beidler's dream of an office copier, that the first automatic photocopier, the Xerox 914, came on to the market.

7. SAFETY RAZOR. The invention of King Camp Gillette, the safety razor went on sale in 1903 after years of teething trouble. But in that first year it was snubbed by the American public, with the result that just 51 razors were sold throughout the United States. The following year, Gillette sold 90,000.

8. TRIVIAL PURSUIT. Formulated in 1982 by three young Canadians — newspaper photographer Chris Haney, sports writer Scott Abbott and ex-ice hockey player John Haney — Trivial Pursuit took 45 minutes to conceive but four years to market. They lost $45,000 on the first batch, to the dismay of 18-year-old unemployed artist Michael Wurstlin who had designed both board and logo in return for five shares in the company. By 1986, the shares were worth $500,000 each.

9. TUPPERWARE. When Earl Silas Tupper first marketed his new product in 1945, he boasted about its unique, water-tight, air-tight seal. However, the seal very nearly proved his downfall since demonstrators at retail stores were unable to operate it. As a result, they hid Tupperware away on top shelves out of harm's way.

10. VACUUM CLEANER. In 1902 Hubert Cecil Booth formed the Vacuum Cleaner Company Ltd. but, rather than sell his new invention, he chose to provide a service to the public. The huge apparatus arrived at a customer's house on a horse-drawn van and was parked outside while long hoses were threaded through the windows to suck up the dust. Apart from being cumbersome, the appliance was very noisy and frightened passing horses, which led to Booth being sued by cab proprietors.

20 PRODUCTS ADVERTISED ON THE FIRST NIGHT OF ITV

1. BATCHELOR'S PEAS.

2. BRILLO PADS.

3. BROWN & POLSON CUSTARD.

4. CROMPTON LAMPS.

5. CROSSE & BLACKWELL SOUP.

6. DUNLOP RUBBER.

7. EKCO RADIO AND TV SETS.

8. ESSO PETROL.

9. EXPRESS DAIRY.

10. FORD CARS.

11. GIBBS' SR TOOTHPASTE.

12. GUINNESS.

13. KRAFT CHEESE.

14. LUX WASHING POWDER.

15. NATIONAL BENZOLE PETROL.

16. OXO.

17. SHREDDED WHEAT.

18. SUMMER COUNTY MARGARINE.

19. SURF WASHING POWDER.

20. WATNEY'S BEER.

ITV opened on 22 September 1955 and the first commercial, chosen by lots, was for Gibbs' SR toothpaste. Viewers saw a tube of toothpaste embedded in a block of ice, a lady called Meg Smith brushing her teeth 'up and down and round the gums'.

10 INVENTIONS OF THE 20TH CENTURY WHICH ARE STILL SEARCHING FOR A MARKET

1. In February 1994 BRYAN PATRIE from Menlo Park, near San Francisco, patented the Watercolour Intelligent Nightlight, a device which reminds men to lower the lavatory seat when they have finished. Nicknamed 'the marriage saver', it only works in the dark when men are apparently at their laziest. If the seat is left up, an infra-red beam reflects back off the seat and switches on a red warning light, shaming the man into action. If the seat is down, a green light glows. During research, one half-asleep tester, seeing the red beam in the bowl, thought it was blood and that he was dying.

2. Travelling on Philadelphia public transport, MRS. NATALIE STOLP had noticed how 'flirtatious young men' deliberately used the crowded conditions as an excuse to press a knee or thigh against their feminine neighbour. Her 1914 patent sought to stem the rising sap by attaching a spring to the lady's underskirt which responded to pressure by releasing a short, sharp point into the offender's flesh.

3. In the 1980s three French women — DOMINIQUE PEIGNOUX, YVETTE GUYS and FRANÇOISE DEKAN — marketed a musical nappy whereby a contraption was tucked inside a baby's nappy and played 'When the Saints Go Marching In' as soon as it became wet.

4. In 1919 JOHN HUMPHREY of Connecticut invented an unusual alarm clock: one which would rouse someone from his slumbers by hitting him. The apparatus consisted of a timepiece attached to an adjustable rod with a rubber ball on the end. When the alarm on the clock went off, instead of a bell ringing, the rod would be activated, causing the ball to hit the desired area of the sleeper's anatomy. Humphrey deemed his device to be of great benefit to deaf people or invalids who might be upset by bells...but who presumably didn't mind being whacked over the head with a ball.

5. Helium-filled furniture was the brainchild of WILLIAM A. CALDERWOOD of Peoria, Arizona. His 1989 patent envisaged furniture floating to the ceiling

when not in use, thereby allowing extra floor space. When required, the furniture would be pulled back down to the floor by a rope.

6. EARL M. CHRISTOPHERSON of Seattle patented a 1960 device to enable people to look inside their own ears.

7. THOMAS FERRY of Wilmington, Delaware, perfected a moustache-guard in 1901. He said it was 'designed to hold the moustache away from the lips and to prevent the lodgement of food thereon while eating'. It consisted of a number of upward-pointing teeth inserted through the moustache from below 'to support the long flowing ends of the mustache which otherwise might droop down in the way'. An elastic tape was then strapped around the lip hair.

8. In 1984 Welshpool publican PHIL LEWIS was discussing potato crisp flavours with some Romany customers. They told him of an old gypsy delicacy — hedgehog baked in clay — and suggested the possibility of hedgehog-flavoured crisps. Using a closely-guarded recipe, Lewis set to work in his kitchen to produce the first packets. Customers likened the taste to smokey bacon but, as the venture attracted more and more publicity, animal-lovers protested and Lewis was forced to abandon the snack for more traditional flavours. Bensons Crisps bought him out in 1988 and kept Hedgehog on as a brand name rather than a flavour.

9. It was in 1966 that America's THOMAS J. BAYARD invented a vibrating toilet seat, acting on the belief that physical stimulation of the buttocks is effective in relieving constipation.

10. To reduce pedestrian casualties in 1960, DAVID GUTMAN from Philadelphia came up with a special pedestrian bumper designed to be fixed to the front of a car. Not only would it cushion the impact in the event of a collision but it also had a huge pair of claws which would grab the pedestrian around the waist to prevent him dropping to the tarmac.